1993

Making Fast Food

Making Fast Food

From the Frying Pan into the Fryer

ESTER REITER

Artwork by Richard Slye

McGill-Queen's University Press
Montreal & Kingston • London • Buffalo

© McGill-Queen's University Press 1991
ISBN 0-7735-0843-0 (cloth)
ISBN 0-7735-0947-x (pbk)
Legal deposit third quarter 1991
Bibliothèque nationale du Québec

Printed in Canada on acid-free paper
First paperback edition 1992

This book has been published with the help
of a grant from the Social Science Federation
of Canada, using funds provided by the
Social Sciences and Humanities Research
Council of Canada.

Cartoons on pages 60, 149, and 170 appear
courtesy of the artist, Matt Wuerker.

Canadian Cataloguing in Publication Data

Reiter, Ester
Making fast food
Includes bibliographical references and index.
ISBN 0-7735-0843-0 (bound)
ISBN 0-7735-0947-x (pbk)
1. Fast food restaurants. 2. Convenience
foods. 3. Food industry and trade. I. Title.
TX945.R44 1991   338.4'764795   C91-090225-9

This book was typeset by
Typo Litho composition inc.
in 10/12 Palatino.

To the memory of my parents Herman and Sarah Reiter

and to my sons Joshua and Daniel Koulack
(may they never forget the taste of Sarah's chicken soup)

Contents

Acknowledgments

Many people assisted in the research and writing of this book.

The workers and managers at all levels of the Burger King corporation made this study possible. I would like to express my appreciation to Debbie Techlowicz for her help and friendship. Brian Cooper and Barbara Reid of the food and hospitality division of George Brown College allowed me a glimpse of how the restaurant industry worked. The Canadian Restaurant Association opened their library to me. Art Milnes provided valuable assistance through the material he collected from the Strikes and Lockout files of Canada.

Family, friends, and colleagues all provided various kinds of help – they cheered me, cared for me, teased me, and also listened incesssantly to hamburger talk. I couldn't have managed without them. Thanks in particular to Meg Luxton, Susan Berlin, Bonnie Fox, and David Rapaport. Jim Turk, as my Ph.D. thesis advisor, was instrumental in the launching of the adventures of the "Burger King queen," as he used to call me. Miguel Murmis nourished me with his insightful guidance and his kindness in seeing this project through to completion.

I benefited from the intellectual input of a number of people. Meg Luxton was always to be counted on, providing encouragement, help, and advice. David Rapaport's critical views on academic research and writing influenced the final product. Susan Berlin generously contributed her time and editing skills in going over an earlier version. Judy Wittner, the Labour Studies group, Bonnie Fox, Harriet Rosenberg, Wally Seccombe, Sedef Koc, Barbara Neis, Roberta Hamilton, and my feminist reading group all offered criticisms and insights that helped in shaping this book. It was my good fortune that Jane Springer agreed to edit the manuscript. I thank her for her careful editing and thoughtful criticism and for dragging these hamburger pages all the way to Mozambique! I also appreciated the cooperation of the crew at McGill-Queen's, in particular, Joan McGilvray.

The research was supported by a Social Science and Humanities Council research grant. The financial assistance of the SSHRC's Aid to Scholarly Publications helped it to see the light of day.

Making Fast Food

Introduction

As a teenager in the 1950s, I remember how eager I was to find a part-time job. I wanted money that I could spend as I wished, without having to consult my parents. My brother became a delivery boy for the local "fruit man" when he was eleven years old, but I had to wait until I was fifteen, when I finally got a job in a specialty chocolate shop. A few years later I got a summer job in the kitchen of Schraft's, a large restaurant chain in New York City. My co-workers thought it was wishful thinking when I said I was only there temporarily, and would return to college in the fall. Everyone else was either an immigrant (Irish and Puerto Rican were the dominant nationalities) or black, and the younger workers dreamed of some day escaping from Schraft's kitchen into a nice clean office job.[1] Kitchen work was at the low end of the respectability spectrum.

My mother, an immigrant woman, had given up her job as a "salesgirl" (that's what they were called and that's how they were treated!) in Macy's department store when she became pregnant with my older brother and she never looked back. She worked hard, very hard, cleaning and cooking and caring for us, but I think she felt that she had a better deal than my father, who as a drug salesman, drove around in his car all day long. The meaning of paid work for family members is not uniform.

I too was a dependent wife when my children were born in the early 1960s. I remember the pleasure I felt later, when amidst the many challenges of managing as a single parent, I at least had the freedom to spend "my" paycheck as I pleased. The individual ideology of the wage – the notion that the wage "belongs" to those who "earn" it – also worked to my younger son's advantage. At age eleven, he had $120 saved from his paper route which, over my strenuous objections, he decided to spend on a banjo-making kit. He had never played the banjo, and as I am useless at do-it-yourself projects, I hated to see him waste his hard-earned money. The money, however, was "his," and so I had to respect his decision. (He was playing banjo in the Winnipeg folk festival by the time he was thirteen, and is now a professional musician!)

For women and young people, the economic independence gained from earning money can help minimize the gender and age subordination built into our family/household system.[2] It's easy to see why for many young people and women, any job is initially very appealing. But industries that employ these workers on a part-time, minimum wage basis don't do so out of altruism.

In 1986, one out of twelve Canadian workers earned $4.00 an hour or less. Forty percent of these low-wage earners were young people, between the ages of sixteen and nineteen, and another 24 percent were under twenty-four years of age. Most (85 percent) of these young people were also full-time students. Women were almost twice as likely as men to be working for $4.00 an hour or less. Most jobs paying these low wages were in the service sector; one in three jobs in the accommodation, food and beverage services – the census industrial classification with the highest percentage of low-wage jobs – received minimum wage or less.[3] Students attending school and under eighteen years of age can legally be paid at a special rate that is lower than the minimum wage for other workers. Thus, in 1986, when the minimum wage for adults was $4.00 per hour, students could be paid 85 cents less or $3.15 per hour. This helps to make young people a particularly desirable labour force.

How did an entire industry develop that relies on the work of this particular labour force, which now drafts retirees as well? What are the nature of these part-time, minimum wage jobs that people who do not see themselves as "really" workers take on?

This book is about the fast food industry, the development of a market and a labour force for that industry and the kind of jobs created there. Since my teenage years, the giants of the industry, such as McDonald's and Burger King, have grown into companies with sales that are counted in the billions and empires that extend throughout the world. Indeed, eating fast food and working in a fast food outlet have become symbols of life in contemporary society. This book examines the processes that led to the prevalence of this way of life and, through entering the kitchen of one of the large fast food chains, the reader will share my first-hand experience of how the work is organized and what it involves.

Theories about what happens at work and why workers behave as they do have, until very recently, treated the worker as a uniform creature of no particular gender or race.[4] However, it was assumed that this ungendered, raceless worker was really an adult white male, settled in a factory where he could expect to remain for long stretches of time with some job security, and where, if lucky, he would move up the job ladder a few rungs. Researchers who considered the influences of life outside work on the paid workplace usually studied "attitudes" or "orientations to work."[5] Women, involved in a demanding labour process at home and in their paid workplaces, were neither considered nor respected as workers. Young people still attending school who had part-time jobs never entered the literature.

Some scholars critical of the pro-business orientation of industrial sociologists noted how gender, race, and ethnicity were important in making sure workers got jobs deemed suitable for their particular attributes.[6] Their focus however, was on labour market segmentation and job assignment, and they didn't explore what happens after that. Some Marxist critics who looked at what happens at work assumed that paid work experiences were most important, and treated workers as influenced only by the flows of capital and the social relations at the point of production.[7] It is only very recently that some writers have begun to explore the effects of gender and race in the workplace itself.[8] The challenge is how to incorporate these important concepts without losing sight of what we have learned from previous analyses.

Anyone who has held a job can testify to the influences of workplace culture and workplace organization, and thus the value of the insights provided by early industrial sociologists and their critics. Our observations confirm the findings of the labour market theorists. Despite pay equity and employment equity legislation, women and visible minorities in Canada have fewer opportunities than other workers to decent, well-paying jobs. Some economists, noting the low labour market entry wages of young men and women, predict that they will not be able to find substantially better paying jobs when they get older. The unionized industrial workplaces of their fathers are disappearing.[9]

This book begins in the home as a reminder that "real" life and "real" work encompass both private life and paid work. After a sketch of how the market entered the family and why more family/household members took on waged work in the post-World War II period, it moves into the realm of business and describes restaurants in Canada earlier in this century and the growth of the fast food industry. With this background, we can then walk through the doors of a Burger King in Mississauga, Ontario, to take a look at life in a fast food outlet. At this point, the book takes a more personal turn.

In Chapter 5, I describe participant observation research as a methodology and the challenges of putting this methodology into practice. After some initial difficulty, I managed to work in a fast food outlet with the knowledge of management. I spent five months there, full time, as an unpaid crew person and another seven months after that, returning for one shift a week. Thus, I provide a view based on my experiences and observations of how the developments described in the first part of the book translate into life inside a fast food outlet. The themes intertwine – what the dominance of corporate capital means to the restaurant industry, its effect on the organization of work, people's experience of such a work situation, and how factors related to gender and age enter the workplace. Behind what I hope is a readable account lie some big issues.

Exploring the question of the relationships between the world of paid work and the world of consumption is a major challenge. Why is the nuclear family the dominant ideological form? How has this form of family influenced the development of markets in services and labour? Why do we persist in treating the world of production (where paid work occurs) as an entity separate from the world of consumption? How do we acknowledge and document the enormous range and variability of people's experiences without losing sight of the continuing impingement of a macro world – the world of the transnationals. As Marx reminded us so long ago, while we can struggle and make choices, we do not create our history exactly as we choose.[10] I hope that considering the case of the fast food industry will bring these questions to the fore.

The family gathering around the dinner table for a home-cooked meal is becoming a much less regular occurrence. Mom, the teenaged kids, and even the grandparents are recruited for work in fast food outlets where families can go to eat breakfast, lunch, or dinner. Market inroads into these areas is a new development that has taken place only in the last half of the twentieth century. The growth of the fast food industry represents the successful unfolding of a particular vision of contemporary life.

Most of us assume that what is familiar is natural and inevitable, yet there is no natural or right way to live. Throughout the twentieth century, there have been contending visions of how contemporary life should be organized. What we do at work, when and how we play, what we eat and who prepares it, when we sleep and how much sleep we get are all aspects of daily life shaped by a social organization that is historically created and constantly changing. Views on who should live together, who should contribute to material and emotional well-being, and what form these contributions should take vary. Social and economic forces set the parameters for the relationships between men, women, and children and how they interact within a kinship unit called the family and live together in an economic unit called the household. The flourishing fast food industry represents the dominance of one particular blueprint for how to live.

Business views identify the market and a healthy "bottom line" as the motor for social and economic growth. Others would like to see a society where human need rather than profit is primary. Pointing out that women have been excluded from the classic philosophical discussions as well as from important areas of economic life, feminists are committed to working for women's full equality.

In this age of neoconservatism, business logic most often influences Canadian public policy. Social conservatives of the New Right celebrate the heterosexual nuclear family living together as the only proper way to organize private life, and elevate motherhood to a state of natural grace. However, a pro-business economic policy where expenditures on social programs such as day care are kept to a minimum, together with a regressive tax structure, make life very difficult for many families, in particular for women who are mothers. Women need to take on paid work, but continuing responsibility for their families' welfare and the lack of universally available services limits their job choices. For women with such restrictions, part-time work with hours that allow them to be home after school hours is all that they can manage. Some of them, along with their teenage offspring, find jobs in the outlets of huge food conglomerates that grew through unchallenged mergers and acquisitions.

Most Canadians claim to want a society where all citizens have formal legal freedom, justice, and equality. Our laws, in the post-World War II period, support a notion that women deserve equality with men – at work and in political life. Each individual is entitled to pursue self-fulfilment. For women, this means participation in public life on an equal basis with men, and not doing all the unpaid work involved in running a home and raising children.

How then will that work get done? Who will do the cleaning, the cooking, the child minding? Women with salaries pay for such services through the marketplace. They hire other women to do that work for them in their homes, or they look to commercial services, often staffed by other women. The emphasis on formal equal rights enables some to have a chance to compete for positions of influence in politics and business. Some women have increasing opportunity to partake in the rewards of success in industry, commerce, and the arts and end up with comfortable and interesting lives, serviced by less fortunate women. Today, some women have made major inroads into the well-paid professions as doctors, lawyers, and college professors, and they are no longer so rare in corporate life. However, the lives of most women have not changed very much. They end up in the same low-paid, dead-end service jobs as they did earlier in this century, only in greater numbers.

Formal legal equality can and does exist along with profound inequalities in actual living and working conditions. The classical liberal idea of autonomous individuals competing for their own success leaves the contemporary structure of work and family unchallenged. Freedom in the marketplace and formal political equality have gone hand in hand with fewer rights and more management control of the workplace.[11] Looking at paid employment and domestic life as two separate worlds that do not intersect creates difficulties for everyone, especially women.

This book tells a story of how family members took on waged work in the post-World War II period and how the fast food industry grew in a world driven by private enterprise. By investigating the consequences of these developments the reader is asked to consider – are there perhaps better ways to organize our lives? Is this the best we can do?

CHAPTER ONE

The Market Moves into the Family and the Family Moves into the Market

Betty Friedan, whom many consider the American "mother" of the second wave of liberal feminism, and Vladimir Ilyitch Lenin, the Bolshevik architect of the 1917 Russian revolution, were both concerned with women's subordination, and both thought the solution lay in increasing women's participation in paid labour. When Betty Friedan wrote the *Feminine Mystique* in the late 1950s she, like Lenin some forty years earlier, advocated that women should enter socially productive labour to free them from the stultifying atmosphere of the kitchen and the nursery. Each, however, had a different proposal for who would take over the household chores. Friedan's solution was for women to hire a maid – an option not available to many women for economic reasons, and morally not acceptable for those with egalitarian sensibilities.[1] Lenin believed the socialization of housework was the route to follow – bringing housework into paid production. In early 1990 Soviet citizens were celebrating the arrival of McDonald's in Moscow as they looked for models of how to provide more consumer goods and services and ease the burden on their women.

Some of the theories of these early thinkers have become reality. In Canada in recent years, new workers have been drawn into paid work in great numbers. The single most dramatic increase in the labour force has been of married women with children. In 1986, six out of ten women with children (60.8 percent) also held jobs for pay; in the age bracket thirty-five to forty-four years of age, these percentages were even higher (69.7 percent).[2] In some areas of the country, such as Ontario, over half (54.5 percent) of teenagers fifteen to nineteen years of age were in the labour force in 1989.[3] The female labour force in Canada increased 64 percent in the decade since the 1971 census while the male labour force increased only 28 percent.

More than seven out of every ten of all women in Canada between the ages of fifteen and forty-five were in the labour force in 1986.[4] How and why this process occurred needs to be understood not only as the triumph of the new, free woman but also as the extension of opportunities for business to find new profitable areas – creating pressure for more members of the family to enter waged work to pay for these recently developed consumption habits.

CREATING THE CONSUMER

Since the 1920s, the challenge for many industries has been not just to meet existing demands, but to create a market for the abundant goods and services produced, changing the relationship between the domestic economy and waged work. The mass production of goods and services has cheapened costs, so that it makes more economic sense to earn the money to buy those goods and services than to produce them in the home. The price of precut and pre-cooked fried potatoes has increased more slowly than the cost of raw potatoes, which still need to be peeled and cooked.[5] Knitting sweaters or sewing one's own clothes is a hobby rather than a money-saving activity.

The goods and services considered necessary for subsistence have changed: many more are "needed" and these must be bought. By 1981, over 97 percent of the population had electric or gas stoves, refrigerators, telephones, and at least one television set. Eighty percent or more had record players and/or tape recorders, at least one car, and a colour television. Over 75 percent had their own washing machines.[6] Equipment for the majority of Canadian families in 1988 included a microwave, a video cassette recorder, and cable TV.[7]

The effect of this movement of the market into the sphere of the family has been varied. New technology applied to a household task may at first remove the activity from the home; then later, still newer technologies return the activity to the home in an altered form. By the late 1930s, for example, many families sent a good part of their laundry to power laundries. Later, when washing machines were widely available, the decentralized, small residential-service power laundries could not compete with the growing corporate concentration in washing machine production for the home market. The laundry was returned to the home – to be washed, most often, by women.[8] At the same time, advertisers promoted a raised standard of cleanliness, and the sale of a host of new products to make one's wash "whiter than white" and eliminate "ring around the collar."[9]

Similarly, the development of the movie industry during the first half of the twentieth century drew people out of their homes in search of entertainment. Once television was developed, however, the at-home entertainment market proved more lucrative and now, virtually every Canadian family has at least one television set. The movie industry, as measured by the number of paid admissions to theatres and drive-ins, has been declining since the 1950s.[10] In addition to the profits from selling TVs for the use of individual families, the advantages to advertisers of a home installation of a "blinking neon sign"[11] are considerable.

Distinguishing between necessities and luxuries is difficult. For example, private car ownership in many areas of Canada is virtually indispensable, given the location of shopping centres, the lack of adequate public transportation and the elimination of home deliveries as a service. Necessities have frequently been created. For example, the decline of public transport in major US cities occurred in the 1930s and 1940s because companies such as General Motors found the short-term gains from investment in private transport more profitable than long-term investment in maintaining a public transit system. With the growth in suburbs after World War II, living quarters were located far from work and shopping. People had no alternative but to look to the private automobile.

In the late 1980s, the Canadian government withdrew its commitment to a publicly supported national transportation system. Air Canada was privatized and transcontinental Via Rail service discontinued. If servicing northern areas of the country interferes with private companies' profit margins, will Canadians in Churchill need to buy their own airplanes in order to get around?

Clothing purchase illustrates a more blurred distinction between necessities and luxuries. With the invention of the sewing machine in the latter half of the nineteenth century, garment construction moved from the home to the factory. There, the use of machines and an increased division of labour permitted the mass production of cheap clothing. With the help of lowered costs and massive advertising, fashion – previously the domain of the wealthy – now became a concern of every woman. Women were encouraged to "express themselves" within the limits of the season's current styles, colours, and hem lengths.

Wives and mothers were told that their job security rested on maintaining sexual attractiveness. Still dependent on husbands for economic survival, they now had to seek eternal youth through appropriate foundation garments and glamorous attire. Young people are a particularly vulnerable target for this sort of propaganda. The puffed-out crinolines and cashmere sweater sets of the 1950s and the designer jeans and name-brand running shoes that are de rigeur in the 1980s represent far more than mere physical necessity.

For the young teenager stepping out into the world, appropriate attire is the pre-condition of acceptance by her peers. The awkwardness and self-consciousness about one's body common among adolescents have been seized upon and translated into the promise of a sense of security, love, and friendship for a re-designed teenager – and into a fortune for the manufacturers. [12]

Marketplace entry into food preparation and consumption has had the effect of moving food preparation out of the home and into the factory. It has also set up a battle between supermarkets and fast food restaurants over where ready-to-eat foods will be bought and whether they will be eaten at home or in public places. At the turn of the century, food preparation in most Canadian kitchens involved few manufactured products. Although bakeries were common in urban areas, most meals cooked at home were prepared from unprocessed raw foods: chickens had to be killed and plucked, oatmeal soaked, and nuts shelled. Bread, potatoes, and some meat formed the staple of most working people's diets. [13]

People were not aware of the health advantages of a more varied diet, which might include fruits and vegetables, until the early part of the twentieth century. It was at that time that canned fruits and vegetables and prepared cereals made their way into Canadian kitchens. In the 1930s, techniques were developed for the quick freezing of foods, but these techniques were not perfected on a commercial scale till the need to feed armies abroad in World War II. In the 1950s and 1960s, an increasingly diverse assortment of ready-made foods, needing only to be defrosted and served, became available in stores. Mechanical conveniences such as refrigerators and gas or electric ranges also gained wide distribution in Canada in the post-World War II years. [14]

By the 1950s, the combination of technological advances in preserving and storing food, the growing ownership of automobiles and the development of vast new suburbs transformed both shopping and eating habits. Shopping plaza supermarkets overwhelmed grocery stores, putting many small, independent grocers out of business. Families made less frequent shopping trips in their cars to buy larger supplies of groceries. In the supermarkets, shoppers gathered the groceries themselves instead of being served by clerks. Caring for one's family became "consumption work," carried out in shopping and service centres organized to increase the profit margins of the seller, not the convenience of the consumer. [15] The predictions for the future are that consumers will be cooking even less. Some analysts maintain that food preparations skills may soon be limited to defrosting and microwaving! [16]

The market has moved into the family. In the past twenty-five years, the rise of the fast food industry, together with the advent of other businesses aimed at the family market, have appeared to make some of the early visions a reality. However, this socialization of the domestic sphere has occurred primarily in the interest of maximizing profit. For example, care for one's children can be arranged in a "Mini Skool," while breakfast, lunch and dinner can be served up in less than three minutes at the local McDonald's or Burger King. Mini-maid services will clean your home, and Vacation Watch will check your house when you go off on your Uniglobe packaged vacation trip.

Caring for Profit: The Commercialization of Human Services in Ontario,[17] finds that many services, such as care for the elderly in nursing homes and retirement homes, care for the handicapped, and even hospital management are increasingly being provided by profit-making enterprises. Thus, 90 percent of our nursing homes, half of our beds for the elderly, almost half of all licensed day care places, and half of the contracts for homemaking services and special care homes are given over to entrepreneurial management. In situations where workers have managed to organize and blunt the edge of management's prerogatives, we see management respond with contracting out, thereby removing services from the nonprofit sector into opportunities for private corporations. Since the completion of the free trade deal between Canada and the United States in 1988, daily headlines report more and more of these instances.

Fast food was designed to lure families out of the home, by providing a meal at a price that everyone could afford. As eating out became more popular in the late 1960s and early 1970s, the eating habits of the population were transformed. According to the Canadian Restaurant and Foodservice Association, 39 percent of each food dollar was spent on food away from home in 1988. The estimates for the United States are even higher. *Advertising Age* claims family meals are fast becoming a thing of the past. "In one generation we have gone from a traditional food producing society to a food grazing society – one where we eat wherever we happen to be."[18]

Eating out in fast food places is influenced by a number of factors. People who live in large urban areas spend more money on restaurant food than people who live in small cities; as well, smaller families eat out more frequently than larger ones.[19] While the amount of money spent in restaurants varies with income level, a study by the National Restaurant Association of the United States found that there was little relationship between income level and the number of away-from-home meals eaten at fast food restaurants. While in the past, patronage in restaurants seems to have been a class-distinct phenomenon, fast food has proved to be the great leveller.

One of the important determinants of the frequency with which a family buys ready-to-eat food to be eaten either in restaurants or at home is the wife's employment status. Families in which the wife is employed full time spend almost twice as much money on restaurant food per week as families in which the wife has no outside job.[20] An article entitled "Ready to Eat Revolution" describes the pattern: "Americans are finding there is simply no time or energy left to cook a meal after all the work, personal improvement and social activities of a typical "New Age" day ... When those pressured people do get back to the sanctity of their homes complete with microwaves and VCRs, the last thing they want to do is prepare a meal."[21]

FAMILY MEMBERS ENTER THE LABOUR FORCE

Since the 1930s, the dollar amount constituting a minimally adequate income has more than doubled (using constant dollars).[22] At the same time, it has become increasingly difficult to stretch a paycheck by intensifying unwaged work. As prices for pre-prepared products rise more slowly than the price for prepared and partially prepared foods, more hours in the kitchen do not free up much money for other goods and services.[23]

Many women must take on waged labour if their families are to live as other families in Canada do. The National Council on Welfare pointed out in the 1970s that one worker earning the minimum wage could not earn enough to keep even a two-person family above the poverty line.[24] They estimated that in Ontario, 65 percent more families would have been poor in 1975 had the family been forced to rely on the husband's earnings alone.

The result has been the steady influx of women into the paid labour force. Since the 1970s, this flow of married women with families into the ranks of the employed has included considerable numbers of mothers with young children: by 1980, well over half the women with preschoolers were in the workforce. Without the necessary support services – such as day care and adequate care for aging family members, women must take on the kind of jobs that still allow them to meet their domestic responsibilities.[25]

For young people, the story is somewhat different, but parallel. The combination of a decline in farming, the introduction of the assembly line into industry, and the influx of a large immigrant population rendered many young workers superfluous by 1930. School attendance became compulsory and youngsters increased their secondary school attendance, which reached record-high levels in the 1970s. At first, this trend was accompanied by a decline in the number of young people in the labour force; beginning in the late 1960s, however, there has been a steady influx into the labour force of young people still attending school. By the late 1970s, when statistics on employed students began to be collected on a regular basis, more than one out of three fourteen to nineteen-year-old students in Canada were in the labour force.[26] By the late 1980s, more than half of the teenagers still attending school were in the labour force in the more industrialized areas of the country such as Ontario.

These variations in labour force figures reflect the availability of work, as well as teenagers' desires for jobs. In A.B. Hollingshead's well-known study, *Elmtown's Youth*, first published in 1949, the author describes the great variety of jobs traditionally performed by adolescents in farms, businesses, and industries. He notes that "from the frontier days to the present, the economy has had need for the labor of adolescents, and just as important, the vast majority of the adolescents need the jobs the economy provides to earn the money they all have to have in order to participate in the commercialized forms of recreation available to them."[27]

A survey conducted by the Toronto school board in 1978 found that by the time students were seventeen years old, 59.3 percent had had a part-time job while attending school. Even more (74 percent) reported looking for work.[28] Both this study and a Statistics Canada survey done in 1974[29] found, as might be expected, a higher frequency of part-time work among older students (grades 11, 12, and 13).

While women's labour force participation (when education levels are held constant) is related to how much husbands earn, there seems to be little relationship between socioeconomic status and young people's working patterns. One Canadian study found that in schools in some better-off neighbourhoods, a higher proportion of students was working than was true for their counterparts in working-class neighbourhoods. The authors felt that perhaps these students had better contacts and so were able to find paid work more easily.[30] Youngsters generally have minimal say in how family income is divided, so even teenagers from well-off families need to earn money.[31]

Working-class households in the twentieth century have consistently required the work of all household members in order to survive.[32] However, in cities as on farms, much of this work in the first three decades of the century took unwaged forms. The efforts of some members of the family (women and older children) to scrounge fuel and building supplies and to look after very young children made it possible for others to take on waged work and stretch an inadequate wage.[33] The economic activities of family members outside of regular jobs rarely entered official statistics. Women, with the help of their children, cleaned and cooked for boarders, took in washing and ironing, did home work for the garment industry, and worked in family businesses. Children earned money with paper routes and as clerks and delivery boys for small stores. When they took on regular jobs for pay, women earned about half of what the men received, children about one quarter. Certain industries (such as cigar making and clothing manufacture) had high concentrations of child and female workers.[34]

Thus, while women and their teenaged children have always contributed to the family economy, in the past twenty years there has been a growing number taking on paid work. Both groups, however, enter the labour market at a disadvantage: women with families must still be available to care for their needs, and teenagers are expected to attend school full time, at least until the completion of high school.

This means that they can work only during certain times of the day and for limited periods of time. They need to look to part-time employment, and this is available in only a few types of jobs in some industries. The two largest groups of part-time workers are married women over twenty-five, and students of both sexes fifteen to twenty-four years of age.[35] Members of these groups occupy the lowest-level positions, earn the least money, and get the fewest benefits of any workers.[36] Thus, married women and students available for part-time work are welcomed as a source of cheap labour by a growing number of industries.

Poorly paid, non-union part-time job opportunities, particularly in the service sector, are increasing. While the number of full-time jobs increased by 25 percent in the period from 1975 to 1986, the number of part-time jobs increased by 83 percent.[37] The 1981 census figures show that employment in restaurants, caterers, and taverns (one of the largest categories of employment for part-time workers) has more than doubled since 1971. Almost half a million people (470,680 to be exact), worked in this area.[38] In their brief to the Commission of Inquiry on Part Time Work, the Canadian Restaurant and Foodservice Association (CRFA) made clear the conditions they thought were appropriate for foodservice employees. They stressed the "great number of opportunities available to part time employees ... created by the flexible nature of the working conditions." They maintained that any restrictions on hiring, terminations, or other procedures involving part-time employees would result in fewer jobs: "It is our experience that part time workers are not looking for greater benefits from their employers but are mainly concerned with working convenient hours for immediate remuneration."

The CRFA noted that their industry is a "top employer of students in Canada." Over half the industry workers are women. CRFA representatives strenuously opposed making any benefits, even unemployment Insurance, available to part-time workers: "If increased unemployment insurance were extended to part time employees, they will become aware that they can apply for benefits when unemployed. This will lead to increased instability among this category of workers, since so many are secondary income earners."[39]

The influx into the labour force of women with families has created a generation of weary women. While most would not choose to return home full time, the burden of doing two jobs takes its toll. Recognizing that paid work is now a question of necessity, rather than choice, we seek relief through purchasing consumer goods and services. Sometimes, as in the case of the fast food industry, as we shall see, the solutions are also part of the problem.

The incursion of corporate capitalism into the home has occurred in a way that enhances profits, rather than benefits the consumer. It has produced a situation in which more wages are needed in order to buy more goods and services. All members of the family, from young children to aging grandparents, are the targets of a variety of marketing strategies geared toward increasing consumption.[40]

Many families have a sense of being on a treadmill, driven by the pressure of always needing and wanting more. The tedium and insecurity that many people feel is exploited by advertisers to sell even more products.[41] Thus things that "money can't buy" are put on sale indirectly – through the promise that the purchase of enough products will make you desirable and lovable. Or if you want some fun, you must buy a meal at McDonald's, where you can "give yourself a break today."

Both the money for relief from the pressures of commodified life and the expanding market for social commodities comes from the family. Wages can now be earned by more family members in paid work, while promising the family relief in purchasing comfort and luxury through things such as an "exciting dining experience offering people more than just food."[42]

Changes in the restaurant industry illustrate this process. We shall see how the "interchangeable worker" has been created to service the mass-produced consumer. Fast food is one common work situation for family members drawn into paid labour. What does this development signify for our future as workers and as consumers?

CHAPTER TWO

The Restaurant Industry in Canada

We may live without poetry,
  music, and art;
We may live without conscience
  and live without heart;
We may live without friends and
  live without books,
But civilized men cannot live
  without cooks.

We may live without books, what
  is knowledge but grieving;
We may live without hope, what
  is hope but deceiving;
We may live without love, what is
  passion but pining;
But where is the man that can live
  without dining?

From the menu at Dan's Cafe, Aurora, Ontario (circa 1920)

Dining out was neither a common nor a very important activity for our forefathers and mothers. Most people ate at home. The restaurant industry in Canada provides an example of how an activity that used to take place at home for household consumption became a business undertaking. There were two major phases to this process: the first was the development of restaurants as separate eating establishments, and their growing patronage by people away from home at mealtimes; this began in the late nineteenth century in Canada and extended until the 1950s. The second phase was the development of the fast food industry, which sought to expand the market by actively encouraging people to eat dinner out instead of cooking at home; the beginnings of this phase occurred in the late 1950s and early 1960s.

As the restaurant industry developed, both the technology for producing a meal and the market for eating out changed. The industry sought a different kind of worker to produce and serve the meal, and developed suitable techniques for managing the new workforce. Management techniques reflected not just the current thinking at the time, but the nature of the industry and the kind of workers who were used. Workers were sought who would be in plentiful supply and not cost very much. Thus production was geared to using as many low-paid, unskilled workers as possible. However, even in this industry, traditionally reserved for the most easily exploitable workers, restaurant workers attempted to organize to protect their interests.

A technology that enables a more unskilled worker to produce meals in turn produces cheaper meals. And cheapened production allows the market to expand because more people can afford to eat out.

In this chapter, I only touch upon a rich and still untold history. The restaurant industry is varied in its products, in how they are produced, and in who buys them. All sorts of restaurants co-exist, serving many different clienteles. Filling the stomach is only one of a number of purposes they serve – they also perform a variety of social functions.

THE BEGINNINGS – RESTAURANTS UP TO WORLD WAR I

The first commercial eating places in North America were associated with inns located on travel routes.[1] As transportation systems developed, so did eating facilities. When the Canadian Pacific Railway (CPR) was completed, people began to travel more, for pleasure as well as business. Sir William Van Horne, the first general manager of the CPR developed a hotel and feeding empire by making use of the railway's monopoly on all land north and south of the railway line. The CPR constructed luxurious hotels to which wealthy people were transported in comfort, and where they were fed grandly.

As one might expect, the facilities for the well-to-do bore little resemblance to those available to poor immigrants and other working people. The tooled leather benches, white linen, and expensive silverware of the dining car on the Holyrood, one of the first transcontinental trains, were a far cry from the dining halls, also owned by the CPR located at division points along the route. There, immigrants and other poor travellers streamed out of the train to be "refuelled" (along with the locomotive) in the short time allotted, generally twenty to thirty minutes.[2] Eating places were not only marked by strong class distinctions, but also served different social functions. As a rule, only the wealthy *chose* to eat out. For the working-class person, food available at home was far preferable to the fare served in affordable eating places where the food was often barely edible.[3]

On the other hand, working-class and immigrant centres often provided more than just a meal. Joe Beef's tavern, located on the Montreal waterfront, was one of the establishments where poor men and boys ate in the 1870s and 1880s. It provided not only cheap meals, but job referrals, strike support, and entertainment and included a menagerie of monkeys, bears, and parrots. Joe Beef also had a separate room where newspaper boys and other homeless men could sleep; he charged twenty cents a day for room and board and took in all in need. McKiernan, the Irish sovereign over this waterfront kingdom for the poor, proclaimed that when helping the unemployed, he did "not give a damn whether he is an Indian, a Nigger, a Cripple, a Billy or a Mick."[4] A bottle he kept on display in the tavern had a bit of beef preserved in it, which had lodged (fatally) in the windpipe of one of his patrons. Joe Beef's menu, great piles of bread, cheese, and beef heaped up at one end of the bar, was in marked contrast to the sumptuous delicacies such as mock turtle soup and chicken truffles offered patrons of the CPR hotels.[5]

Restaurants that were separate establishments date back a little more than one hundred years. Although the restaurant industry began in Canada before the turn of the century, the total number of separate eating places remained small. Only 891 restaurant keepers were reported in the Canadian census of 1891, the first year in which restaurants are identified as a category distinct from hotels and boarding houses. Almost all of these places were to be found in the larger urban areas in Quebec, Ontario, and Nova Scotia.[6] With the increase in immigration to Canada in the early twentieth century, the number of people in the restaurant business grew. By the 1911 census, 2,720 people were listed as restaurant keepers and they employed 7,283 people, largely immigrants; over 50 percent of the male restaurant keepers were foreign-born, and over 78 percent of the male employees were born outside Canada.[7]

Restaurants sprang up as cities did. The connection between the two was noted in this 1884 article on restaurants in the newspaper, the *Toronto World*:

Nothing is more indicative of the metropolitan growth of Toronto than her restaurants. And it may be said that it is an industry that has had almost a spontaneous growth. Six years ago it was almost impossible to get a dinner in a restaurant on Sunday, and during the week a person was limited to two or three bills of fare a la European. In those days Thomas' English chop houses and the St. Charles were the only restaurants near the centre of the city, and they monopolized nearly all the trade. But a different story can be told now ... It is just something astonishing to see the number of business men, clerks, lawyers, workingmen, boy reporters and beggars that "lunch down town" now in this city. The number cannot be less than 5000.[8]

The article goes on to list restaurants by "class"; about two dozen places in all are noted. The fanciest places are for commercial travellers and local businesspeople. The author considered the lowest to be those with a clientele of bootblacks and newsboys, or those run by "coloured" people on Queen St. West.

What were the interiors of such restaurants like? How was the food prepared and served? In *The Search for America*, a novel by Frederick Grove that is set in Toronto in the 1890s, the author takes us inside a commercial eating place. The hero, a young gentleman from England fallen on hard times, describes his experiences as a waiter in one of Toronto's second-rate restaurants. Phil, the hero, approaches a restaurant that is part of a Toronto chain with a clientele of businessmen, old people, and travelling families. He enters the restaurant dining room by walking past a long, mirrored corridor, then goes up a few steps and through a set of swinging doors. Before him are rows of booths, their high-backed benches covered with leather; as well, there are circular tables that seat eight, and beyond these, a counter. A row of electric fans hangs overhead. The waiters wear white jackets and black ties. The manager warns Phil that this place is in business not to please the customer, but "in order to get their money out of their pockets into our own ... We want our waiters then to serve our customer as quickly as possible and we want our customer to eat as fast as he can in order to make room for the next one."[9]

Our hero is warned to be careful about offering customers things that they are not paying for, such as ketchup or Lea and Perrin's sauce. "He (the client) is apt, if he is given the chance, to take ten cents' worth of catsup with an order that yields only ten cents profit. We prefer not to give him that chance. And besides, to put it cynically, he will linger too long over his plate, if he enjoys his food beyond its mere filling powers."[10]

Phil is offered a chance to start as an omnibus (busboy). His hours are 10:30 AM (10 AM if he wishes a free breakfast) till 2:15 the next morning. Wages are $4.50 a week. Arriving at his job for the first time, he is directed to the locker room, located down a narrow, pitch-dark staircase to "an excessively dirty subterranean room." Grove describes the litter, the stifling air "saturated with the odor of human sweat, foul with the exhalation of slow, dry decay."[11]

The restaurant proper ends at two sets of swinging doors, beyond which is the dishwashing room, a low-ceilinged room oozing with steam where "two fat, Slavic-looking women dressed in heavy woolen garments are busy." Down another corridor, Phil arrives in the low-ceilinged kitchen in which "the heavy odors of frying fat, boiling gravy, and cooking roasts filled the atmosphere in veritable layers."[12] A counter separates the waiters from the cooks. Behind the counter are four ranges, each about twenty feet long. The attendants (about a dozen) are either naked down to their hips, or wearing thin undershirts. Greasy aprons cover their lower bodies. During the lunch rush, everyone, including the manager of the restaurant, works madly:

Behind the counter a casual observer would have seen half naked maniacs dancing and jumping about in crazy lunacy. In the corridor, waiters were bustling each other, reaching up into the dish-rack, flinging plates on the counter and bellowing orders at the top of their voices. From out of the reeking pit behind me came yelling shouts, repeating every order that was given. Plates full of food were thrown back on trays held by the waiters. The swinging doors in front kept opening and slamming shut in every accelerated pulsation. Whoever passed through gave them a vigourous kick. The checker stood on a chair behind his desk, roaring for checks, swinging his arms, jumping like one possessed; but in reality he did nothing but spear the checks onto spindles, although he sometimes tried to keep up the pretence of verifying an order which passed out on a tray.[13]

Restaurant work was not considered a particularly glamorous way to make a living. Gus Boukydis, a successful Toronto restaurateur now past his seventies, describes how his father came to start Diana Sweets back in 1912:

I suppose the reason my father got into the business is because he was an immigrant. He got into it, I presume because he couldn't do anything else ... The interesting fact is previously the only people that would agree to work in the industry were immigrants – sort of low-income, low expectation people. Now the industry has acquired a certain amount of glamour. All sorts of people are in it that wouldn't be caught dead in it even ten, fifteen years ago.[14]

Aaron Ladowsky, another immigrant, also went into business in Toronto in 1912. He was a young baker who had arrived in Canada in 1906. He was earning twelve dollars a week, and his wife worked at Eaton's. The Ladowskys, along with two other bakers, opened United Bakers Dairy on what is now Dundas Street, in the heart of the Jewish area, near the Jewish theatre. The partnership between the three bakers lasted only a month, but United Bakers Dairy run by the Ladowsky family is still in business. At first, the store was a bakeshop and coffee shop, a takeout for pastries, bread, and buns. People on their way to work would stop in for coffee. Herman Ladowsky, who was born in 1911, says he remembers the first store; the family lived above it:

My father was the baker in the back and my mother ran the operation in the front ... Yes, we had hired bakers and hired waitresses too. My father was a community man. He organized the Jewish bakers' union. He was president of societies, he was president of the synagogue. He had a wonderful gift of speech, and he was able to devote all this time to his social activities because my mother looked after the business. She was always the businesswoman. We stayed open till late. We used to be sitting outside our supposedly front door, which was our veranda, till 11, 12 o'clock in the summertime. (There was no air conditioning in those days.) We lived above the place. You rolled out of bed into work, and rolled back into bed when it was closed. [15]

In the early days of this century, Canada was still a largely rural country. Thus the population density which is needed for a large restaurant market did not exist. For the average family in small cities and towns, dining out was an infrequent experience. In the eyes of a restaurateur reminiscing in 1951 about pre-World War I days, the restaurant business was not quite respectable. "[M]ost good citizens went home for lunch or ate in a hotel dining room. The restaurant business as we know it today did not exist." [16]

Labour supply was a problem. Although the hero in Grove's book found it hard to find work, he comments that the restaurant was constantly short-staffed; restaurants drew on a pool of labourers who could not find any other way of supporting themselves. Hours in this industry were long and wages for even unionized workers were very low. While a skilled male cook in a first-class hotel could be paid over twenty-five dollars a week, wages for waitresses and busboys were less than seven dollars per week. A female head cook could expect about fifteen dollars weekly. [17] In labour disputes from 1910 to the 1920s, the common issues were wages and hours of work. Workers, in a number of the cases reported, had to strike for the reduction of the work week to fifty-four hours, and for the right to one day off a week. In several instances, workers struck when management hired Chinese or Japanese workers. The fear was that these workers would work for even lower wages.

The technology for transporting and keeping food was just beginning to emerge; while refrigerated cars for transporting meat had been developed by the late nineteenth century, it was not until after World War I that the technology for the freezing or cold-packing of fruits and vegetables was available.[18] Some canned goods were produced, but food costs were still quite high. Restaurants for the wealthy, which provided varied menus, could not profit from the meals they served; their losses were made up through the sale of liquor, or for some, through their hotel operations.[19]

THE 1920S AND 1930S

By the 1920s, mass production was well underway in a number of industries. In compensation for the loss of craft skills, workers were offered higher wages and the chance to become consumers.[20] The transition from craft-based to mass production technologies coincided with the development of scientific management, and a new philosophy of workplace organization. Frederick Taylor, in 1911, laid down the basic principles of scientific management.

Scientific management elevated obedience over independence. For the first time, management claimed the right to decide how work ought to be done, down to the smallest detail. Through workers' adherence to the "one best way" of performing the work, decided by management, it was believed that material wealth and social harmony would be simultaneously promoted. As this new system was introduced in industry in the early decades of the century, more women were entering the workforce. They were to be found in areas where the work had been reorganized by these new principles and therefore required less autonomy and less skill than previously.

At this time, the process of urbanization was accelerating. In Toronto, for example, huge office buildings were built to accommodate the new financial institutions and the head offices of growing manufacturing firms. Many more people were employed in the downtown area, and, of these, many more were women. In 1891, only 14.3 percent of Canada's clerical workers were women; by 1931, this percentage had grown to 45 percent.[21]

Public transportation systems were developed to get working people to their jobs downtown and shoppers to the growing number of retail stores. In 1920, the city of Toronto took over transit services, thereby improving public access to the city from the suburbs and from nearby cities.[22] The effect of these numerous and interconnected developments was to make eating out more acceptable for the middle-class urbanite. Diana Sweets, which had originally served only pastries, started serving full course meals, and a number of moderately priced restaurants (such as Murray's, Ellen Bradley's, Muirhead's and Fran's) opened their doors in Toronto and Montreal. Stores such as Woolworth's and Kresge's expanded and modernized their luncheonette counters. By 1928, the year the Ontario Restaurant Association was founded, a rosy future for the industry was predicted:

There is a prosperous time ahead for the restaurant business, as there has never been a time when so many people were taking their meals in public places. Our modern industrial life, the increasing employment of married women, the interest that women are taking in civic affairs leading them more and more out of their homes, the small apartments in which many families live, the convenience of entertaining outside of the home. All these factors contribute largely to our business and it seems improbable that there will be a return to former conditions. [23]

During these years, marketing and personnel policies designed to enhance the sale of food began to be promoted in the pages of the restaurant journals. Murray's, which started as an "outlet for the idle capital of the parent company, Crawley & McCracken," congratulated itself on its successful formula "good food" and standardization of the menu, portions, and service. Indeed "Miss Murray" became the model for the standardization of waitresses as well. "Wholesome in appearance, friendly in attitude, and efficient in service, the Murray's waitress has a personality that harmonizes perfectly with her setting."[24] Murray's had reason to celebrate. The company was doing extraordinarily well.[25] In the midst of the "bitter thirties," the company took in two million dollars in sales.

The Boukydis family also did very well during this time: "During the Great Depression of the thirties, we profited immensely. We did better during the thirties than we are doing now. My father had two restaurants, and there were four of us, myself and three sisters. We all went to private schools, we lived in Forest Hill, we had a maid ... I think that was fairly unusual ... Murray's and Basil's up the street also did very well. There wasn't a hell of a lot else."[26]

The prosperous restaurants that fill the pages of the journals, as Mr Boukydis noted, were the exception. Most establishments were very small operations. Of the 5,534 eating places enumerated by the census for 1930, only 1.4 percent took in $100,000 or more in gross sales. The largest number, 2,522 stores, grossed less than $5,000 for that year.[27]

Sarah and Aaron Ladowsky, Rose Lieberman and Rose Green, Bakers's Dairy
Restaurant, Spadina Avenue, Toronto, 1920's. Courtesy of the Ladowsky family.

Small owner-operated restaurants, such as United Bakers Dairy,
were largely invisible to the restaurant journals. These places were
more than just places to eat.

The success of this restaurant is the intimacy and relationship we have with
all our customers that span all the years. I have people who come here that
tell me that when they arrived in Canada, and the bus brought them to the
Labour-Lyceum, they had their first breakfast in United Bakers. They met
one another, they got to know one another, and they found *landsleit* (fellow
countrymen) while sitting with one another. "Where do you come from?
What's your name? Oh, I know so and so." Next thing you know some of
them were even related and didn't know it. This was the intimacy of United
Bakers.

Bowling groups used to gather here – Jewish bowling leagues. The bowling place used to be down at Elizabeth St. The family people, husband and
wife couldn't eat their dinner (at home) fast enough because they had to

go the Friday night play at the Jewish theatre which would bring them back stories of their days in Europe. Then they'd come here for a Friday night *glayzl tay* (glass of tea) and a piece of cake. I used to say this was the only place in the world where you could find a bookmaker and a rabbi sitting at one table. Whatever you wanted you could get around here.[28]

Immigrants ate in restaurants and other groups that faced discrimination in the job market found jobs in the restaurant industry. Often, as at United Bakers Dairy, the work was done primarily by family members in small family-owned businesses. In 1931, when the Chinese made up less than one percent of the Canadian population, one out of every five restaurant, cafe, or tavern keepers was of Chinese origin. More than one out of every three male cooks was Chinese.[29] Mr Boukydis, a former president of the Ontario Restaurant Association, remarked that "Every small town in Canada had a Chinese restaurant."[30]

Food costs were high in those years; profitability came at the expense of workers' wages. The cost of labour was very low and hours of work impossibly high. Despite the terrible general economic conditions, there were attempts to unionize. The Food Workers Industrial Union, part of the Workers Unity League (WUL), claimed the most successes. In 1934, they managed to organize twenty-one locals, situated in every major city throughout the country.

The trade union philosophy of the left-wing Workers Unity League was very different from that of the larger craft-oriented, American Federation of Labour. Mr Sims, WUL general secretary, expressed the difference to the *Financial Post*: "We believe in united action to organize the workers to be ready to fight. The A.F. of L. believes in depending on the good sense of the boss. We don't do that. Depending on the good sense of the boss never gets you anywhere. The A.F. of L. believes that the worker and the boss can get along together if they have the right sort of agreement. We don't believe that. All that the working class has got and will get is through showing a united front."[31]

In 1931, skilled workers in Canada earned on average just over $1,000 year, at a time when a study by Leonard Marsh found that $2,000 was minimally necessary for an "American standard of living for a family."[32] Restaurant workers, at the minimum rates proposed by the Hotel Association, fell far below the norm for skilled workers, and were earning nowhere near enough to support their families. Even assuming they were able to work full time all year long, earnings would amount to 41 percent of the estimate for a decent living.[33]

Labour disputes during the 1930s often involved workers objecting to a seven day work week of ten to twelve-hour days. In February

1934, the waiters, the cook, and the dishwasher walked out of Preston Lunch, in Toronto. The workers asked for recognition of their union, the Toronto Restaurant and Hotel Union Workers, and a 10 percent increase in wages, which stood at ten dollars per week for waiters and sixteen dollars for others. They wanted their eighty-four-hour-a-week job (twelve hours per day, seven days a week) shortened to fifty-four hours a week for waiters and sixty hours a week for others.[34]

Another dispute involved the cooks, waiters, and waitresses at the Blue Goose Cafe in Vancouver. The *Vancouver Labour Statesman* described the strike in an article from September 1933.

After several conferences extending over a month, the members of the Hotel and Restaurant Employees Union, Local 28, walked out of the Blue Goose Cafe, Granville Street, in protest against unfair wages. The union reduced its scale to $12 per week – the lowest in twenty years – but the cafe decided $8 for girls and $10 for men was plenty to pay them. The waiters and waitresses had to supply their own uniforms, some of them for the girls costing as much as $15. Girls, of course, are expected to work 48 hours a week and keep their self respect on these wages and conditions.[35]

In an era where craft unionism was still the dominant form, the Workers Unity League, which began its activities in 1934, posed a threat both to employers and established trade unions. The WUL believed in organizing workers according to industry, rather than craft. Thus all the workers in a restaurant, whether they were cooks, waiters, or dishwashers, would belong to the same union. This gave the union more power in the event of a strike.

When the Restaurant Employees Union, of the Food Workers Industrial Union of Canada, a WUL union, organized at the Carleton tea room, the workers found that they were opposed by both the employer and the American Federation of Labor union. The owner pointed out that the restaurant had been non-union for eleven years. He called upon the American Federation of Labour-approved union, the Hotel and Restaurant Employees and Beverage Dispensers International Alliance, to collude in smashing the strike in progress.

Four employees – the day and night chefs, the soda fountain clerk, and the counter man – were fired for "insubordination" on 1 May 1934. They began picketing the restaurant on 3 May for eleven hours each day, from 11. AM until 12 midnight carrying a sandwich board on their backs and chests that read: "We are on strike at the Carlton Tea Room against long hours and seven days a week. Restaurant Employees Union FWIU of C (Food Workers Industrial Union of Canada)."

An injunction was quickly obtained against picketing. It was extended twice. By 19 May the fired workers decided to ignore the injunction and renewed picketing of the restaurant. In the meantime, in an effort to break the strike, the proprietor joined the AFL Hotel and Restaurant Employees Union. "I told the picketers Condos and Capasto, who were parading with the last mentioned sign in front of my restaurant, that I and my employees had now joined the International Union, that the sign which they were carrying was untrue and contrary to the injunction order, and requesting that they remove such signs forthwith. They just laughed and kept on parading with the signs."[36] The picketers were arrested and let out on bail. They again picketed the restaurant, aided by demonstrations of 100 to 150 people. By early August 1934, there had been seventeen arrests, but regular mass demonstrations were still being held. The outcome of the strike is not reported.

An article in the *Financial Post* lays most of the responsibility for labour unrest (or successful organizing efforts – depending on one's point of view) on the Workers Unity League. Strenuously objecting to the league's tactics, the *Financial Post* describes the story of one such organizing effort at the Two Minute Lunch on Adelaide Street, owned by Mrs Margaret Shyka. Mrs Shyka had "never had any trouble" with the six or seven "girls" she employed until the shadow of the WUL fell across her path.

One day, about a month ago, during the noon hour rush, three men entered the restaurant, and walked through to the kitchen where Mrs. Shyka was working. They told her her employees wanted to join the W.U.L. Union, the Industrial Food workers union. She had never seen the three men before and cannot read English ...

Mrs Shyka started to cry. She called in her employees and asked them what the matter was. She found that unknown to her, every employee had been canvassed by the W.U.L.

Mrs Shyka, however, had help to protect her from the "bullies" of the WUL. By the end of a month of picketing, she managed to secure a court injunction to make further picketing illegal.

The *Financial Post* maintains that this is a case "being duplicated in hundreds of restaurants across Canada." In Toronto alone, by May 1934, there were three locals comprising all workers in thirty restaurants in the city. In the words of the *Financial Post*,

this adolescent organization has in its brief career, instigated no less than nine strikes in the city of Toronto. Not one of these strikes has been started, or aided by the A.F.L. unit, the Hotel and Restaurant Employees Union. And the aim of the W.U.L. is to link every restaurant in every city across Canada in their union. [W.U.L. general secretary] Sims complained to the *Financial Post* that while these strikes were in progress, the A.F.L. union allowed their men to work for the restaurant.[37]

In 1937, the Hotel Association of Ontario put forward a minimum-wage proposal for male employees. Thirty cents per hour was recommended, for a regular fifty-four-hour week, and an allowable deduction of twenty-five cents for each meal eaten. When Quebec introduced a Fair Wage Act with a forty-eight-hour work week, the industry reacted vigorously. Such a limitation was declared "not only absurd but impossible," and "a menace to harmonious labour conditions."[38]

Because of the depression, there were plenty of workers available to work at low wages and production of a meal remained a very labour-intensive process even though, by the 1930s, much of the equipment currently used in restaurants was already available. Both Mr Ladowsky and Mr Boukydis had refrigeration in their restaurants.[39] Dishwashers, ranges, potato-peeling machines, and meat slicers were advertised in the trade journals.

Efficiency, portion control, standardization – similar principles to those used in large production industries – were beginning to be stressed. An article in the *Canadian Hotel and Restaurant* praising the kitchen and luncheonette in the "handsome new" Woolworth's on St. Catherine St. in Montreal describes the production line principle in the organization of the food service and notes that this "has lately become a highly developed feature in the mechanical layout of manufacturing plants."[40] In contrast to the kitchens described in the novels of an earlier period, this kitchen, with its stainless steel foodservice equipment, is described as "immaculate."

Each restaurant was a small manufacturing centre; meals were produced from raw materials with the help of both skilled and unskilled workers. In larger operations, machinery assisted in this process but the labour process remained reliant on the collective effort of the workers in a restaurant.

Eating out was still more expensive, and therefore not competitive with the dinner produced at home. By the 1930s, however, Canada had become predominantly urban and cities and towns had the population base necessary to support restaurants. Adequate transportation facilities, refrigeration, and cooking equipment were available so that a variety of foods could be obtained to be stored and cooked in restaurants. However, the same economic conditions that provided a labour force for low prestige, low-paid restaurant work also limited the size of the market. Most people did not have sufficient disposable income to make eating out a regular substitute for cooking dinner at home.

Gross sales in the restaurant industry declined during the first half of the 1930s; although they rose a bit by the beginning of World War II, sales in 1939 were still below what they had been at the start of the decade.[41] For most people in those years, making ends meet involved spending as little money as possible by doing more unpaid work at home. Family members took in boarders, cooked inexpensive meals from raw materials; in other words, stretched the budget by intensifying the work done at home.

Thus, during the 1920s and 1930s, eating out had become more acceptable but was effectively limited to the middle class. More restaurants offered full meals, and more people found themselves away from home during mealtimes. Judging from the articles in the restaurant journals, soda fountains and luncheonettes had become very popular. The *Canadian Hotel and Restaurant* magazine developed a special section for the magazine in the 1930s entitled "Soda Fountains in Canada."

The industry however, we must remember, has always been multilayered. Thus, in the second and third decades of the century, the restaurants in elegant hotels, or Murray's with its gleaming equipment, were only part of the restaurant picture. The small ethnic restaurants played a different role from those servicing the middle classes. They provided, for those without families, a supplement to boarding arrangements. These small restaurants also served as a focus for community life – places where people could meet, socialize, discuss politics, and bring their families.

THE EXPANSION OF
THE WORLD WAR II YEARS

Canada at war presented particular challenges to the industry. On the one hand, business was booming; by 1942, restaurant sales had doubled since the prewar days. By the end of the war, in 1946, industry growth had almost quadrupled since 1939. [42].

Many men were in the armed forces. Women were encouraged to help the war effort by leaving home to take on paid work or to do volunteer work. The labour force participation rate of women increased 50 percent in just five years: from 20 percent in 1938 to 30 percent by 1943. Many people worked swing shifts, instituted in factories to increase production, and many families were forced to share accommodations because of housing shortages. All these factors tended to increase restaurant patronage. Jobs were plentiful, and people had money in their pockets. Those living in crowded conditions and those who could not eat with their families ate out frequently. Butter, milk, sugar, and meat were in short supply in the grocery stores and so people turned to restaurants to provide variety in their restricted diets.[43]

While the demand for restaurants mushroomed, restaurant owners had a difficult time finding the materials with which to meet the newly expanded market. They too had to contend with restricted food supplies. Menus had to offer foods not deemed suitable for shipping abroad to feed soldiers; thus fresh fish, lobster, and salmon replaced the ham and bacon that could be sent overseas. Restaurants were allotted food on the basis of their prewar volumes, not their present customer numbers, which had expanded greatly. Equipment was difficult to acquire, and repairs were problematic – steel was needed for wartime use. The government put limits on practices involved in serving customers as well. A law passed in 1945 limited discriminatory practices in restaurants. Owners had to remove signs indicating "gentile clientele only," but they were still allowed to declare that they were catering to a "restricted clientele only."[44]

Labour supply, of concern to restaurant managers even in the midst of the depression, became a major problem for restaurant owners. A restaurant association official deplored the "class of help restaurants are forced to hire these days." Many of them were "practically useless," he complained, tending to work two or three days and then leave. Dishwashers were hardest to find, but skilled cooks and waitresses were not easy to come by either.[45] An Ontario Act proposed in 1944, limiting maximum hours to forty-eight a week, was seen as "adding straw to the already ladened camel." The industry's vigorous opposition led to a compromise: split shifts remained illegal, as originally proposed in the bill, but a maximum of one hundred hours of overtime every four months was allowed.[46]

Another response to the scarcity of labour was a plea for improved working conditions. The supervisor of Eaton's restaurants, Miss M.M. Ryley, felt that more humane treatment of restaurant workers was in order, particularly in the food preparation area. For example, she felt that tables and chairs could be provided so that workers cutting up vegetables could work while seated.[47] She pointed out that food workers were most often women who had households to maintain when their job at the restaurant was over.

Paying better wages was apparently not a strategy that was seriously considered. Labour remained very cheap. One American restaurateur recollects that "we didn't concern ourselves with productivity because at those wages, thirty-five cents per hour, we didn't have to. Productivity meant only one thing – the speed with which you got the order to the customer."[48] Mr Boukydis, the proprietor of Diana Sweets, recalls:

Restaurants were extremely profitable during the war. The competition was limited because before things started to boom, nobody could build restaurants. It was extremely difficult to get staff. I don't remember distinctly, but the quality must have suffered terribly. There just weren't any people around to do the work. The most vivid memory of the war and the postwar years was a tremendous shortage of people. In those years, nobody would work in the industry except immigrants and of course there weren't any immigrants during the war and for quite a few years after.[49]

The industry, faced with the serious shortage of labour, searched for ways of organizing the work so that those people already employed would not move elsewhere. They sought to use management strategies that had been developed in industrial manufacturing situations. If spontaneous interest was not a natural outcome of what employees were doing at their jobs, a way must be devised to make employees feel pride in their work. Employers were reminded that it was their job to create a sense of cooperation between workers and their employers, to get workers to feel as if their personality and dignity were respected. The management advice in a magazine published in the 1920s was to "treat workers as human beings. Show your interest in their personal success and welfare. That is, if the work holds no interest, show your interest in the worker."[50]

Sociologists and psychologists developed a new approach to this problem of workers' morale known as the human relations approach to industry. Industrial sociology dates from the work of Elton Mayo and the famous Hawthorne experiments of the late 1920s. Concerned with the causes of output restriction and low productivity, Mayo "discovered" the importance of the solidarity of worker relationships.

Mayo operated from the conviction that industrial conflicts were harmful and could be eliminated through the cooperation of employers and workers. The Hawthorne experiments supposedly demonstrated how the informal social groups that develop at the workplace can be used to minimize conflict, and thereby to increase productivity.[51] The Hawthorne General Electric studies provided the "scientific" basis for attempts to manipulate workers' attitudes, a practice subsequently explained and justified as management "theory."

Everett C. Hughes, one of the prominent sociologists studying work during that period, pointed out the value assumptions in industrial sociology's study of restriction of output. He noted that it is implied "that there is someone who knows and has a right to determine the right amount of work for other people to do."[52] Nevertheless, proponents of the human relations approach to industry, Hughes included, saw no necessary contradiction between making the workplace better for workers and increasing a company's profitability. Indeed, they felt the contrary was the case.

Everett C. Hughes, along with William F. Whyte, W. Lloyd Warner, Robert Havighurst, Burleigh Gardiner, and Frederick Harbison, organized the Committee on Human Relations in Industry at the University of Chicago in the early 1940s. In December 1943, the National Restaurant Association and the University of Chicago entered into an agreement to further the development of education and research in restaurant administration. The restaurant research carried out from 1944 to 1945 under the leadership of William Whyte was one of the projects undertaken by the Committee on Human Relations in Industry.

William Whyte's study, *Human Relations in the Restaurant Industry*, found that the division of labour in the kitchen constituted a status system in the restaurant. The kitchen staff in the chain restaurant he studied (Stouffer's later bought out by Nestle's) was large, consisting of forty-five workers, excluding dishwashers. Staff members had arranged themselves into a complex prestige hierarchy, which according to Whyte was only partly related to the skill of the work done. Those dealing with more desirable materials in the cooking stages were at the top. The most prestigious workers were those who cooked on the range. Next came the people working at the chicken and meat preparation stations. Those who worked on the fish station were at the bottom of the status hierarchy. The successful running of this restaurant was a complex affair. From the kitchen, runners took the food to the service pantry where it was portioned out by pantry workers to the waitresses. A checker was stationed at the exit of the service pantry to make sure that the right portions of food were provided. William Whyte comments:

Timing and coordination are the keynotes of the operation. If the customer does not get his food when he wants it, he is upset. If the waitress cannot get it from the service pantry, she chafes at the delay. And so on down the kitchen. A breakdown anywhere in the chain of production, transfer and service sends repercussions through the entire organization. No one can fail to feel its effects, for the restaurant is an organization made up of *highly interdependent parts*. If one part fails to function, the organization can no longer operate. The parts are the people who handle the food and adjust their work to each other. But cooks, pantry girls, waitresses, and other workers are not the only important parts. To keep this delicately adjusted machine functioning requires supervision of a high order. At each important point there must be a supervisor helping to organize the work of the employees and to organize their relations with each other to eliminate friction and build up the cooperation essential to efficiency.[53]

This view of a community of interest between workers and management, and the notion that management can learn to ease conflict and behave humanely towards workers, is one that informs Whyte's view of the restaurant industry. At the time of the research, when wartime conditions had created a labour shortage in the industry, strategies designed to lessen labour turnover were welcomed. Minimizing conflict was seen as helpful for all parties concerned and conflict was not considered basic to industrial organization. Problems that resulted from a change in the organization were presented as challenges for management to solve.

In the introduction to *Human Relations in the Restaurant Industry*, Whyte presents the case of Tom Jones, the restaurant owner who "starts at the bottom and reaches the top."[54] At first Tom Jones and his two employees work together as countermen and dishwashers. Business improves, and Jones moves to larger quarters. A differentiation of tasks is instituted, and some employees work in the kitchen, some serve the food, and some wash the dishes. Jones continues to maintain a close relationship with his customers, and is there to smooth over the coordinating problems in the work of his staff. As business continues to prosper, a more extensive division of labour occurs, which includes the employment of an elaborate supervisory staff, and the delegation of direct supervision to Jones' subordinates. Mr Jones' personnel problem changes from how to get the cooperation of the workers to how to get the cooperation of the supervisors, who in turn will get the workers to cooperate.

Finally, as the restaurant organization expands, Jones "discovers" that it also tends to move towards standardization. The passive term indicates that this growth and change in organization is removed from Mr Jones' decision-making power, or, for that matter, from that of any human agency in the restaurant business.

New problems present themselves. Mr Jones enters the chain restaurant business. This expansion requires that both food and service must be standardized, or in other words, the restaurant must use "standard recipes as well as standard service procedures."[55]

Jones approaches the chef of his first large restaurant, promises him job security, and asks him to write down his recipes.

The chef did not respond well to this request … Operating without written recipes, the chef was king of the kitchen. The manager might find fault with some of the dishes but, not knowing how they were made, he could only bring the matter to the chef's attention and hope for the best. If recipes were furnished, the manager could then supervise the chef much more closely. He could check to see that the recipes were being followed. He could bring in new recipes and revise old ones. Furthermore, this standardization would tend to take the skill out of the job and much of the prestige with it. It had taken the chef years to learn his craft, and now, in a small restaurant down the street, cooks were being trained through standard recipes in a matter of weeks. And women were taking over those jobs too. It all went against the grain, and the chef did not want to be a party to it. So he balked. And Jones wondered whether it would be possible to change the chef, or whether a kitchen with standardized recipes required a fresh start, with inexperienced workers and a college-educated food production manager to train them. That was a major problem but there were others like it. Jones came to the realization that every standardization of procedure involved important changes in work routines and human relations. Unless these changes were skillfully made, the morale of the organization would deteriorate. Within limits, standardization was clearly necessary for business reasons, and so he faced another problem. How can I gain the benefits of standardization without losing employee morale and cooperation?[56]

Certain unquestioned assumptions run through Whyte's descriptions: that growth in the scale of business to maximize profit is natural and inevitable, and attendant conflicts are undesirable and avoidable. These assumptions, like those in the Hawthorne studies that provided the model for Whyte's research, come from a view of industry and its role in society heavily influenced by the ideas of Durkheim. From this perspective, there is no conflict between finding ways to improve the company's profitability and creating a better place for employees to work.

Many working people interviewed told us that they made their friends in their places of work. This means that if a restaurant is not a good place for employees to make friends with each other, then it will not be considered a good place in which to work. Furthermore, the behaviour of workers in actually doing their jobs is strongly influenced by the group of cliques that form. This was borne out in the trail blazing Western Electric study. After years of scientific experimentation, unparalleled in this field, the researchers concluded that these informal organizations among workers were a greater influence upon the rate of production than money incentives, rest periods, and a number of other material factors.[57]

The results of the Hawthorne studies signaled to management the need to find ways of getting the informal groups that exist in any workplace to identify with management. This led to a concern with the emotional life of employees. Managerial philosophies based on the work of social psychologists such as Maslow and Herzberg stressed the need for satisfied employees.

Restaurant expansion during the war years was limited by the same factors that led to increased demand. People had jobs and they had money; given a choice, few wanted to work in restaurants. Crowded housing conditions made people want to frequent restaurants, but new restaurants could not be constructed, nor existing ones expanded. Food on the grocery shelves was rationed, but restaurants also had to cope with limited supplies. As Mr Boukydis recalls, the constraints under which restaurants operated during the war years did not disappear overnight when the war ended. Equipment was still hard to obtain, and meatless days when restaurants could only offer vegetarian menus stayed in effect as late as 1947. A suitable supply of labour remained a serious issue. The war years had transformed eating out into a major industry; but restaurant owners were not optimistic about how long the boom would last.

Relatively small operations, with working proprietors, still characterized the restaurant industry in the post-war years. In the 1951 census, 10,191 restaurants were enumerated with 12,378 working proprietors.[58] Although eating out in the 1950s was still restricted to the few who had no choice, rather than a way of life for most people, the seeds for a transformation of the industry were being sown.[59]

SEEDS OF CHANGE – RESTAURANTS IN THE 1950S AND 1960S

Money by the Roadsides

The noisy, hard-riding auto of yesteryear has become the sleek, powerful family car of today. Muddy roads have become superhighways and the ranks of car owners legion. Indeed this is a country on the move and because of this, road-side services have increased not only in number but, like the automobile, sleekness and comfort. Motels, restaurants, service stations hedge our busy main roads, jostling for the business and the favours of the passerby.[60]

At the end of World War II, approximately 10 percent of the population owned cars.[61] Ten years later, in 1955, not only had the population increased by 25 percent, but there were now four million vehicles on the road – an increase of almost 400 percent. In 1952, television had not yet come to Canada; three years later, families all over Canada were tuning into thirty-three channels on a total of 1.5 million TVs.[62]

The transportation and communication facilities developed after the turn of the century became widespread in the post-World War II period. New industries established during the war (e.g., aircraft, manufacturing, diesel engines) continued to grow, while the capacity of other industries (such as steel) permanently expanded.[63] These developments led to the concentration of large labour pools in small geographical areas, and at the same time, concentrated consumer markets.[64]

The level of urbanization increased substantially; by 1961, 70 percent of the Canadian population was classified as urban. Government policy and low mortgage rates along with continued economic growth and the revolution in transportation contributed to the massive suburban migration and growth of metropolitan areas during the 1950s.

Restaurateurs discovered a new market – the average family at home. Whereas previously restaurant patronage was seen as respectable only for those away from home at mealtimes, now something else was happening that looked "like magic." "It's a magic that enables any restaurant to be as big as a city, to gather profits as big as the operator's imagination and to do these things without major capital outlay."[65]

This market is to be lured by take-out menus. The food must not suffer from jostling, a system must be arranged for patrons to easily give and pick up their orders, and most importantly, patrons must know they can obtain food to be carried away. Here the take-out dollar must compete with the supermarket. The restaurant meal must look better to beat the grocer's TV dinners.

The meal cooked by the housewife nevertheless remained the most challenging competition: "She puts love into her cooking." Advertising "using all the gimmicks and approaches you can think of" was necessary to counter this competition. One suggested approach was: "Tired of spring housecleaning? Don't cook dinner, call us." Another, "Save your pep for the picnic." A really good one, "Too hot to cook?"[66] Strategies were also suggested for attracting the teenage market with their limited pocketbooks. Restaurant proprietors were encouraged to cater to this group by placing inexpensive items on the menu, and to turn the inconvenience of having noisy teenagers around into a profit-making activity:

Teenagers love noise – loud raucous noise. The high pitched gabble, the teenage version of small talk can drive an adult almost to the brink of insanity ... Yes, teenagers are a problem, a headache, but their patronage can be turned from a hindrance to a help. Eventually even the youngest become an adult – and a legitimate customer. Even in their somewhat metamorphic state, they can prove to be good, though not affluent, customers when handled with imagination, determination, restraint and authority.[67]

With an eye to exploring how well this element of the market – those who had be lured away from home cooking – was being served, *Restaurants and Institutions* magazine investigated the eating places in the small Ontario town of Bowmanville. The results were disappointing. The menu was too long, not merchandised properly, and although meal prices were low, the food was much too plain, without the attractive garnishing that would appeal to those weary of home cooking. Actual production of the meal was termed too "primitive." Cooking was done on a coal stove, dishwashing and food preparation were done by hand. Only one of the restaurants had a slicer.[68] These problems were not the only ones limiting the growth of the market in suburban areas. In 1959, Diana Sweets restaurant in Don Mills reported a shortage of workers to be the most difficult problem in the new suburban expansion. "Perhaps the greatest single factor that had to be considered was labour. Lack of staff is the bane of most suburban food service operations. It costs them dearly in actual loss of business."[69]

Now that the opportunities for expanding restaurant operations were broader than ever before, how was the industry going to meet this challenge of labour supply? At first, mechanization was pushed. Machines that had actually been available since the 1920s and 1930s were seen as a means not only of saving labour, but of improving morale. Thus potato and vegetable peeling machines, slicers, mixers, and dishwashers were recommended in order to improve efficiency but also to increase a restaurant's "ability to hire help at all."[70] With jobs plentiful in most parts of the country, and wages going up, getting a dishwashing machine was recommended so that the "Help Wanted" sign could be changed from "Dishwasher Wanted" to "Dish Machine Operator Wanted"[71] and a "better class of worker" attracted. Another restaurateur argued for paying people more, and charging them for restaurant meals. Making workers *feel* important, the human relations approach to industry described earlier, was stressed.

The vice-president of the Canadian Restaurant Association noted that "I have purchased many pieces of fine equipment just to make the staff work a little easier. Make them feel that it has been purchased for them ... Make them feel that you cannot continue without their help and cooperation."[72] However, this approach had its limitations. Mechanization may lead to happier employees, but it will not guarantee increased profits to the employer. A restaurant manual made this clear.

In a restaurant which served guests for lunch, one employee, working at a sink, washed all the glasses, china, and silverware. To increase efficiency, the restaurant operator installed a single tank dishwashing machine. Later, he was advised to install a conveyor type machine to save the work of opening doors and pushing the racks through. Still later, the restaurant operator replaced the conveyor type with a flight type machine, to eliminate the work of handling racks. After all these improvements at the company's expense, how much labour was saved? The restaurant is still using one employee to wash the tableware for 100 customers. True, their employee's work has been made easier and time has been saved. But the time has been saved for the employee – not for the restaurant![73]

By the mid-1950s, more successful approaches to the labour problem were found. As the title of one article phrased it, "Labour costs leave you no choice."[74] Use of paper products and plastic wraps was suggested as one way to keep labour costs down; getting the customer to do the work was also recommended. One restaurant man, Mr Spence, claimed that what customers objected to was inactivity; just as they do not mind serving themselves in the supermarket, they would not mind carrying trays if there was no delay in service. A limited menu restricted to items with a short preparation time would make fast service possible and would also be useful in streamlining operations.[75].

Suggestions for the use of pre-prepared foods began to appear. The Institutional Sales Manager for Kraft Foods Ltd. urged restaurant owners to "throw away the jam pots."[76]. Food manufacturers were encouraged to look beyond the supermarkets to the institutional market for food sales. Products such as pre-sliced cheese and portion-control packs of jellies and ketchup were introduced in 1952, and actively promoted by the end of the decade. In another article, the same Kraft official noted that food consumed outside the home represents a multimillion dollar market and "rich rewards await the food manufacturer who realizes the peculiarities of the institutional market."[77] By 1960, one author reported that developments in the freezing process for fruits and vegetables were so far advanced that they represented an important consideration in the profitable operation of food service.[78]

Thus technology was seen as a potential solution to the problem of ensuring an adequate labour supply. By the mid-1950s, *Restaurants and Institutions* magazine was asking, "Is the manufacturer replacing the chef?" "In more leisurely times, the restaurateur, his chef and his staff could satisfactorily meet the requirements of customers in food preparation and service. The demands were perhaps fewer and certainly less urgent. But today the demand for both speed and excellence in food preparation has overtaken many a restaurant operator."[79]

Only a few years later, the solution to the perennial problem of the industry – lack of skilled labour willing to work for low wages – had been found. "Convenience foods," foods prepared in central locations by food processors, had become part of the bright future of the industry. These, together with frozen and dehydrated foods, would transform the industry. One restaurant official declared in 1967 that "custom-made food will soon be as luxurious as custom-made automobiles and shirts." He predicted that as food processing was done more and more by manufacturers, restaurant food would become increasingly similar in quality and variety within the competitive price area. The result would be less competition based on quality, more based on service and atmosphere.[80] The president of the National Restaurant Association in a speech in Montreal viewed these developments as the "answer of the little man's plight against the chains in a new area of 'total retailing.'"[81] The small restaurateur was reassured that his special knowledge of his clientele would outweigh the size advantages of the larger chains. When labour costs rise, then the industry must turn to preprocessed products.

To go the heart of the labour problem, management must concern itself not just with attracting workers to the workplace but also with what happens while at work. "Successful restaurant operation depends on complete cost control, based on time and performance factors that are *exact and unwavering*. That means the use of automatic equipment, a mechanical labour force."[82]

Thus, we see how in the earliest days of restaurants, neither the population concentration for a large market, nor the technology and raw materials needed to serve them was available. By the 1930s, immigration and urbanization had provided a population base, but not a very extensive market, as most people could not afford to eat out during the depression years. The technology for the restaurant as the site where food was manufactured was well developed. A supply of labour was available, and the organizing principles of scientific management were applied in the larger establishments. However, economic conditions limited industry growth during the 1930s.

The prosperity of the World War II period made the demand for restaurant services high, but the difficulty of finding cheap workers and the scarcity of materials made it difficult for restaurant owners to take full advantage of the demand. In the post-war period, a qualitative change in the industry occurred: previously, restaurants were built to meet an existing demand – of travellers, or others away from their families at mealtimes. Now, for the first time, advertising encouraged the family that might otherwise eat at home to buy their dinners in a restaurant. Thus, the potential was created for an enormous market expansion. However, availability of workers remained a serious problem. Although at first technology had been suggested as a means of luring workers into the industry by improving working conditions, by the 1960s a more profitable avenue was discovered: World War II developments in paper products, plastic wraps, freezing foods, and dried foods began to be used in restaurants to minimize the need for labour. Thus the pressure to find skilled chefs and enough dishwashers was lessened by the application of new technology to the restaurant industry, and by the discovery of a plentiful labour supply in the same area targeted as a growing market – the family.

CHAPTER THREE

The Fast Food Invasion

It is ridiculous to call this an industry. This is not. This is rat eat rat, dog eat dog. I'll kill 'em before they kill me. You're talking about the American way of survival of the fittest.

Ray Kroc, founder of McDonald's[1]

Since the late 1960s, the map of Canada, once full of regional disctinctions, has been transformed. Fast food restaurants of a handful of chains have colonized the suburbs from coast to coast, obliterating local differences in taste and style. Each town displays the familiar logos of the fast food stores themselves – neat, clean, and orderly, all offering the same menu items, prepared the same way, from Nova Scotia to Vancouver Island. By the 1970s, fast food restaurants had ventured downtown; urban as well as suburban residents had a number of fast food restaurants within easy reach, often located side by side. For example, by the mid-1980s, the Yonge Street strip in Toronto, between Bloor and Queen Street and under a kilometre in length, boasted five McDonald's, three Burger Kings, two Wendy's, and two Harvey's.

The restaurant business in Canada has grown enormously. While the number of eating establishments increased by 50 percent from 1961 to 1986, in that same period sales grew from $795 million annually to over $12 billion.[2] People are spending almost five times more of their money in restaurants than they did a generation ago. The concentration in the industry is such that gross world sales for McDonald's alone were $17.3 billion annually by 1989, more than the entire Canadian restaurant industry.[3] In Canada in 1988, McDonald's grossed over $1.4 billion. This one company accounted for over 30 percent of the market share for fast food restaurants in the country.

McDonald's total sales amount to more than the gross national product (GNP) of many countries. Foodservice sales in the top 100 U.S.-based companies amounted to $82.4 thousand million. The three largest companies – McDonald's, Pillsbury, and Pepsico accounted for more than 37 percent of this revenue. Half a billion dollars was spent by McDonald's and Burger King (owned by Pillsbury at the time) just in television advertising in 1987.

How did the phenomenal growth and concentration of this industry occur? Several features, distinct but interrelated, need to be identified to understand what fuelled these giants and what made this growth possible. I will begin by discussing why growth is so important for business in general, and for this industry in particular.

In Canada, as in the United States, large corporations harnessed the capital and energies of small entrepreneurs through franchising arrangements. Giant food-processing multinationals then entered the restaurant business directly by buying out a number of these chains. This provided the financial base for aggressive advertising strategies which, in turn, developed a broader market for fast food. The ingredients were in place for the implementation of a different kind of labour process, one that replaced the "erratic elegance of the craftsman" with the "munificent predictability of the machine-tender."[4]

WHY GROW?

Marxists and management theorists alike agree that a business that stays still, content with its current development, is a business that will soon die. The need to maximize profit propels capitalists both to expand the market by growing larger, and to employ less skilled labour, that is at once cheaper and more easily controlled. It is not "human nature," but a particular organization of industry that explains the desire for more profitability, at the expense of worker, the consumer, or both. Individual businessmen have only two choices – to compete, to grow and to increase their profits, or to fold.

The imperative for growth was identified by Marx as intrinsic to industry under capitalism. The driving force for enterprises is the accumulation of capital. Capital must lead to more capital. Goods are produced not to be used but to be sold. Their use is only a supplementary aspect in their ability to sell. Thus, even when these products prove damaging to our health, there is resistance to controlling their distribution. Tobacco is a glaring example of this, but there are others within the restaurant industry. Although the use of sulphites can cause severe allergic reactions, and even death to people with asthma, both the United States and the Canadian restaurant associations objected to requiring large fast food companies to list the ingredients used in their food on the wrappers, as a protection to those sensitive to these substances.[5]

Owners can improve their profits in several ways. The first is to get workers to work long hours for low wages. When there is a scarcity of work, and starvation is the alternative, this remains a desirable strategy. We saw these conditions in the early days of the restaurant industry, up until World War II.

Another strategy is to find workers who will work for cheaper wages. The restaurant industry employs immigrants who have difficulty finding better paying jobs, women with family responsibilities, and young people. As these groups are in short supply, they now turn to older workers and handicapped people.

Through the introduction of new technology and a reorganization of work, it is possible to eliminate the need for expensive skilled workers, and use cheaper unskilled labour. This also makes possible yet another strategy to increase profits. When labour laws limit the length of working hours, an owner can still develop ways of making employers work harder. This is easier to do with an unskilled hamburger flipper than with a highly paid chef on whom the restaurant relies for the production of a tasty meal.

Although many of us have a vision of history as one of constant progress, when considering the lives of working people, Marx tells a different story. As industry developed from what he characterizes as craft, to manufacture, to large-scale industry, conditions for workers changed, and not for the better. With manufacture, as in the restaurant William Whyte studied, the workers are divided into categories of skilled and unskilled, and inserted into a hierarchical structure.

Skilled workers, however, are more difficult to control. Thus capital must constantly wrestle with their insubordination.[6] With the development of large-scale industry, the difficulties caused by workers are more easily held in check. In place of the coordination of skilled workers required in manufacture, the work is done by the machines themselves. The instruments of labour (the technology used in production) are converted from tools that workers use into machines that workers tend. The same operations that used to be done by hand are now done by the machine. The simplicity of the work means that skilled workers are no longer required. Machine work can be quickly learned by young, inexperienced workers, and a rapid and constant turnover will not interrupt the labour process.

Along with the tool, the skill of the worker in handling it passes over to the machine. The capabilities of the tool are emancipated from the restraints inseparable from human labour power. This destroys the technical foundation on which the division of labour in manufacture was based. Hence, in place of the hierarchy of specialized workers that characterizes manufacture, there appears, in the automatic factory, a tendency to equalize and reduce to an identical level every kind of work that has to be done by the minders of the machines.[7]

This process enables the capitalist to extract more profits, but his profits are useless if they are not invested to increase his capital and his profits still further.* In a society that is based on markets, the only way to retain one's privileged position is to own as much productive property as possible. An owner has no choice but to try to remain competitive. If he doesn't, he will soon be driven out of business by the competition. This means finding ways of extracting more surplus value than his competitors, and also of finding new places where his surplus can be turned into profit. Of course, his competitors will imitate him if they can, and so the race is a constant one. An expanding industry gives rise to other expanding industries. Restaurant expansion benefits the construction industry, suppliers of raw materials, financial institutions, and insurance companies, to name just the most obvious. Advertising agencies, radio, and television also derive profits from the expansionary needs of the restaurant industry.[8]

Strategies for corporate growth, couched in metaphors of "invasions," "battles," and "attacks" are directed towards several fronts. Some of the ways companies seek to grow include franchising, market expansion, mergers, and overseas expansion.

FRANCHISING

Franchising arrangements are advantageous to big business for a number of reasons. The franchise concept has allowed companies to expand rapidly without large outlays of capital. Franchising in-

---

* Business has long been a man's world, although as some noteworthy women such as England's Margaret Thatcher have demonstrated, the ability to be ruthless is not necessarily exclusive to one gender.

volves the right to sell certain products, under a recognized name, in exchange for a fee arrangement. The items are backed by national advertisements and suggestions for standardized on-the-spot promotions. The operator is given protection from same-name competition in his or her area. The products generally are limited in number and are offered together with prescribed ways of preparing them, using specified machinery purchased from the franchisor.[9] To acquire these privileges, the operator pays a franchise fee, a percentage of sales as royalties, and another percentage of sales in payment for advertising. Technically, the franchisee of a large company is counted as an independent businessperson. When Statistics Canada tallies up the number of chains and the number of independents in the restaurant business, they consider a chain a company that owns four or more establishments. By these calculations, Fran's restaurants in Toronto comprise a chain, while the holder of one McDonald's franchise would be counted as an independent businessperson. However, this legal independence does not mean control over one's own business.

Franchising is a good deal for a company interested in growing larger without investing its own capital. Individual entrepreneurs put up the money and the parent company benefits. Through royalty payments, companies profit from the successful operation of their franchisees, without needing to involve themselves in day-to-day business decisions.[10] However, the imperative for continued growth is strong. An ever-increasing number of franchises must open in order to continue to maintain growth.

Most importantly, franchising is a way of controlling managerial labour. The entrepreneurial energies of the small independent operator are now linked to a large company; the owner-operator has a vested interest in the profits a store makes.[11] Thus, from the point of view of a capitalist, franchising presents a route to meeting some of his competitive challenges, as well as meeting needs for devoted management.

Franchisees need to have two qualities: they must be willing to work hard and they must be able to take orders. The requirements for a desirable franchisee are contradictory. For example, she or he must have plenty of initiative but also not exercise it too much. Dick Dinelle described his criteria as director of franchising for Burger King Canada: "I am looking for free thinkers, entrepreneurial types. But I'm not looking for anyone who is going to try to change the system on me."[12]

Willingness to use the entire family and to put in long hours is another requirement. The franchisees must have the "backing of the whole family ... We are looking for the kind of person who is going to devote 110 percent of his energy into the business," said George Cohon, president of McDonald's of Canada.[13] Mr. Mills, a Burger King franchisee from Brampton, Ontario, described the seven-day-a-week schedule he and his wife undertake: "Judy would open the restaurant at 8 AM and I'd do the backroom work. Then we'd switch, and I'd stay in the restaurant until it closed at midnight."[14]

Given the nature of the restaurant business, bringing local operators together into large chains does not substantially improve productivity. (Productivity is measured as the output per unit of labour input.) Restaurants are very labour-intensive businesses, and fast food franchises remain labour intensive. Someone still has to sweep the floor, clean the tables, serve the food, and cook the hamburgers and fries. If bulk purchasing presents an advantage to an operator because of its simplicity, most of the cost benefits generally accrue to the parent company, not to the franchisee. Why would an independent operator choose to become part of a large franchise operation?

The answer lies in marketing. Where one small store is limited in the amount of advertising it can afford, systemwide promotional campaigns can have great persuasive power. The industry recognizes the crucial role of advertising in selling fast food.

It's been obvious ... that the top chains were following the lead of industry's major packaged goods companies who long ago turned to colorful wrappings and heavy advertising to establish a brand identification which would promote consumer allegiance to what, without the hype, could be seen as relatively dull, undifferentiated products.

As blind tastings have proven, it's easier to tell a Whopper, Big Whopper, Big Mac or Wendy's Single apart in television commercials than when you're eating them.[15]

THE FRANCHISED RESTAURANT COMES TO CANADA

The franchise came to Canada as a United States import,[16] first used by automobile manufacturers and oil companies for the distribution of cars and the selling of fuel in gas stations.[17] Howard Johnson's and A&W pioneered franchising in U.S. restaurants in the 1920s.

A&W first entered Canada in the 1950s; by 1960, 20 percent of the 2,000 A&W outlets were located in Canada.[18] By the mid-1960s, Kentucky Fried Chicken had also become a major investment franchise in Canada. Unlike A&W, where only the root beer was standardized, the franchise for Kentucky Fried Chicken required the operator to buy the cooking equipment as well. Mr. Boukydis, owner of Diana Sweets restaurants, recalls: "They'd buy the Colonel's system and recipes, and so on and put in his equipment, his pressure fryers, and that was it. Actually, the colonel made more millionaires in Canada, particularly western Canada, than anybody else. He made a revolution. He made millionaires in about ten cities in western Canada. They weren't really restaurants, they were takeout places."[19]

Franchisors were, for the most part, companies located in the United States. One Canadian exception, Gentleman Jim's Steaks, did well in the mid-1960s; taking no chances at placing "itself at a competitive disadvantage by revealing its Canadian origin," the company got itself a Detroit address from which to promote its product.[20]

Fast food franchising seemed like a bottomless gold mine in the early years: the promise of big money lured some small businesses into investing all they had and losing everything. Would-be investors were warned that "several of our American cousins have been badly bitten."[21] Nevertheless, in an industry with a very high failure rate, entrepreneurs sought out the reduced risks a franchise could provide.

Franchising, even in the 1980s, remained an area where some colossal frauds were pulled off. One, which was exposed in 1982, involved a company called Global Franchising, established in 1980, with a head office in Weston, Ontario. On paper the company was the third largest franchise operation in Canada, with 338 units in Canada and 1,093 in the United States.

Included in the list of seventeen chains owned by Global was Burger World, which claimed it would open a "robot" restaurant in Sarnia, Ontario. For this chain alone, apparently forty franchise units were sold at fees ranging up to $200,000. All of these chains were fictional! Only one restaurant ever opened in the entire Global empire. It was a steakhouse in the Toronto area that soon closed.[22]

Even when the franchise was legitimate, the advantages did not come cheap. In addition to royalty payments and advertising levies, capital expenditure was usually required, and could be quite steep.[23] In 1989, McDonald's franchises required an investment of $650,000.[24]

Fast food franchising had to contend with a tarnished image in early 1970, according to a speaker at a fast food seminar sponsored by the Ontario Region of the Canadian Restaurant Association. "Unfortunately, franchising has received a bad name, a very black eye because of dishonest, deceitful, deceptive practices of a few so-called franchising companies ... We have no use for the fast-buck fly-bynighters who give franchising the bad reputation it seems to have in the minds of so many."

Nevertheless, another participant in the fast food seminar remarked,

Fast foods are becoming popular things to write about, and discuss. They're becoming the hottest thing in the food service industry ...

You have your patrons – largely from the silent majority – Mr. and Mrs. Middle Canada, who whether by choice or the necessity for convenience, have by now partaken of your food many times. Perhaps, they were first enticed into your operation as they were driving out with the kids one Sunday afternoon.

This same Mr. and Mrs. Middle Canada may well become part of the great fast food boom, by investigating the possibility of buying a franchise, or investing money in the stock of fast food companies which have gone public.

You have have the growing and all-important youth market – 50 percent of the population is now 25 or under. They're the ones who used to clamour for a hamburger on Sunday afternoon, and now borrow your car to take the girlfriend down to the drive-in.

Franchising grew rapidly in the 1970's. In 1968, the *Canadian Hotel and Restaurant* magazine estimated that fast foods represented approximately 12 percent of all restaurant sales. In 1986, the *Financial Post* observed that half of the 40,000 commercial restaurants in the country specialize in fast foods, and half of these are franchised operations.

The US dominance of restaurant chains in Canada, noted in the early years of fast food growth, continues today. "Most franchisors here are affiliated with a u.s. chain, and as the u.s. market becomes saturated, an increasing number of franchisors look north ... One franchise manager for a United States fast food chain states, 'Canada represents the greatest franchise opportunity outside the u.s.a.'"[25]

Franchising was a way for us-based companies to take hold of the Canadian market. In 1982, the *Financial Post* reported: "u.s.-based franchisors could never have broken into the Canadian market had they not sold whole territories to local investors. Now the federal government is concerned Canada is losing out in terms of franchise fees and royalties flowing out of the country vs. the inflow."[26]

MERGERS AND ACQUISITIONS

During the late 1960s and early 1970s, large multinational food corporations entered the restaurant business directly. By 1970, 66 percent of the fast food business in Canada was in the hands of fourteen companies, and the predictions were for growing dominance of fast food by a handful of companies.[27] The greatest competition in the restaurant business was from the suppliers: "The food manufacturing giants are fighting for shelf space in the supermarkets with house brands manufactured by the grocery chains. They want new markets for their products, and they are going into the restaurant business."[28]

By the early 1970s, General Foods, United Fruit, and Lever brothers (a subsidiary of Unilever) all owned restaurant chains. Burger King became part of the Pillsbury empire and the second largest hamburger chain in the world. Kraft, a major food supplier, exercised strong control over the industry through its merger with Dart (the owner of Tupperware) and the acquisition of major restaurant equipment manufacturers such as Hobart and Kitchen Aid.

A new spate of mergers occurred in the 1980s. Kentucky Fried Chicken, previously owned by Heublein, then taken over by the large tobacco conglomerate RJR Reynolds, became part of Pepsico. In 1988, Pillsbury was taken over by an even larger company, Grand Met PFC, a British-based company.

Pepsico is the largest food conglomerate in the world with its ownership of Pizza Hut, Kentucky Fried Chicken, and Taco Bell. Added to this, of course, are the more than four hundred soft drink plants it owns or controls in over fifteen countries. Throw in a few transportation companies such as North American Van Lines, add a pinch of something different like the Wilson Sporting Goods company, and what you have is formidable concentration of wealth. Thus when the company decided to move into Canada with Pizza Hut restaurants, within one year Pizza Hut became one of the largest foodservice presences in the country.

Once the initial expansion of fast food was completed, the next step involved companies buying back the more successful locations from their franchisees. Thus George Cohon, who held the Ontario rights to McDonald's, purchased the western franchise and sold the entire Canadian territory back to the parent company. He, in turn, was made president of the Canadian subsidiary.

Permutations and combinations spin off from these major players in fast food. Horn and Hardart, for example, became a Burger King franchisee and at one point almost took control of the entire company.[29] Woolworth's and Greyhound food services are now Burger King franchisees.

A new twist are joint agreements made between two different franchise companies, such as a chicken and hamburger company, or supermarkets and a fast food chain. St. Hubert's Bar-B-Q had an agreement to sell chickens in Loblaws, while coupons for Swiss Chalet dinners were distributed in Dominion Stores. While buying gas for your automobile, you may be offered a discount to a fast food restaurant. In 1987 McDonald's started marketing a new line of children's clothing, called McKids, in an arrangement with Sears. It is also possible to buy a Fisher Price Toy McDonald's outlet, with a carrying case or a stand-up Fisher Price McDonald's "drive-thru" stand. The plastic food and McDonald's cap are extra.

Today, large conglomerates owning businesses unrelated to food service control most of the foodservice industry. (McDonald's is the exception.) The top three food chains, McDonald's, Burger King, and Kentucky Fried Chicken together account for more than 60 percent of sales of the top ten fast food restaurants in the United States. In Canada, by the mid-1980s McDonald's alone controlled over 50 percent of the hamburger market and 25 percent of all fast food business.[30]

EXPANDING THE NORTH AMERICAN MARKET

Fast food companies use a variety of techniques – media advertising, local promotions, games, coupons, giveaways, price discounts – to attempt to lure consumers into their stores. They also become involved in community activities in order to create a benign image of themselves.

For example, McDonald's in Canada is highly visible through its Ronald McDonald houses, although McDonald's is actually only one of the donors. Ronald McDonald houses are places designed for the families of sick children who live outside the city to stay in while the children are in hospital, or for children who are hospital outpatients. A new children's wing in Queen Elizabeth Hospital in Charlottetown, PEI, received a $35,000 donation from McDonald's towards the $2.86 million required to equip and furnish it. In turn, McDonald's was given the right to decorate the interior of the lounge, playroom, and some of the rooms. The *Globe and Mail* noted, "it's a likely bet that those interiors will bear at least a passing resemblance to a McDonald's restaurant and that Ronald McDonald and other corporate symbols may grace the walls."[31]

McDonald's drinks are donated to school picnics and community fairs. McDonald's gift certificates are promoted at Hallowe'en as a "safety" measure. Pepsico and McDonald's are now sponsoring fast food literacy programs for primary school children in Winnipeg. Students earn free fast food through Pizza Hut's "Book It" and McDonald's "Leading Road" programs. More than 15 million US schoolchildren are already getting their pizza coupons in this way.[32] All these approaches provide relatively cheap and effective advertising for the company.

One of the more inventive corporate charitable activities was dreamed up by a Burger King franchisee in the US mid-west. He organized a contest for elderly people; the two lucky winners would have their heating bills paid for the winter months of one year. Thousands entered the contest. Burger King workers raised the money by donating one hour of their time after their shifts doing extra chores such as washing the windows of cars in the Burger King "drive-thru." The contest was a big success. Sales and profits went up, and the promotion cost the store nothing. In addition, the idea was promoted that a heated dwelling in winter was the bounty of the lucky winners, rather than a right of all older people.[33]

McDonald's of Canada's support of Rick Hansen, the young athlete who travelled across the country in his wheelchair to raise money for paraplegics, carried the same message: What a generous company! McDonald's got some free publicity – the photographs of Hansen all included some McDonald's paraphernalia – and another message came across as well. The extraordinary efforts of an extraordinary young athlete are necessary in order for paraplegics to get a few necessary services. While strenuously opposing the raising of the minimum wage in the United States, or legislation giving employees medical benefits and maternity leave, in 1989, 700 restaurants in 48 cities raised $750,000 for food banks, three-quarters of their $1 million goal.[34]

McDonald's advertising has been so successful that the "awareness level" in North America for Ronald McDonald was quoted as being 96 percent, only slightly behind Santa Claus.[35] In Canada, Peter Newman reports that an Information Canada poll of primary school students on the identity of Sir John A. Macdonald found that 70 percent of the kids thought he had started a hamburger chain.[36]

The large fast food chains have also sought to increase sales by finding areas of expansion within the country. Doubling back on existing markets, such as people travelling on highways, is one strategy. When it was announced that Howard Johnson's had signed a deal with Burger King to change their highway restaurants into fast food outlets, even the industry newspaper expressed concern about the fate of the small businessperson in food service in the 1980s.

Remember the good old days when mom and pop franchisees dominated much of the industry with an entrepreneurial spirit? But the realities of

Burger King on Campus

economics and a maturing business have made it much harder for the moms and pops to operate as franchisees or otherwise.

The result, as highlighted by the Howard Johnson-Burger King deal, has been a proliferation of major corporations becoming franchisees of other major corporations ... Something is lost when the old-time or the new-fangled entrepreneur is unable to contribute an individual pioneering spirit to franchising.[37]

Today, the major highways in Ontario are dotted with McDonald's and Burger Kings.

Expansion into institutional markets is another lucrative route. In 1984, Burger King signed an agreement with the Army and Air Force Exchange Service (AAFES) of the US Defense department, considered a coup by the industry. Burger King now has outlets on military bases throughout the world.

In addition to the military contracts, Burger King also has food-service agreements on college campuses. McDonald's has military contracts, and also services a number of schools, hospitals, and museums. One advertisement for investors for college campuses declares the Burger King to be "more popular than the football hero, the student government president or even the homecoming queen."

Even the expansion of the prison population in the United States is now seen as a suitable arena for market expansion by the large fast food companies. More prisons mean more meals, and feeding the large US prison population approached $100 million of business in annual revenue in 1989.[38]

In Canada, McDonald's holds exclusive foodservice rights at the Metropolitan Toronto Zoo. Explorations are being made to serve more food in schools and hospitals. McDonald's also won similar rights for the multimillion dollar domed stadium in Toronto, where they built eighty-one Skydome outlets in 1989.[39]

OVERSEAS EXPANSION

The need for new markets has chased the owners of capital over the surface of the globe. "It must nestle everywhere, settle everywhere, establish connections everywhere," Marx stated in 1848.[40] A 1988 *Fortune* magazine article concurred. "Today the competition for goods, services and ideas pays no respect to national borders."[41] In 1987, a *Globe and Mail* Report on Business article agreed that "overseas markets have become a necessity for the North American chains." [42] With one restaurant for every 400 people in the United States, the industry must search for virgin territory.

McDonald's now operates in forty-seven countries, including Yugoslavia and the Soviet Union. McDonald's sales in foreign countries doubled in the five-year period from 1982 to 1987, going from $1.4 billion to $2.8 billion annually. It is estimated that 40 percent of all new units will be in overseas markets.[43] Russia and China are only part of the worldwide areas McDonald's anticipates will help them reach their goal of "totally dominating" the foodservice business in the next fifteen years. The search is for countries with a strong middle class and disposable income.

In the meantime, four pizza chains, including Pepsico's Pizza Hut, have expanded into the Hong Kong market. Kentucky Fried Chicken, another Pepsico-owned company, has a 500-seat outlet in Beijing's Tiananmen Square, as well as outlets in Japan. The European Economic Community (EEC) is another enticing area. With only 7 percent of food dollars now spent there on away-from-home food, the potential for growth is very attractive.

Fast food expansion outside North America is not problem free. In Britain, for example, getting workers to say, "have a nice day" is tough. "It's a totally alien concept to them." In Spain, labour laws require all workers to be full-time employees, while in Germany advertisers cannot make false claims, offer incentives, or name com-

petitors in advertising.[44] Even more serious are provisions in franchise agreements that conflict with the antitrust laws of the EEC – particularly those preventing a franchisee from expanding into new territories. Ironically, one of the attractions of the East European market is the absence of strong trade unions, which are anathema to the fast food industry.

Mexico is the most recent territory to open up for expansion. Reduction of trade restrictions in 1990 is now making it possible for US firms to insist that their Mexican franchisees import specific equipment from the United States or elsewhere. Mexico's lowering of trade tariffs also makes it more feasible for products to be imported, as required by American Franchisees.[48]

New Excitement in Val d'Or —

CHAPTER FOUR

Burger King: A Case Study

There are only two things our customers have, time and money – and they don't like spending either of them, so we better sell them their hamburgers quickly.

James McLamore,
founder of Burger King[1]

Burger King is a useful case study to understand how franchises helped to expand the growth of fast food, and how the vast resources of a huge corporation influence the organization of work. With such a broad empire to administer, this transnational company can and needs to establish standardized rules for the training and deployment of both managers and personnel for all its outlets from one central location.

The Burger King company was founded in 1954, by two marketing and financial entrepreneurs, James McLamore and David Edgerton. By 1959 their strategy of selling a limited menu of hamburgers, fries, and soft drinks worked well enough that the partners had succeeded in expanding their business to five stores in Miami, each one a small building surrounded by a large parking lot. The owners then set out to form a nationwide chain of Burger Kings, all selling the same hamburgers, fries, and drinks quickly and cheaply.

Similar to other fast food pioneers, such as Ray Kroc of McDonald's and Harlan Sanders of Kentucky Fried Chicken, the Burger King founders sought to attract investors by giving away exclusive rights to large territories through franchise arrangements. Franchisees could then do as they wished. Some subfranchised sections of their territory, others bought land and built stores themselves, while some diversified into other fast food businesses, buying rights in a number of franchised chains. A Burger King franchise originally cost $25,000 including equipment, plus 1 percent of gross sales. By 1984, the standard investment was about $400,000, with 4 percent of gross sales on top of that.

The chain had grown to 274 stores by 1967, 35 of them company-owned. Then, during the first wave of mergers between food processors and restaurants, Pillsbury, the large food conglomerate, bought the entire company for $28 million. The Pillsbury empire extended to more than 85 countries, including holdings of canned and frozen goods such as Green Giant, Haagen Das ice cream, flour, and rice products.[2] In 1983, 50 percent of Pillsbury operating profits came from its restaurant operations.[3] In the fiscal year 1988, Burger King grossed $5.3 billion in its 5,500 units around the world. This enormous company was taken over by a still bigger one – Grand Metropolitan PFC, based in Britain – in early 1989.

Burger King's early franchising arrangements, made in the 1960s and early 1970s, sometimes proved troublesome. At first the company owned only a fraction of the restaurants, fewer than 20 percent. Some, known as BKLs (Burger King Licensees), were operated on land and/or buildings that belonged to Burger King. The largest and most difficult group to control were the DTLs (Direct To Licensees). The Direct to Licensees often held franchises to entire territories. Both the land and buildings were owned by them rather than the parent company. Thus, in 1972, one franchisee, Chart House, grew big enough that it attempted to take control of Burger King.[4]

Horn and Hardart, which held franchises for twenty Burger King restaurants in New York, also presented problems for the parent in the early 1970s. It attempted to expand by purchasing new Burger King outlets in California and including Arby's roast beef sandwiches along with Burger King products in its New York stores.[5] Through a series of court battles challenging the power of existing franchises, and imposing tighter regulations on new franchises, owners' powers were limited. By the late 1970s, franchisees had to live within an hour's drive of any of their Burger King stores, a policy that limited the number of restaurants any single operator could own. Although this new policy was publicized as an attempt to improve operations, it served effectively to curtail challenges to Burger King's power.

Burger King has had it ups and downs. In the mid-1970s, sales were sagging, and the company needed to do something drastic. They hired a new president in 1977, Donald Smith, who had been the third-ranking executive at McDonald's. (Smith was lured away from Burger King to Pepsico in 1980.) In a massive overhaul called "Operation Grand Slam," franchising arrangements were changed, marketing strategy was altered, and food production and labour operations overhauled to increase profitability. In 1974, Burger King wanted all its stores changed from conventional lineups to multiple lineups, using many cash registers, a system that had boosted sales in McDonald's. This new arrangement, called the "hospitality" lineup, was resisted by franchisees, who were reluctant to pay the cost of the additional cash registers and the extra help that would be required to operate them. The increased sales revenue from such expenditures directly benefitted the parent, who did not pay for upgrading the store. It did not necessarily increase profit for the franchisee, who had to foot the bill for the improvements; however with Smith's prodding, all outlets eventually converted to the new design. Company-owned outlets were renovated and Smith succeeded in convincing franchisees to do likewise by demonstrating the advantages of the remodelled Burger Kings. Stores became more elegant, with real shrubbery and soft lighting. The stores' new design boasted an open kitchen. The new units had no walls, and so customers could see what was going on. Smith felt that this arrangement improved productivity, as workers would work harder when they were in full view of the customers.[6]

"Drive-thru" windows were installed to increase sales. Fry preparation was changed to resemble McDonald's more closely. Fries were now made from potatoes with less moisture in them, sprayed with sugar to make them brown nicely, and cooked in shortening made from a mixture of animal fats and vegetable oils.[7] As part of the effort to turn Burger King around – that is, make the company more profitable – advertising was redirected to children. Although males aged twenty-five to forty-four were seen to be the single largest group of customers, Burger King management found that children have the biggest influence on where their parents take the family at dinnertime.[8] A new cartoon character called the "Magic Burger King" challenged children's loyalty to Ronald McDonald. Like the McDonald's character, the Burger King makes personal appearances at store openings and is featured in media advertising.[9]

Although Smith managed to reverse the company's sagging sales and profitability, the early high growth period of fast food ended in the United Stated by the mid-1970s and market saturation started to become a serious concern. In the five-year period from 1977 to 1982, McDonald's, Burger King, and Wendy's all lost ground in unit sales.[10] Burger King launched aggressive marketing campaigns to increase its position in the market. For example, the "Great Burger Wars" in 1982 claimed that Burger King's whopper hamburger was preferred by consumers over McDonald's and Wendy's. Both companies responded with lawsuits for "false and misleading advertising." One industry observer, noting that the taste test had never been used before for advertising for a national food chain commented, "Who are they fooling? No one goes to any of those places for a good hamburger."[11] Media coverage of the "Battle of the Burgers" gained Burger King an estimated five million dollars of free publicity.

While Burger King gained over Wendy's and McDonald's during the advertising campaign, all three companies increased their share of the hamburger market. Burger King unit sales increased 10 percent during the first month of the campaign, McDonald's unit sales went up 3 percent, and Wendy's 6 percent.[12] These wars, however, made some foodservice commentators nervous. Exalting Burger King's cooking at the expense of competitors could open a Pandora's box that would destroy "customer confidence" in fast food. The fear was that concentrating on the quality of the product would lead "to more health scares, more fads, more discoveries, more board of health restrictions and government rulings ad infinitum regarding food and its production, preservation, processing, cooking and serving."[13]

Burger King introduced new products and launched an aggressive effort to secure new markets. In the late 1970s and early 1980s Burger King sought to increase sales by expanding its menu to include a new meal – breakfast. In the wake of McDonald's success in this area, a number of fast food chains extended their hold to embrace the morning meal market, at the expense of independently owned coffee shops. Here again, the fast food chains were credited with "effectively creating the eat-away-from home breakfast market."[14] Franchisors were more enamoured of the expansion than the franchisees as the increased sales would increase their commissions. "The biggest breakthrough fast-food made was shovelling it down the throats of franchisees – because it was not profitable and in some places still isn't."[15]

BURGER KING CANADA

The first Burger Kings in Canada opened shortly after the Pillsbury buyout in 1969. Two were in Windsor, Ontario, and two in Toronto. These southern Ontario stores were administered through the northern United States regional offices in Detroit and Buffalo. In 1974, Burger King Canada was established, and in 1976, it became an independent division within the corporation rather than part of the Burger King International grouping.[16] Burger King expansion into Canada began in earnest in 1979. The similarities between the two countries are strong enough to make Canadian expansion far simpler than it would have been in other parts of the world, where it would have had to deal with the complexities of foreign customs, laws, and regulations. The expansion plan for the late 1970s and early 1980s called for the opening of fifteen new restaurants per year.[17] Plans for the 1990s had increased this number to twenty.

Taking a tip from the McDonald's real estate successes, the company prefers to control both land and building by leasing out the stores under Burger King Licensee agreements where possible. By the end of 1981, there were eighty-two Burger Kings in Canada, bringing in a total of $70.5 million in annual sales. Two years later, there were 113 restaurants and sales had increased to $124 million, making Burger King the tenth largest foodservice company in Canada.[18] By 1988, Burger King was the fifth largest foodservice company in Canada. When Pillsbury, the parent company, was swallowed up in a takeover by Grand Metropolitan PFC, Burger King was sold for $5.68 billion. The Canadian office, explaining that the new management is even more concerned about tightening up labour costs, confirmed that hundreds of people in the regional offices were fired in 1989 and 1990.

Some employees had no need to worry. Philip Smith, the departing chief executive officer of Pillsbury, earned nearly $8 million for the five months he spent with the company. His annual salary of $1 million doubled for liquidation damages. He received annual retirements benefits of at least $200,000 and in addition was able to tender his 75,000 shares in Pillsbury for $66 each for a total of $4.95 million. If he had difficulty finding a buyer for his $1.53 million house, Pillsbury offered to guarantee the equity.[19]

Although concentration of fast food chains by American-owned firms is increasing, the restaurant association does not view this as a problem. On the contrary, Burger King's growth of the past few years earned Burger King Canada an award from the Canadian Restaurant Association for "Hospitality Leader."[20]

While Burger King Canada is allowed some regional autonomy in its marketing campaigns, decisions on equipment, organization of the labour force, and principles for site selection are all made using formulas established at head office in Miami. There is now a National Training Centre located in the Toronto area, to train new managers for Canada. However, the courses offered are organized by Burger King University in Miami, Florida and senior managers (first assistants and head managers of outlets) are sent directly to Miami. Let's take a look at how the training is organized.

Burger King University

BURGER KING UNIVERSITY

Burger King University was set up in 1978, replacing the first training
establishment, Whopper College, established in 1963. Burger King
University is located in what the company calls the "perfect setting
for learning," a converted art museum in Miami. An elaborate fountain outside spews forth water that emerges in the shape of leaves.
A secretary-receptionist sits guarding the locked entrance to the
classrooms and offices. Behind her are two larger-than-life size
seated statues similar to the one of Abraham Lincoln in Washington
D.C. – homage to the founders, James McLamore and David Edgerton. The building is equipped with the latest state of the art
technology.

Inside are training rooms that include facilities for simultaneous
translation, small conference rooms, and an elaborate audiovisual
system that the company claimed in the early 1980s had the world's
largest rear-projection screen at that time. The computerized equipment can handle the programming of up to sixty slide projectors as
well as complete audio recording, remote control systems, and colour video taping. These are used for role-playing situations, for
example, between customer and manager.[21]

The university features what may be the only library in the world
with a television set at its centre. The books in the one-room library
and reading room include management literature and some Burger
King material. The administrative offices of the Burger King faculty
are designed on the open office concept, which means that every-

thing everyone says can be heard by others, and commented on with a hearty cheeriness.

The professors in the early 1980s were all white men, mostly in their forties.[22] They came from the field and had to reach the rank of franchise district manager for the company, which involves responsibility for about one hundred stores, before they were eligible to teach at Burger King University. Becoming an expert in any one area is discouraged as all the professors are expected to teach all the courses. The BKU faculty are charged with the responsibility for developing training programs for every level of employee in the system. These include three- and five-day courses for upper management and franchisees in areas such as franchise development, site selection, real estate, and marketing. The longest and most frequently given course is called AROC, the Advanced Restaurant Operations Course, which is an eleven-day program for head managers and first assistants. Attendance varies from sixty to ninety people for each course. About half the time is spent on management skills, with the remainder of the time divided between equipment maintenance, labour scheduling, and products. In each of the areas, consistency is the key factor. In this university, "profit is not a dirty word."[23]

In addition to the Advanced Restaurant Operations Course given in Miami, a Basic Restaurant Operations Course (BROC) is prepared at Burger King University and offered in the district offices. In Canada, the training centre is in Mississauga, Ontario. The crew training kit, entitled "The Basics of Our Business," was also prepared at the school, as were the film strips with accompanying tapes used in crew training at each local outlet. By the late 1980s, these were replaced with videos and each outlet equipped with a VCR.

At Burger King University, the greatest emphasis is on what Burger King calls "preventive maintenance" through "The People Game." This means teaching managers how to deal with their crew, as discussed in detail in Chapter 6. At one time, training of restaurant managers required instruction in many different areas. Accounting procedures used to involve hours of careful calculation to keep track of incoming orders, inventory levels, sales, customer counts, and so on. Now, store managers only need know the correct program entry number to access this information from the computerized cash registers.

The one important task left to managers is hiring and supervising a crew of workers. While the computerized machinery for assembling the meal has simplified the tasks workers must do, it has not yet replaced them. Thus the Burger King University curriculum for managers places more emphasis on how to control workers, and less on the actual skills needed for operating a restaurant. Managers must be proficient at selecting workers who will be available to work when needed, and trained to operate according to the rules and regulations of Burger King. They must be able to schedule and agree to come in or leave as needed, generally for three-hour shifts.

KEEPING THE UNION OUT

Although there have been sporadic attempts to organize in the fast food industry, the superior resources of these large companies, combined with a part-time high turnover labour force, makes unionization extremely difficult. Nevertheless, these large employers pay careful attention to the possibilities of unionization in their organization. At Burger King University, for example, managers are told that unionization efforts only occur as a result of "poor management." Furthermore, the running of a good restaurant is threatened when a union is organized. The following is a schema supplied in the Burger King University Advanced Restaurant Operations Course that demonstrates the pros and cons of a union from Burger King's point of view.

With a Union	Without a Union
• Contract causes wage levels to go up	• Reward good employees, your choice
• They control job assignments, cashiers must stay on cash	• You control moving staff around, from cashier to boards, etc.
• Forbids cross-training	• Manager cross-trains people
• Senior crew choose their hours	• Manager controls schedule
• Can't call in anyone (seniority)	• Call in anyone you please
• Counselling done by a steward from a union	• Manager provides counselling
• Can't change policy	
• Union doesn't like productivity	

In line with the notion that managers are the ones who have the power to motivate crew and make them feel that they and their jobs are worthwhile, managers are told that people who organize are not standing up for their rights. Rather they are "voting against management." Burger King cautions that one must be particularly careful with teenagers and housewives, because they are "more inclined to be upset."[24]

Thus it is argued that a union threatens company workplace control. Managers are warned that wages, job classification, and job discipline will all be determined by the union; the restaurant will be a changed place, where managers will no longer have access to the grapevine. The signs will be different; union notices and union newspapers will predominate, and there will be an increased curiosity about things like pension plans. Even vocabulary will change. People will start using phrases such as "workers' rights."[25]

If managers are faced with such a terrible prospect, they are warned that they must nevertheless obey the law. The acronym they must abide by is "don't SPIT" – don't spy, promise, interrogate, or threaten. Instead call head office if there is a union organizing drive, because this is a situation that must be dealt with by senior management. The notion of a collectivity with rights, rather than a group of individuals with needs and wants, to be urged on by a manager "coach," is very threatening to Burger King's organization of the labour process.

Handout from the Ontario Restaurant Association booth, Hostex Convention, 1984

Burger King's position on this is not unique to the industry. Management and unions agree on one thing – the key issue is control over the work. At Hostex 1984 (the foodservices exhibit held annually in Toronto), the Ontario Restaurant Association display offered a handout entitled "Unions are not inevitable." The pamphlet states that there is hope "if you start right now to follow a course of sound Positive Employee Relations" to "help you preserve your union-free position."

With a union present, the pamphlet warns, employees will no longer have the right to control their own businesses. Furthermore, the union is very expensive! Not only do unionized payroll expenses rise by 25 to 30 percent for "unwarranted wages and benefits," but unions also introduce expensive and cumbersome machinery through the constraining provisions of a union contract. The stress however, is on control. "You, the owners, directors and managers of their company, will lose the right to manage your business."

Thus, a union will challenge the tight centralized control that large fast food companies maintain over their empires. The increased wages are feared, but even more is the idea that workers may begin to think collectively and to develop the notion that they have rights in the workplace.

Photomontage   Richard Slye

CHAPTER FIVE

Working in a Burger King Outlet

The growth of the restaurant business and the expanded market for eating out can be viewed as the successful realization of the liberal vision of the good society. Business prospers, jobs are available for whoever wants them, and women need no longer be tied to the stove. Eating out is affordable and thought to be an enjoyable experience. Yet while the marketplace flourishes, and individual freedom reigns in that arena, the constraints that exist behind the scenes at work tell a less cheery story. For many people, in particular women and young workers, the kind of jobs available to them and the ability to use their creative abilities at work are very restricted.

Theodore Levitt, writing in the *Harvard Business Review*, describes how many jobs are now essentially "machine tending." From a business point of view, this is a brilliant innovation – applying the methods of the assembly line to the service industry. Thus, a McDonald's retail outlet is admired as "a machine that produces, with the help of totally unskilled machine tenders, a highly polished product. Through painstaking attention to total design and facilities planning, everything is built integrally into the machine itself, into the technology of the system. The only choice available to the attendant is to operate it exactly as the designers intended."[1] Karl Marx, in the *Communist Manifesto*, written over one hundred and twenty years earlier, described essentially the same process. "Owing to the extensive use of machinery and to division of labor, the work of the proletarians has lost all individual character, and consequently, all charm for the workman. He becomes an appendage of the machine, and it is only the most simple, most monotonous, and most easily acquired knack, that is required of him."[2]

What businesspeople celebrate as an advance, and the embodiment of freedom, others describe as the precise opposite. The conditions for freedom, from a socialist or Marxist perspective, are not free selling and buying in the marketplace, but the abolition of the ability of one group of people – capitalists – to appropriate the work of others in order to make a profit.

GETTING FIRST-HAND EXPERIENCE

Machine tenders are people, with hearts and minds. How do they feel about the work that they do? I wanted to explore what this job felt like from the inside. What is it like to be a machine tender?

Getting first-hand experience in order to do a study is a particular kind of fieldwork in sociology – called participant observation. It has certain advantages. Rather than deciding in advance what the important questions are, involvement in the situation allows researchers the opportunity to learn something they didn't know before. In other methods, such as surveys, findings are limited to confirming or disproving previously decided upon hypotheses. Yet reducing phenomenon to measurable operationalized variables, necessary with more quantitative approaches, often oversimplifies and distorts what we want to study. Reality is complicated and changing. The ongoing process that can be experienced when one actually goes into a setting more accurately captures what goes on than the static snapshots gathered through quantitative methods.

Data gathered through interviews or questionnaires give a certain kind of information – people's perceptions or attitudes about what they do. People's answers can be influenced by many factors and may not necessarily shed light on what the researcher assumes is the subject of the investigation. For example, an answer to whether one likes one's job or not could depend on any number of things: whether or not this was the only job the person could get, how it compares to other jobs she or he could expect to get, where the question is asked, what the respondent thinks the interviewer wants to hear. Sometimes answers do not jibe with what people actually do or think when they are in a situation. For example, one worker I knew would insist on how much she loved her job at Burger King, but when I saw her at work, she always looked bored and unhappy. A friend of mind who works with computers complains about going to his "cage" each day. Co-workers tell me that he almost always seems engrossed in his work, joking and interacting in a manner that miserable people who feel trapped could never do. Both responses give information that is useful. According to Mitchell, the intimacy one gains of the connections linking a complex set of circumstances is a good way of getting new insights.[3]

That's fine, but is it "scientific"? In many people's minds "science" can only tell us something if it presents itself as "objective" and

comes in the form of numbers, sample surveys, or statistical infer-
ence. Feminists, as well as Marxists, have pointed out that since
descriptions of the world come from men and women who also live
in it, scientists, like other human beings, invariably have a point of
view influenced by their gender, class, and race, among other things.
Rather than pretending to embrace a false objectivity, a good scientist
lays his or her cards on the table.

Fieldwork, as opposed to survey research, has its own rigour. The
in-depth knowledge gained from first-hand experience needs to be
put into context. If information is carefully and systematically gathered and documented, if there is suffcient related knowledge, and
the underlying theory is adequate, then a case study, using participant observation, is the best way of observing how general principles manifest themselves. [4]

When I decided to study work in the fast food industry, I realized
that the most suitable approach was to enter the setting and interact
as normally as I would in any situation. Sure, my presence would
make things a little different, but not substantially so. A fast food
restaurant would not reorganize the work because I was observing
it. Observing in a setting, without engaging in interaction with the
people around me, seemed to me to be deluding myself. I couldn't
be invisible, and so I would stand out even more. Besides, acting
as the removed observer would not only limit the information I
would have access to, but would give off the message that I thought
I was somehow "better than" or "above" the people I was studying.
I know I am luckier than many of the adult workers who have fast
food jobs but I certainly don't consider myself "better."

My first major challenge in doing this kind of research was getting
into a fast food restaurant, or gaining access to the field. The larger
fast food chains compete with each other constantly to increase their
share of the market. In addition to the fear that they will steal each
other's "secrets," there is the constant worry that labour organizers
will try to infiltrate their business in an attempt to unionize the
outlets.

I first attempted to approach McDonald's, since they are the largest
chain in Canada. I got as far as the comfortably furnished suite of
George Cohon, president of McDonald's of Canada. Carefully
watching the Ronald McDonald clock on the wall to make sure I
didn't overstay the fifteen minutes I had requested, I asked
Mr. Cohon for permission to work in a McDonald's outlet and to
attend their training school in Chicago, Hamburger U. I explained
that I wanted to know how McDonald's managed to take inexperienced teenagers and transform them into productive workers. He
responded that since I was not from a business school, he would

not turn me down outright, but would think it over. After considering my request, he wrote and said no. Figuring that I had little to lose, I wrote him again, asking just for permission to work as a crewperson. The reply was more than I had bargained for. Mr. Cohon sent a letter to the university where I was studying informing my adviser and the chair of my department that I was to cease and desist from all efforts to enter McDonald's.

My next step was to try the chain that used a labour process very similar to McDonald's, Burger King. With Burger King, I modified my request. I asked for as little as possible. I requested work as a crew member to better understand what the industry was like from the ground up and I indicated that it would not be necessary to put me on the payroll. I tentatively enquired about attending their local management training course "if they could arrange it." I left out any intention of interviewing anybody or asking questions that might make them defensive about the "secrets" of their operation. (I stuck to my bargain about not formally interviewing crew members, although I later regretted it. It is very difficult to capture the colourful way people have of commenting on their own situation without pen, paper, or tape recorder handy.) I was referred to the director of operations, and told that January and February were slow times for the store. If I wished I could ask again in the spring, when perhaps they could use me.

I was feeling pretty discouraged. Six months had gone by and all my plans seemed to be leading nowhere. I spent my time reading back issues of the restaurant trade journals in the George Brown Community college library. I found out that George Brown offered a ten-week training course to become a fast food supervisor. I enrolled, and it provided a valuable overview of how fast food businesses are run. This was later useful in determining how generalizable my findings in the Burger King outlet were. The course had an advisory body to which the major fast food companies, with the exception of McDonald's, sent representatives. (My teacher explained that because McDonald's has such a large share of the Canadian market, their main interest is in maintaining their leading position. They can afford all the company training they want, and don't find it in their interest to participate in cooperative efforts with other fast food operations. Burger King at the time was just beginning expansion plans for the Canadian market and didn't hold themselves so aloof from these cooperative efforts.) I attended the advisory committee meetings as a student observer. Mr. Cooper, director of the foodservices division at George Brown, who had been head of the Ontario Restaurant Association and had a long career in the field, shared some of his observations about the industry with me.

The George Brown experience helped in another way. The ninth week of the course was spent in "hands-on" experience. Students were sent to work in a fast food outlet for the week. A number of companies agreed to provide placements for the George Brown students and we could give our preferences as to where we would like to work. Burger King was on the list, and so I finally had my first introduction to the store.

When I arrived at the Burger King outlet, I was put through a fifty-hour course similar to the one they provide for prospective franchisees. I was trained each day at a different station and wore a crew uniform, brown polyester top with a yellow and brown stripe, a brown orange and yellow baseball cap, and brown shoes. Other workers were quite friendly, if a little unsure of exactly what I was doing there. They were used to prospective franchisees working beside them as trainees, but this was their first experience with a student from the George Brown course. Since I was going through the steps a potential franchisee would take in learning store operations, the final day was spent on supervisory functions, and so I was asked to dress like a manager, in brown slacks and a white shirt. When I appeared in this getup, I was no longer treated as just another new worker, and people seemed to keep their distance.

The week spent at Burger King helped when I once again contacted the Burger King director of operations at the conclusion of the course. I was able to show by my fast food certificate that I had a serious interest in foodservice. I was allowed to continue working in the same store I had been assigned to for my course, but was told it would not be possible for me to attend the management school. I worked full time for no pay until the end of the summer, and then part time until the following spring.

How did my experience feel? I remember feeling uncomfortable and frustrated most of the time. I felt that I was neither fish nor fowl. My position at Burger King was ambiguous. Despite my acceptance by other crew members both on the kitchen floor and in the informal camaraderie in the crew room downstairs, I was always different. My reasons for being there and my background were not like the other workers and most of the managers. I made it known that I was writing something about fast food. Everyone wanted to know if they would be in it.

I had to do whatever the managers told me to, but I hated it when their orders made no sense to me, and began to feel very sorry for myself. When I first started working on a daily basis after the George

Brown course, it seemed as if everybody had a right to tell me what to do. I tried to laugh at myself by comparing my research – which sometimes involved emptying trash cans in the Burger King dining room – with that of a colleague who spent two years in a lovely mountain village in the south of France doing her fieldwork. I bet I had more years of schooling than any other garbage collector in the whole fast food empire.

I had ways of bolstering my ego, of convincing myself that I was not just my Burger King identity. Only at Burger King, in this situation, was my status likely to be lower than the manager ordering me around. Even though I knew that, the managers could still make me feel pretty low.

Keeping detailed field notes was very difficult. The crew uniforms had no pockets, and so it was not possible to keep pen and paper handy. We were not allowed to leave the floor during the busy lunch and dinner rushes, and at other times one had to request permission. In any case, writing implements would have had to be kept in a locker, and it would take a suspiciously long time and be much too noticeable to attempt to write anything down during working hours.

I had to keep reminding myself that I might as well not be there if I wasn't going to make the effort to carefully record my observations. After nine hours a day on my feet, this took some effort. I also found that during the five months in which I was working full time, I became very disoriented. I was constantly forgetting appointments with friends, and housemates complained that I was not around either physically or emotionally. Leading a double life is difficult and, I later found out, my confusion was not uncommon.

I was always concerned about the one-sidedness of my relationships with other workers. Committed to a praxis model of research, which involves doing things *with* people rather than *to* them, the ideal situation would have been one in which the workers had invited me to participate in a project documenting their work with the aim of collectively working out strategies to improve their conditions. This was not the situation I was in, unfortunately. Therefore I was constantly agonizing over how limited was my ability to work together with the other workers. When people felt unfairly treated by a manager, or scheduled to work at inconvenient times, all I could do was sympathize. On occasion, I provided some information. For example, I brought in and passed around the handout from the Ontario Ministry of Labour on Employment Standards so that workers could see for themselves that they could refuse to leave early, if managers asked them to stop work before a three-hour shift was up. I explained how Burger King was organized, how the chain of command operated, and how profitable it was. However, I always had to be careful, because if I were suspected by management of being a "bad apple" (as one manager put it), I would soon be out on my ear.

A few months before I left Burger King, a new labour system was implemented. It was designed to increase efficiency by the time-honoured method of getting fewer people to do the same work. Where there had been a few women scheduled to work six- or seven-hour shifts during the weekdays, all crew were now, without exception, assigned work for only three hours at a time. This made a more intense work pace possible and eliminated the need for management to schedule breaks. Each week, I was working with new people whom I was unable to get to know very well. The changeover in managers was also rapid and by the spring, not one manager was the same as when my fieldwork had begun a year earlier. Thus, rather than the graceful exit from the field recommended in the how-to manuals on fieldwork, my work at Burger King faded away.

I know, from the George Brown course and the industry journals that I still read, that the principles used to run the Burger King outlet I worked at are standard throughout the industry. Nevertheless, in the summer of 1989, I decided to check to see if things had changed much since I first worked in a Burger King. This time, I simply applied for a job at one of the franchised restaurants on Yonge Street in Toronto. A manager interviewed me and asked no questions about my application. He only asked if I minded cleaning. I started the training all over again and a few hours into it I was convinced there was no need to worry. There were some minor changes, such as replacing the individual packaged condiments with plastic bottles of ketchup and mustard placed near the napkins and straws, but even the crew room notices could have been taken from the restaurant I had worked in several years earlier.

ORGANIZING THE CUSTOMER "EXPERIENCE"

The Burger King restaurant in which I worked, which I'll call Briarwood, was a company-owned outlet, located within a shopping mall in a suburb of Toronto. The mall is set at the intersection of a highway and a main thoroughfare; the Burger King sign is quite visible as one approaches from either road. The store is surrounded on three sides by a large parking lot, with space for several hundred cars. A "drive-thru" window occupies the fourth side, where customers may be served without leaving their cars. Approximately 35 percent of the store's business uses the "drive-thru."

A large porch, with round stone picnic tables for the use of customers in mild weather, fronts the brick and glass Burger King building. A small, professionally landscaped garden borders the store. Cement receptacles lined with garbage bags are liberally provided to handle the debris of the meals, which are completely packaged with disposable materials. Crew members are sent outside periodically to make sure that there is no garbage strewn about; keeping the parking lot clean is considered important for business. This company is convinced that if customers see a clean lot, well-maintained landscape and building, and sparkling glass, they will have a positive mental image of the food and service.[5]

Customers enter the restaurant through glass doors that lead directly to the serving counter, where they can line up to give their orders at one of several cash registers. To the left, in front of a mirrored wall, is a live potted tree, and a large display featuring the "Burger King" with his latest giveaway. Most of the giveaways are aimed at the under-six set. Cleverly designed, inexpensive plastic games, cars, planes, or whistles shaped like pickles are offered for limited periods (in addition to the Burger King crown, which is always available). Young children, when they are brought into the store, often ask what the Burger King has for them this time.[6]

Sometimes, Burger King holds contests aimed at teenagers and adults. For example, the restaurant offers peel-off coupons, making the lucky person an "instant winner" of fries or a drink, or (less frequently) a hamburger. Thus, these are enticements to all family members to leave the private kitchen and come to a public place for the family dinner. Eating at Burger King is promoted as fun, and affordable.

When entering Burger King, customers find themselves in a clean, brightly lit place, with the soothing sounds of muzak in the background. Walking up to the long serving counter to place an order, they know that it won't take long, and that they can expect the same thing they get from other Burger Kings in other places. As they look up, the menu overhead displays the various items available. In the centre is a technicolour picture of one menu item, usually a new product displayed to whet the appetite. An illustration can improve sales of that item as much as 40 percent.[7] The entire menu is printed twice, once on each side of the picture.

Menu items are limited to foods that can be pre-prepared. Any additions to the menu do not involve new equipment. The trend is to cut down on labour costs by getting the customer to do as much of the work as possible. This begins by having the customer walk to the counter to place his or her order.

There are seven varieties of hamburgers with different garnishings, and four sandwiches, three of which are deep fried. Fried potatoes are available in two sizes, as are carbonated soft drinks.

Picture of Burger King worker

The larger cup for the soft drink is the "regular," so that if a customer wishes the smaller amount, she must learn to ask for a "small." One dessert – fried apple pie – is offered, and a variety of beverages – milk, juice, tea, coffee, shakes, and hot cocoa. By the late 1980s, many stores had salad bars, and some had the customers serving themselves drinks.

Next to the menu, a photograph of the "Employee of the Month" smiles down upon the customer. The employee chosen receives a $20 bonus in addition to the honour of being so displayed.

The customer's order is taken by a "counter hostess", or cashier who, like the menu, follows a standardized format. First, a smile and the greeting. She says, "Hello, welcome to Burger King. May I take your order, sir?" or a minor variant of the above. Chances are this greeting will be offered by a young pretty teenager. If it is lunchtime on a school day, adult women in their twenties or thirties or older women and men in their fifties and sixties can usually be seen working at the various work stations.

If a customer orders only two items, the cashier will suggest a third to fill out "the food triangle." What the company calls "the food triangle" consists of a sandwich (or hamburger), fries, and a drink. The profits on fries and drinks are largest, so cashiers are trained to gently convince customers to include these items with their order.

Profitability in menu items varies. Drinks, particularly soft drinks, tea, and coffee are the most lucrative. They are sold at about 600 percent of their cost, excluding the price of the cup. Fries are the next most profitable item, with a 400 percent markup. The lowest margin markup is the chicken sandwich, at 100 percent.

Added to the cost of the ingredients is the cost of packaging and condiments. Food wasted because it is not sold in the specified time period (ten minutes for sandwiches, seven for fries) is also included in the calculations. Total food costs at Burger King are similar to other restaurant operations, taking up 40 percent of actual sales. A more precise breakdown of food costs as a percentage of sales is as follows:

Item	Percent of Sales
Food	32.2
Condiments	2.0
Paper	5.2
Waste	.9
Total	40.3

While the order is being made up, the cashier takes payment for the meal. She places the money on the register, rings in the amount handed her, and then presses the AMOUNT TENDERED button on her computerized cash register. The required amount of change then appears on the register.

The cashier inside the store does not need to know how to make change to operate the register. At the "drive-thru" window, there is a time delay between ordering and payment, so that a number of orders may be taken before one is paid for. Here, the ability to make change is a necessary skill because the amount in the register may not be the same as the transaction at the window.

Fickle customers do not present a problem for the cashier. If a customer changes her mind in the middle of ordering, items can be deleted or altered so that a new bill does not have to be made up.

After payment is made, the cashier assembles the order in a specified fashion: first the drinks, then the sandwiches and dessert if one is ordered, and last the fries. If the order is to take out, the cashier knows from previous instructions which size bag to use. During the course of my fieldwork, one of the economy measures taken by the company involved putting items in a smaller size bag. Those cashiers who persisted in doing things the old way were reprimanded for the waste.

Condiments (salt, vinegar, ketchup) are given on request only. The company stresses the importance of saving money by obeying rules and giving out only one packet of ketchup at a time and only when there is a special request for it. After the order is presented, the cashier is instructed to invite the customer to return by saying, "Thank you, call again please," sincerely and with a smile.[8]

In Burger King's training manual for employees, the emphasis on smiling is explained. The attitude of the crew people and the management creates what is called an "atmosphere" or "personality" in each Burger King restaurant. Since the "counter hostess" has the most contact with the customers, she in particular needs to present a "good attitude." This attitude reflects not only her positive feelings for the job and for fellow workers, but for superiors as well.

Smile with a greeting and make a positive first impression. Show them you are GLAD TO SEE THEM. Include eye contact with the cheerful greeting.

If a customer is eating her meal at Burger King, she is handed her order on a tray. Each part of the meal comes wrapped in its own disposable package, to be separately used and consumed. The condiments – salt, vinegar, ketchup – are also provided in their own individual, disposable packages. Only the tray, covered with a disposable tray liner, is not to be discarded. Tray liner designs are changed periodically as they are used for advertising purposes. They are decorated with slogans such as "Hop on the Whopper Wagon," featuring smiling young people in and near a jeep, holding hamburgers. The captions explain why these young people seem to be having such a good time: "The best tasting Burger that ever filled a bun."

A maximum of three minutes elapses from the time the customer enters the restaurant, decides what to order, and leaves the counter with the meal.[9] During busy times, when each cash register is staffed by both a counter hostess and an "expeditor" who helps the cashier by collecting the orders, it is not uncommon for the meal to be ready for the customer before she has had a chance to pay for it and receive her change. Quickness of service is known as SOS (speed of service), and is stressed as one of the most important elements in restaurant profitability.

The customer, with the meal neatly arranged on the tray, leaves the counter and helps herself to straws and napkins. She then looks around for a place to sit. The dining room is divided into sections, with the tables arranged for seating groups of two to four people. The arrangements for four people are two small tables located close to one another with a small separation so that two groups of two can also use them and still maintain some distance. The seats are hard plastic and uncomfortable enough to encourage adherence to the posted notice that maximum seating time per customer is twenty minutes. Garbage receptacles located in four different parts of the dining room remind customers that they are supposed to dispose of their leftovers themselves. Burger King "dining room hostesses" wipe the tables clean and keep the floor underneath tidy. They also check the bathrooms regularly and clean them if necessary. The hostesses also control any rowdy young customers.

Eating at Burger King is referred to by the company as a "dining experience." It is constantly stressed how important it is that the restaurant be a pleasant place so that customers will want to return. A sign in the crew room downstairs framed and enclosed in glass reminds employees of this:

Why Customers Quit

1% die

2% move away

5% develop other friendships

9% competitive reasons

14% product dissatisfactions

68% quit because of *attitude of indifference towards customer by restaurant management or service personnel*

"Counter hostesses" or cashiers are impressed with the importance of making the market setting resemble as much as possible life outside the cash nexus. Customers are called "guests" and doing a good job means not just serving them the food they ordered but making them "happy." Employees are told, "Your job is a sort of social occasion. You meet people – you want these people to like you, to like visiting your restaurant." The first and last duty of the counter person is to make the customer feel that they are not just paying cash for a service but that they are genuinely welcomed.

If a customer does not wish to step outside the car, he can go to the "drive-thru" window. At any time of day, people are parked in the lot, eating their meals in their cars. "Drive-thrus" have recently been installed in almost all Burger King restaurants, except in the urban downtown locations where there are no parking lots. They flourished in the early days of fast food, but were replaced in the 1960s by in-store facilities. By the late 1970s, Wendy's discovered how lucrative "drive thrus" could be and the other chains quickly followed suit.

The customer drives up to the menu billboard. This sets off a bleeping noise inside the store and a crew person welcomes the customer and takes the order through a microphone system similar to a walkie-talkie. If the window of the customer's car is rolled down, his voice can be heard from inside the car. He then drives to the pickup window to pay for the food and get the bagged meal. Burger King standards for window-time transaction are thirty seconds maximum.

The "birthday party package" is another option available from Mondays to Thursdays at all but peak business hours. The birthday party guests are given free drinks, free cake, the giveaways for the week, and free coupons to return to the store. The children sit sporting Burger King crowns, and their orders are taken by a Burger King server who also sings "Happy Birthday." Four or five of these were held each week at Briarwood. Thus, with the help of big business, one of the jobs of mothering is expedited with a minimal amount of effort, and no cleanup is necessary. The birthday rituals of "Pin the Tail on the Donkey," balloons, other games, and the general ruckus of these annual occasions are gone and birthdays are made into an orderly and predictable event. Celebrations are mass-produced and easily available for a price.

The clientele at a Burger King varies according to the time of day and the location of the store. The outlet where I worked was situated near office buildings and a shopping mall. During the weekdays, the lunchtime customers were predominantly adults, mostly businessmen. During the supper hours, particularly Friday nights, families with children were much more prevalent. A not uncommon sight were toddlers, under two, sitting in the high chairs Burger King keeps on hand for its very young customers, contentedly stuffing french fries into their mouths.

Burger King keeps careful count of who its customers are. Slightly more men than women eat at Burger King. Young adults aged eighteen to thirty-four constitute the largest group of customers and also spend the most. They come an average of once or twice a month. Youngsters twelve to seventeen years of age visit the store an average of once a week or more, and thus are more frequent customers. Since 1978, the number of young children at Burger Kings has increased until the proportion visiting the store is the same as that represented in the population as a whole (about 10 percent). [10]

Burger King's presentation of itself as a happy, clean, efficient place where the customer will be well treated is thus designed to divert attention away from the food it serves. All elements of the service are geared towards maximizing Burger King's "bottom line."

RECRUITING WORKERS AT BURGER KING

Finding new workers is a perennial problem in the fast food industry. "Kids today just don't want to work," said one manager in his early twenties who was wearied by the constant search for new workers. The front-page headline for a May 1989 issue of *Restaurant News* is the same as forty years previously – "The Labor Crisis." The industry is on the lookout for creative solutions to this crisis – hiring retirees, the handicapped, and in the United States, visible minorities. One Burger King in Michigan is helping with day care – paying $1.50 an hour to local day care providers for employees with young children. [11]

The need for workers is constant enough so that even the paper placemats on each tray are sometimes used to recruit workers. Invitations to become part of the "Burger King family" are offered: "If you're enthusiastic and like to learn, this is the opportunity for you. Just complete the application and return it to the counter." The application form is on the right-hand side of the placemat.

In the fall, when there had been unusually high turnover because of the beginning of school, a sign placed in the Briarwood crew room asked,

---

Wanna make $20?

It's easy! All you have to do is refer a friend to me for employment. Your friend must be able to work over lunch (Monday-Friday). If your friend works here for at least one month, you get $20.

Availability is the most important criteria for being hired by Burger King. Second to availability is something called "good attitude." The head manager defined this as displaying an eagerness to work, enjoyment of the work, and appearance. "Some people," Helen, the assistant manager, informed me, "are turned down because they are overqualified, or want too much money. Sometimes they want too many hours, and we just can't give it to them."

Burger King successfully uses young people in its advertisements. Handsome, wholesome smiling teenagers are pictured serving food that we are all encouraged to buy. I assumed that there were particular reasons for finding teenagers desirable workers. However, what I found was the industry's capacity for making a virtue out of necessity. When teenagers are in plentiful supply then their youthful, healthy appearance can be used to market the product as well as serve it. The main concern is with finding a labour force that is plentiful and will work for minimum wage. Linda, the head manager of the store I worked in, professed a preference for the adult women workers. They were thought to be steadier, and more reliable. "They come in. They have a certain pride in the job. They like things to run smoothly and well, whereas the part-timers don't care as much. They are young kids, and they keep a job maybe three to eight months."

Nevertheless, she would never station older workers at the cash register when younger ones were available. "Our customers expect a certain image, and the older people wouldn't look right," she explained. She used "older" as a term relative to the high school students. These women were not teenagers, but many of them were still in their twenties and thirties. All managers agreed that for Burger King's requirements, teenagers are the most available labour force at the lowest cost.

The industry is increasingly looking to much older workers, people of retirement age, as the supply of young people seems to be running out. There are fewer young people in the population and more job opportunities available to them. At the time I worked in the store, Burger King head office personnel in Miami were interested in hiring retirees, because of the high percentage of older people in that area. Now, this trend has come to Canada. McDonald's has a program called "McMasters" – geared toward hiring retirement age workers. Burger King too advertised for older workers at a job fair for seniors in Toronto and also has an arrangement with a school for the retarded to hire workers with special needs.

Fast food has also been a place where new immigrants with limited command of English can find jobs. Some of the most reliable workers at the Burger King in which I worked were young people newly arrived in Canada. Most of the workers in the second Burger King I worked in briefly years later spoke Spanish.

Just as Burger King's hiring criteria have to do with availability rather than the job itself, people take jobs at Burger King because it fits in with their other obligations. For young people, the reasons are straightforward. The only kind of work they can do is outside school hours. For many, it is a first and they start work feeling excited to be holding down a job. One young fifteen-year-old said, "it's prestigious to be working." The work at Burger King is for many young people the best of the limited alternatives available. It pays better than baby sitting. The hours (although inconvenient) are preferable to those of a paper route and the work is less isolating than a job in a donut shop or a convenience store. There is a larger workforce of young people at Burger King, and thus more socializing than at most alternative work sites.

There are special difficulties to contend with in relying on a teenage labour force. Managers, acting in Burger King's interests, often find they must deal with parents who are acting in their children's interest. Interfering parents plagued the head manager.

We have a lot of interfering parents now. When kids are hired, they are read the riot act with respect to being available for closings. (This means staying till 12 on weekdays, or 1 on weekends.) Then mothers call to complain. They call head office, the labour board.

If they are responsible enough to have a job, they have to do the hours too. There is a communication problem between the kids and their parents.

We get the silliest calls. I got one this afternoon from Karen's mother saying she was up late last night and couldn't work tonight's shift. What does one have to do with the other? She didn't even go to school today. She had exams for one hour. Or Joanne, who's quitting because school is ending in two months and she has to stop work because of her marks. It's more likely too many late nights with her boyfriend.

The women with families who worked in the daytime also took the job for reasons that had little to do with the actual work. As one woman put it, "It was a job, and it was steady, and it was close. I could ride my bike to work. They were actually fairly good with me about the hours they would give me." Another woman explained, "With this job, I could be home when the kids returned from school. Babysitting is so expensive that it really doesn't pay to get a full-time job."

Adult women need the money but are restricted to jobs that still allow them to meet their family obligations. One pregnant worker was hoping to hold on to her job long enough so that she could afford a crib, carriage, and playpen for her new baby. The younger daytime workers are unskilled, school dropouts. One young girl said, "This is the only job I can do."

Thus people take jobs at Burger King for a number of reasons. Jobs are hard to come by, particularly for those people with limited skills and training; they don't have many options. Pressures from other spheres of life restrict students and women with families to certain kinds of jobs. While these other obligations make work at Burger King one of the few options they have, they also serve to limit Burger King's power over them. The job at Burger King does not encroach too much on their responsibilities to their families or their schoolwork.

TAKING ON A JOB AT BURGER KING

New employees enter Briarwood through the back door, which is also used for deliveries. The entrance door is easy enough to find. It is located just opposite a free-standing enclosure for the garbage. Getting in is another matter, as the door, for security reasons, has no outside handle. There is a buzzer, and eventually someone opens the door to let in the new employees.

The workers find themselves facing a narrow staircase that goes down to the basement where the crew room is located.[12] A sign posted on the stairwell congratulates an assistant manager on completing his Basic Restaurant Operations Course, welcomes a new manager, or wishes good luck to one who has been transferred.

Down the stairs in the basement is a small, windowless room almost completely taken up by an oblong table approximately three by eight feet. Built in-benches line two sides of the wall, and a long bench has been placed along the third side. On the walls above the wall benches are signs announcing store policy, upcoming Burger King events, and a row of hooks for overcoats. The signs change every few weeks. At the far side of the room is a small alcove, and on either side bathrooms, one marked "boys," and the other "girls." A notice in the "girls'" room reads as follows:

Ladies!

Finally our bathroom is fixed.

In order for us to keep this bathroom in operating condition we need to follow these rules:
1. No hair in sink or toilet.
2. No make-up on walls, e.g. lipstick.
3. Private materials to be put in dispenser provided.
4. The bathroom must be kept as clean as it was when you first came in (and that's supposed to be clean). The rules need to be followed for sanitary reasons. Also toilet should not be clogged again. It shall not be fixed again.

LET'S SHOW THEM WE CAN KEEP IT CLEAN. IT'S UP TO US.

Thanks, mgt.

The bathroom was usually a mess. The threat that another broken toilet would not be fixed is in violation of Heath Department regulations, which require two working washroom facilities for crew use.

A stereo is playing rock music, and about half a dozen people are seated around the table making conversation. Two of the workers are part of the day crew. (During the time I did my fieldwork, three or four workers were scheduled for long shifts during the day. Subsequently, there was an attempt to eliminate all long shifts for crew members.) One is on her fifteen-minute break, and is drinking pepsi from a small paper cup. The other worker is waiting for the bathroom to be free so she can change out of her uniform and go home. The rest of the people in the crew room are young high school students waiting to start their shifts. They are chatting about a disco place where one of them is planning to go dancing Saturday night.

The new workers are told to wait in the crew room for the training manager. They come in and seat themselves. All but one of the seven trainees are young, under eighteen years of age. One woman looks to be in her late twenties and has an infant son. Two young women recognize each other from school and strike up a conversation. It is now 4:25 PM, and the training session was supposed to begin twenty-five minutes ago. The woman with the baby at home says she hopes this won't take too long, as she has to get home.

Conversation is temporarily interrupted when the music on the radio in the crew room starts blaring so loudly that talking becomes impossible. One of the crew waiting to go on shift has recognized her favourite song and wants to hear it at full volume.

Two young girls dressed in tight jeans – the kind that need to be zipped up lying down – come downstairs and examine a sheet of papers posted on the side of the wall opposite the long table. The papers are protected by a locked glass case. They are looking at the work schedule to see when they are scheduled to work that week. One of the young women groans. Apparently, she is scheduled to work Saturday night, and doesn't want to. She asks around the crew room if there is anybody who will take her shift for her. No one volunteers. Finally one of the boys agrees if she promises to do the same for him sometime, which she readily does. She now must get approval from the scheduling manager, who unfortunately isn't working that day. Some of the others tell her she'll never get the change approved, as she generally works as cashier, and her substitute hasn't yet been trained on that station.

The training manager comes downstairs, a dapper young man in his late teens or early twenties. He is dressed in dark brown pants, a beige shirt with brown tie, and light brown jacket with the Burger

King crest. (Burger King has a special tailor who custom makes clothes for management.) The trainer introduces himself as Donny, and apologizes for being late. (I never saw a manager appear on time for either a training session or a meeting). "Something came up and I couldn't come down any earlier," he says, and ushers the trainees into the next-door office, where the training session will take place.

All the new workers are handed out income tax forms, and Donny explains how to fill them out. The trainees are then asked to complete availability forms for Burger King. They are strongly encouraged to indicate that they can work as many shifts as possible. The forms ask for hours available for each day of the week and the number of hours per week full-time and part-time workers want to work. Donny explains that the distinction does not really mean how many hours, but rather when – in the daytime, or after school. The manager tells the youngsters: "You must be able to close two times a week, that is be available from 4 o'clock till midnight on weekdays, or 1 A.M. on Friday and Saturday night. The schedules you fill in apply for the school semester. In the summer we know everybody can work all hours. All part-timers *must* indicate availability for weekends. Any questions?"

Only one question is asked, "Can we get free food tonight?" Donny takes orders for drinks and asks one of the crew sitting in the crew room to get the beverages. The trainees are then handed a three-page mimeographed sheet entitled "Store Policies." It begins, "To insure that a constant policy and efficient teamwork is always present, the following guidelines must be followed by all employees."

The first page of the handout deals with uniform policy. Brown leather shoes are required. One of the workers has brown suede, but they are not acceptable. Only shiny brown will do; vinyl is okay. The boys will be issued a Burger King shirt and hat. They have to provide their own dark brown polyester pants. The girls are issued brown polyester slacks, and a shirt to match with a large yellow and orange stripe down the front. They are also issued a hat – a peaked baseball cap with a yellow and orange stripe. Donny explains that the name tags, which each crew member must wear at all times, go on the left side of the uniform. Anyone who forgets the name tag must pay 75 cents for a new one. The proceeds go into the crew fund. "This way we can afford to have a crew picnic and pay for dances and other activities."

Employees are expected to wash their uniforms. "If you take care of the uniform, we give you a free meal each time you come here. There is no excuse for dirty uniforms." In fact, no worker is ever denied a meal because their uniform is dirty. Sometimes, a worker will be charged two dollars to rent another uniform if they come to work with a dirty one, or forget theirs at home. Each employee has a locker where they may leave their things while working. They must bring their own locks, and may not keep their Burger King clothes in the locker between shifts. They must pay for any lost uniforms or hats.

Donny goes on to ask that employees wear brown socks. The girls' hair must be tucked under their caps. "A lot of girls don't like that but you get used to it." (I was one of the "girls" who disliked that rule. Stuffing a big braid inside a baseball cap was not my idea of glamour.) "Does our uniform policy make sense?" Everyone agrees that it does.

The next section of store policy deals with "Behavior and Attitudes", with a list of twenty-seven rules. The first five have to do with personal hygiene, alcoholic beverages, and "no eating, drinking, gum chewing or smoking in the kitchen." Donny tells the trainees, "It looks sloppy. This is not a greasy spoon. We don't want this place to look cheap." About the rule saying, "No foul language," he comments, "If the manager can hear it, the customer can too." Donny continues to review the rules with the trainees. Payday is every other Friday, and raises are by "merit," not length of service. Evaluations are every six months. (If a crew person receives a good evaluation, he or she will receive an increase of ten cents per hour, unless the evaluation coincides with a legal rise in the minimum wage. In this case, crew members receive only a five cent per hour increase for good performance on the job.)

Off-duty crew will be treated like customers. "When you are off shift, you must go home after one-half hour. This is not a hangout." The point is emphasized again. "You don't see people hanging around factories when the factories are closed. Families are our main customers and we don't want this place to look like a hangout. It will discourage them from coming."

One of the peculiar features of a fast food restaurant is that workers can be customers and customers can easily become workers. Managers are warned to treat rejected applicants carefully when interviewing them because it's good business policy. After all, "Today's rejected candidate may well be tomorrow's customer."[13]

Items 11 to 15 have to do with food. Waste products must be placed in special containers because they are counted after breakfast, lunch, and dinner. Giving out free food means immediate termination. Given the emphasis on treating the customer as a guest, this rule contains some interesting contradictions. One doesn't charge "guests," and one attempts to be as generous as possible with them. In Burger King, however, the non-market setting is stressed only to increase business.

All work stations must be kept clean. Donny comments, "We pride ourselves on that. It brings people back. If you think you have nothing to do, grab a broom and sweep. If there's time to lean, there's time to clean. The time goes fast if you keep yourself busy."

Certainly, workers quickly find that is the case. At first, many people do not like sweeping and mopping. As they become more seasoned workers, they realize that since it is never possible to relax, sweeping and mopping is better than doing nothing, or trying to look busy.

Rule 17 has to do with smiling. "Smile at all times. Your smile is the key to our success." Teamwork is also included in the rules. Donny explains that "teamwork equals better service to the customer."

Back-talk to a customer, fellow employee, or a manager will not be tolerated. "If there's a problem with the manager don't talk back. Things do happen. One manager tells you to do one thing, and another will come along and tell you to do something else. Don't mumble about it, just straighten it out."

Donny pauses to ask for questions. Someone asks, "What if you can't work on a day when you're scheduled?" Getting people to report when scheduled is one of a manager's greatest challenges, and Donny goes on at length about this.

I'm glad you asked about that. We have a line bar schedule tacked on the wall in the crewroom, and you are responsible for making sure when you are supposed to work. If you want to switch a shift because something important comes up, and you can get someone to take your shift, it must be initialled by a manager. Don't do it too often. If you are sick, we want advance notice. Nobody feels too sick to not come in all of a sudden. We're tough on that and we'll give you hassles. We phone back to make sure you're really sick. We're not being mean, but we have to protect our interests.

Tell us two weeks in advance if a special day is coming up and you don't want to work – as long as it's not a Saturday. We hope nobody has problems such as "I have to go to the cottage. My parents insist." Remember, your parents don't work here and don't understand the situation. If you're old enough to look for a job, you're old enough to be responsible for coming.

The scheduling system is the area that generates the most resistance. Crew members find that Burger King demands interfere with their social life, school responsibilities, and family obligations. The unpredictability is particularly difficult, because it makes it impossible to plan activities.

Donny goes on to explain that the shifts are generally three or four hours long. "We're a busy store and it's too tough on a person to work for longer than that." He then plans when each of the new crew members will do their training shifts – each person does three shifts of three hours.

By this time, conversation among the new workers has started up. After the training scheduling is completed, Donny again asks for questions. There are none, so he shows a film called "Best Darn Team." The series of slide-tape presentations put out by Burger King deals with various parts of Burger King operations. They are referred to as the "LaBelle" films and consist of a series of slides that rotate automatically as the tape plays.[14] The film starts with a jingle sung by young people in Burger King uniforms. "Who's got the best darn burger in the whole wide world? Burger King and I. 100 percent beef that's flame broiled, never fried."

The various work stations are introduced – hospitality hostess (dining room and bathroom attendant), counter hostess (cashier), fry station, preparation board (sandwiches), drink station, burger and whopper board, and broiler/steamer. The film merrily declares: "We are all know-it-alls. Everyone knows all the jobs. We're the best darn team. Work hard and have fun too. Get proper training at each station and maybe you can be an assistant manager."

The film is about ten minutes long. Donny concludes the session with a pep talk: "One of the best things about working here is that there's lots of social activities. We have a baseball team, and sometimes play against McDonald's, a bowling team, roller skating parties. Our picnic is great. Head office pays a little, the crew fund pays for some, and we have a good time. Last year we had it at the lake and you could see a whole bunch of angry kids trying to drown the managers." Working at Burger King is promoted as "fun," just like eating there. If there is not much that can be said about the work itself, then Burger King stresses the enjoyment to be gotten from extracurricular activities. The informal social relations that invariably develop at any workplace are now harnessed to make Burger King a good place to work in.

Donny then goes to the supply locker inside the manager's office and tries to find the right size uniform for each person. This takes a few minutes, and he mumbles about how he hates this part of the session. Finally, everyone has a uniform, and the women go to try theirs on. However there is no change room. There used to be two rooms designated for that purpose, and the markings are still on the door. Now, however both rooms are used for storing paper goods and Burger King giveaways. The bathrooms have to double as change rooms, and so the new trainees wait their turn. The woman with the baby at home asks to go first as she is afraid her baby will be hungry. By now it is 6 PM. The orientation session was ended one hour later than planned. For the new workers, this discrepancy has a message. When you work for Burger King, only Burger King is important.

ASSEMBLING THE FOOD

Burger King crew are at the bottom of the Burger King hierarchy. Unlike the status system in some other restaurants, where the cook is considered above the salad maker, and the dishwasher below both, all crew jobs are at the same low level. Position charts for the various work stations are made up by the managers for each meal, and names written in with a grease pencil on an erasable board placed near the time card machine. In the interests of worker "effectiveness," upper management encourages "cross training," although in practice, crews tend to be assigned the same jobs each shift they work. The work has been arranged so that none of the jobs is difficult to learn, but with practice, workers can pick up speed at a particular station.

There are no pots and pans in a Burger King kitchen. Pots and pans are not necessary, because almost all foods enter the store ready for the final cooking process. Large and small hamburgers arrive in pre-frozen patties, the buns are pre-cut and carmelized so they will brown nicely when toasted, the french fries are pre-cut and partially pre-cooked; so are the chicken and fish. Pickles and onions are pre-sliced, and the lettuce is pre-shredded. In the mornings, when breakfast is served, the eggs come in containers that look like milk containers and are pre-mixed. Only the tomatoes are sliced on the premises.

The kitchen design in my Burger King was called the K900 layout, and was planned for a high-volume store. (See the schematic representation of the kitchen on p. 98.) There are a number of different work stations in the store. Three are part of selling the meal: the counter, the "drive-thru," and the dining room. The remaining stations are devoted to the production or assembly of the meal: the cooking and assembly area for hamburgers and buns, the area for cooking fries and some of the sandwiches, the sandwich preparation board, and the area for hot and cold drinks. Anywhere from five to

Kitchen Layout for Burger King

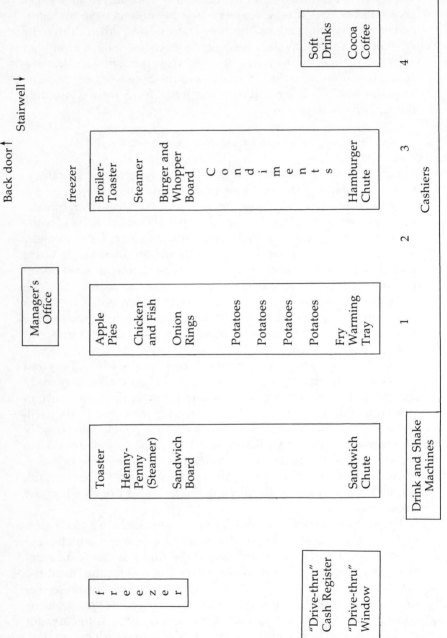

twenty-five workers may be assigned to a shift depending on the volume of business expected. Thus a worker may have responsibility for anywhere from one task to several work stations, depending on how busy it is.

Broiler-Steamer Work Station

The hamburgers are cooked by a gas broiler made by a Burger King subsidiary, Davmor.[15] Internal temperatures reach 1500°F, and the surrounding work area gets quite hot. A conveyor belt runs the meat through the broiler. When I worked there, it took ninety-four seconds from the time a frozen meat patty was placed on the chain to the moment it emerged, cooked, on the meat chute at the other end. The store had two conveyors that could broil up to 835 patties per hour. Near the meat conveyor were two bun chains that toasted the buns and dropped them into a chute near the cooked patties, a process that took about thirty seconds.

A worker keeps the freezer near the broiler filled by hauling boxes stored in the walk-in freezer located on the other side of the kitchen. During busy times, one worker keeps the chains of the conveyor belt broiler filled with meat and buns, while another worker stands at the other end. The worker at the "steamer" end of the belt uses tongs to pick up the cooked patties as they fall off the belt, and places them on the "heel" of a bun (the bottom half). The bun is then "crowned" with the top half and the ungarnished hamburger is placed in a steamer, where, according to Burger King policy, it can remain for up to ten minutes. Jobs at the broiler-steamer are often assigned to new workers as they can be quickly learned.

Burger Board Work Station

The burger board, where the large and small hamburgers are assembled, is made of stainless steel and can be worked from both sides. When the store is busy, the larger hamburgers, called "whoppers" are produced on one side, and the smaller hamburgers on the other. The trays of garnish are placed in a long well or trough located in the centre of the board: cheese slices, pickles, onions, mayonnaise, lettuce, and tomatoes. The ketchup and mustard, stored in plastic bottles, are located near the steamer. One or more workers take the ungarnished hamburgers out of the steamer, add the condiments, place the burger in a box or wrapper, and reheat it in the microwave oven located just above the counter. It is then placed in a chute.

The standard product preparation time for a whopper is twenty-three seconds, or forty-one seconds for two whoppers assembled at the same time. It takes fourteen seconds to heat a whopper in the microwave oven. The MOD (Manual of Operating Data) provides extraordinarily detailed instructions on how to prepare the whoppers. Even the minutest of decisions, such as whether a tomato should be considered small or large, is decided by management. (They were so concerned about waste, they even weighed the tomato cores and ends and recorded the information at Briarwood! This practice was stopped near the end of my fieldwork, however.)

First the whopper cartons are placed printed side down on the table, and the patty removed from the steamer. The bottom half, or the bun heel is placed in the carton, and the pickle slices spread evenly over the meat or cheese. Overlapping the pickles is forbidden. Then the ketchup is applied by spreading it evenly in a spiral circular motion over the pickles, starting near the outside edge. The onions (1/2 oz.) are distributed over the ketchup. Mayonnaise is applied to the top of the bun in one single stroke and 3/4 oz. of shredded lettuce placed on the mayonnaise, holding the bun top over the lettuce pan. Then the two slices of tomato are placed side by side on top of the lettuce. If the tomatoes are unusually small, the manager will decide whether or not three tomato slices should be used that day.

Fry Work Station

The fries arrive in the store in plastic bags, frozen and precut. About two hours before serving, a worker removes them from the bag and places them in a fry rack. As with the making of the hamburgers, there are explicit directions for every step in this process, including how to empty the frozen fries from the bags and place them in the wire baskets. Workers must line up three (or four) baskets in a row and shake the bag six (or eight) times, working their way across the baskets and then back again to create an even distribution.

A worker wheels the rack filled with fry baskets over to the fryer, which contains two vats of oil in which four fry baskets can cook simultaneously. The crewperson on fry station places the fry basket on a lift arm above the hot oil and presses a computer button that causes the arm to lower the basket into the shortening. When the fries are ready, a buzzer sounds and the lift arm automatically raises the basket of fries out of the shortening. A worker then empties the fry basket into the fry bagging station and bags the fries with a special scoop designed to control the portion of each bag of fries.

Each move in the bagging process – how to pick up the scoop, how to hold the bags, how to scoop up the fries – is described in careful detail in the manual.

Each move in the preparation of fries was timed: seven seconds are allotted to placing the fry basket in the fry pot, thirteen seconds to dumping the fries into the bagging station and returning the basket to the holding rack, five seconds to filling the first bag in the bagging cycle, and three seconds to packing each subsequent one.

Fry portioning is watched particularly carefully: despite the special scoop used, the bags can still be filled too much for management's taste. Indeed, most people like being generous because the counter people get complaints if they offer skimpy portions. A sign in the crew room warned us about overfilling the fry bags.

ATTENTION CREW

Fry Yield. Fry yield is the amount of regular portions you get from the total amount of fry use. The ideal amount is 410 portions of fries for each 100 lbs. of fry used.

At the moment, our fry yield is in the unacceptable range of 365–395 portions of fries which is below Burger King standards.

We are the number one crew. So help us bring our fry yield back in the acceptable range.

There are two charts posted in the kitchen to help you along. One shows the names of the people working on the fry station, the yield and the date. There is a graph to show how we are doing each day. There will be a small prize gift to three people who work fry station helping with our cause.

Let's keep
Briarstone
Number One!

The Sandwich Board

Chicken, fish, veal, and ham and cheese sandwiches are made up at the sandwich board. The chicken, fish, and veal arrive proportioned, breaded, and frozen. The worker at this station takes them from a small freezer and places them in a special rack to be cooked. The cooking process is similar to that for the fries. The worker pushes one of several buttons, depending on the type of sandwich and when the cooking time is up, the meat emerges from the oil. The operator then places the cooked item in a warming cabinet called the Henny Penny where it can stay for up to twenty-five minutes. The buns are put through a small conveyor toaster and are kept warm until ready for use.

A kitchen printer located above the preparation table displays which sandwiches need to be made up. As with the burgers, during busy times, a certain "level" will be kept in anticipation of orders in a holding chute behind the cashier. Once the worker assembles the sandwich it can remain in the holding chute for ten minutes before it must be discarded. One again there are detailed directions for how to toast buns, how to take the sandwich meat from the Henny Penny with tongs, and how to make up, wrap, and cut the sandwich. Although none of the operations is difficult, some coordination is involved in ensuring that a sufficient number of cooked meats is in the drawer, and toasted buns are ready when needed.

This station requires the most physical movement. The worker must get the basket for the meats, take it to the chest freezer located nearby, fill the basket, return to the cooking vat, turn around to the sandwich board to make other sandwiches, put down buns in the toaster, return to the vat of oil when the meat is cooked, walk over to the Henny Penny to dump the cooked product, put the fry basket back and return to making sandwiches. Although the freezer, the Henny Penny, and vats of oil are a few steps from each other, at very busy times, two and sometimes three workers are needed at this station.

Drinks and Shakes

The drink station is staffed by a special crew person only during very busy times, from noon to 1:30 PM. At other times, the cashier draws the drinks herself. (More recently, the company has installed portioned drink machines allowing customers to draw their own drinks.) The drink machine consists of stainless steel tanks in which the syrups are kept and CO_2 cylinders to provide the proper carbonation. The production leader checks to ensure that the proper mixture of syrup and soda emerges from the spout, and adjusts it daily. The shake machine has automated shake delivery from a self-contained stainless steel cabinet. The freezer, syrup, and beater units automatically produce any one of the shake flavours (vanilla, chocolate, strawberry) when the button is pressed. As with the carbonated drinks, the proportion of syrup in each shake and the temperature is checked daily.

MOVING UP THE BURGER KING LADDER

The first step up the Burger King hierarchy is promotion to production leader positions. The production leaders are responsible for simple maintenance, and for making sure the restaurant is clean. They look after the small details necessary to keep production smooth, such as making sure there are enough bags for the fries, the salt shakers are filled, and knives, tongs, and grease pencils are in their proper places. They also have front line responsibility for the performance of other workers, much the same as a foreman would. After production leader, one can be promoted to swing manager. Swing managers are in charge during slow times, such as early morning breakfasts, or very late at night. The next steps are to training manager, second assistant manager (there were two at Briarwood), first assistant manager, and finally general manager. The first assistant manager has responsibility for drawing up the labour schedule. One of the second managers positions workers on the floor for each shift.

Beyond the store level, the Canadian organization is run much the same as the US regional offices. Each has vice presidents and staff responsible for field service to franchised and company restaurants, marketing, accounting, training, and new restaurant development personnel. With the takeover of Burger King by Grand Met PFC in 1989, there have been layoffs within the management hierarchy in all Burger King offices. A Burger King official in Toronto estimated that one-third of all jobs in Burger King management have been cut.

No previous restaurant experience is required to enter the lower levels of Burger King restaurant management. For managers, as well as crew, attitude is key. In its management recruitment advertisements, a picture of a race is featured with the caption, "It takes a lot to get there, but it's worth it." The advertisement invites applicants to consider a future at the "Home of the Winner." The job description for managers reflects the most demanding part of a manager's job:

• Must have good verbal communication skills.
• Must possess patience, tact, fairness, and social sensitivity in dealing with customers and hourly employees.

• Must be able to supervise and motivate team of youthful employees and conduct himself/herself in a professional manner.
• Must present neat, well-groomed image.
• Must be willing to work nights, weekends and holidays.

The managers at the Briarwood were all under thirty years of age. They were predominantly male. Turnover was high and of the fifteen managers I got to know, only two were women. Only one, the head manager, had worked her way up from the ranks. The operating manager for Burger King in Canada estimated that only one out of one hundred crew members will ever become a manager.

Burger King policy was to shift managers in company-owned stores around quite a bit. The director explained that they didn't want the managers to become "stale." This was not very clear to me. Perhaps, I thought, managers who got to know their subordinates well would be less likely to stick closely to Burger King rules. For example, Helen, the assistant manager, had told me how badly she felt when new policy required assigning all workers to three-hour shifts, as she knew the hardship this caused some of the women. She, like several other managers, left Burger King for another job. Some stayed in the food industry while others found the regular hours available in other industries more attractive.

The philosophy taught to new managers is of central importance. The Manager Trainee's Curriculum six-week course is offered in Toronto; higher-level managers train at Burger King University in Miami. Going to Miami was an exciting prospect for store managers where I worked.

A PROFILE OF THE WORKERS

During the day, the Briarwood Burger King was staffed by "full timers" or employees who worked a few hours every day. There were, on average, twenty-five such workers during the time I was there. (As the workforce was shifting constantly, I must rely on averages.) Most of these workers were women. Approximately one half of them were married. While most had limited education, a few had completed high school and some had even acquired some additional training. One woman had a nursing degree, another was a college graduate, and a third had started training for nursing. Other daytime workers were women under eighteen years of age who had not completed high school. Only one or two young men worked during the day. One was a high school graduate who couldn't find a better job, while the other had dropped out of school in grade nine to help support his family.

In my restaurant, most of the daytime workers were white. Some of them were new Canadians. One of the most efficient workers in the kitchen was a young woman named Lydia who had recently emigrated from Hong Kong with her parents. When she first started working she knew very little English, but learned her job quickly. She was hoping that she would soon begin school part time. Her family could not afford for her to go full time.

At the beginning of my fieldwork, approximately half of the day-time workers were working more than four-hour shifts. Four worked an eight-hour shift almost every day. These daytime workers, par-ticularly the married women, worked for a variety of reasons. Most of them needed the money badly to help make ends meet. Helen, the assistant manager, and I discussed the impact of a new sched-uling system that would do away with any shifts longer than four hours. Her comments were as follows:

> Julie is saving up for a fancy wedding, she will be fine. However, Sylvia's a single parent, and is badly off financially, Jeanette's on welfare. Darlene lives at home, but her father's sick. Ginnie has saved up and is moving out on her own. She'll be paying almost as much for a month's rent on an apartment as she makes at Burger King. Judith's husband works for a com-pany that is not doing very well and he keeps getting laid off. She has two school-age children, and has been trying to supplement her Burger King hours with another job on Saturdays.[16]

Judith was later promoted to swing manager, and worked all night long till 6 AM. She had two children to look after in the day. As it turned out, she was pregnant at the time. Her baby was born pre-maturely, and weighed less than two pounds. Ida, another worker, miscarried just after a long weekend of hard work in the restaurant. She felt that the arduous work on her feet at Burger King had con-tributed to losing her baby. Both of these women needed to work to pay the rent.

Some of the younger daytime workers also had difficult lives. Ann was a few months short of sixteen and had left home because she said her mother pretended to be an invalid to get her to stay away from school and look after her. She was staying with a friend's parents, and wanted to live with her grandmother and return to school. Cathy, who was fifteen, lived in a foster home. She soon left Burger King to attend hairdressing school. Two Portuguese-

Canadian sisters, who were fifteen and sixteen, had both said they
were a year older than they were because they were afraid Burger
King wouldn't hire a fifteen-year-old. Their father, a restaurant manager, had lost a lot of money. The two girls had dropped out of
school to work, and their mother had also found a job. Their father
was currently waiting on tables.

Despite the difficult circumstances of their lives, and the pressure
to earn money, a number of the women said that they liked coming
to work. One woman who worked three-hour shifts said that it was
a nice break in the day and she was grateful to pick up a bit of extra
money. Another said, "At least when I come here, I'm recognized.
If I do a good job, a manager will say something to me. Here I feel
like a person. I'm sociable and I like being among people. At home
I'm always cleaning up after everybody and nobody ever notices."
Another woman explained that she felt very depressed at home,
and would complain if there was anything she had to do. She enjoyed working. "I go home, and I come here. It's not just the money
because the money is not enough. It's like living in two worlds."

When the full complement of staff was on the payroll, about
seventy-five workers were hired for evening and weekend work.
They were called "part-timers." The average age of these workers
was about sixteen and they were more varied in sex, racial back-
grounds, and socioeconomic circumstances. About half of this group
was male, about one-fourth of the workers were black, and there
were a number of youngsters of Portuguese, Italian, and East European descent. [17]

A number of the black youngsters in my Burger King store were
college bound; three brothers originally from Jamaica and another
brother and sister who subsequently found better jobs elsewhere all
expected to go on beyond high school. Most of the other youngsters
were just expecting to finish high school, and maybe enter a training
course in a community college. Seventeen-year-old Eileen, one of a
pair of Scottish sisters, was one of the few workers in Burger King
who expressed an interest in pursuing a career with Burger King.
She wanted to enter management.

The workers at Briarwood came from varying economic circumstances. Some of the high-school students had parents who were
quite well off and had encouraged their children to work, hoping
they would develop a good work ethic. One head manager thought
that class background did not make much of a difference in the
ability to recruit and hold onto workers. From his experience at
Burger King he felt that while a youngster is in school, she or he
did not feel much pressure to stay at a job they did not like, even

if the parents were not well off. They would just quit. On the other hand, the *Nation's Restaurant News* reported bussing inner city teenagers to staff fast food outlets in wealthy suburban locations. Presumably, some restaurant managers have found that economic background is relevant in recruiting workers.[18]

QUALITY, SERVICE, AND FRIENDLINESS

When workers take a job at Burger King, they are asked to place their responsibilities to Burger King above everything else in their lives: school, family, friends. They are expected to come to work with little advance notice, at irregular hours, and to work as hard as possible for Burger King and Burger King's customers. They are to obey whatever manager happens to be ordering them about, and not make a fuss if they are told to do two contradictory things at once. In contrast, customers are offered consistency and convenience. They and their children will be cared for at Burger King by contented workers.

In *The Cultural Contradictions of Capitalism,* Daniel Bell identifies this phenomenon as a contradiction in values between the ethics of consumption and those of work. In Burger King, the quality of self-discipline required of workers is directly in opposition to the appeal to self-indulgence with which the potential consumer is lured to the store.

Burger King, like all fast food chains, runs on the principles first pioneered by McDonald's: QSC, standing for Quality, Service, and Cleanliness. Quality is defined as standardization and predictability; service is defined as speed; and cleanliness is valued not as a means for ensuring healthfulness, but for its associations with order, which can help promote sales.

The standardization of food is presented as a virtue: the customer knows what she is going to get. However, Burger King's product is not all that different from what can be found at any other hamburger chain. Therefore the selling of the meal, the service part of the business, is crucial. Friendly, fast service in pleasant surroundings will provide the incentive to return that the food cannot. Each Burger King customer, child or adult, is treated as a separate individual. Unlike the situation in a Chinese restaurant where the casserole is shared, or in a family-run Italian restaurant where a whole family digs into one pizza, each fast food customer is given her own burger.

The emphasis on cleanliness has a double function for the restaurant. First, it keeps the customers coming in. Second, since workers are told to use any free time for cleaning, it is used to reinforce the message that workers owe full use of their labour time to their employer. Like the friendliness of the crew, cleanliness is used as a promotion for the store. The image to be conveyed is that Burger King "cares," perhaps to make up for so many other aspects of peoples' lives that are cold and indifferent.

In training workers, management must ensure that the informal work relationships are pleasant enough so that a friendly atmosphere will be created for the customer. They must also make it clear that working at Burger King is different from being a customer. Their task is a difficult one, because the teenagers and the women who work at Burger King are, in fact, both the market and the labour force for the store. Managers know that an important part of the job is to keep the crew smiling, but they must also make sure that workers don't have too good a time.

Photomontage   Richard Slye

CHAPTER SIX

Modern Times in the Hamburger Business

In the 1936 Charlie Chaplin film *Modern Times*, the little tramp's employer tries to increase his employees' productivity by speeding up the line, and in one scene, experiments with a feeding machine that will enable employees to continue working while having lunch. While, thanks to employment standards legislation, most workers can stop their work to have lunch, in almost every other way, Chaplin's vision of a highly controlled workplace has been realized.

Computer technology is used in the restaurant industry to refine and assist in implementing an old method of organizing work – Taylorism. The technology is used to simplify the assembling of the meal so that minimum-wage workers can be used. The investment in training is low enough so that turnover is preferable to the workforce stability that could be created through higher wages. The struggle is to keep labour costs down by paying low wages, while intensifying the work that each employee is expected to do.

THE CHANGES IN WORK

A management manual for the restaurant industry points out that the industrial revolution that occurred in most industries 150 years ago is only now occurring in the foodservice industry. Skills that were once in the hands of skilled craftsmen are being transferred to the machines of the bulk processors:

With unarguable certainty the saucier is being replaced by pre-processed fresh and frozen vegetables, the chef is being replaced by fully prepared entrees, the waiter is becoming replaced by the waitress, the waitress by the cafeteria or fast food counter aide, the server by the vending machine, the executive chef by the food production manager. As the volume of public feeding increases every day, the need for new technologies in foodservice management becomes increasingly urgent. Men [and women] are being replaced by machines for the first time in the history of our industry.[1]

As we have seen, the need to maximize profit propels enterprises both to expand the market by growing larger, and to employ less skilled labour, which is at once cheaper and more easily controlled. Thus the primary purpose for introducing new technology is not to improve workers' conditions, but to simplify work by making the worker into a machine-tender. With the development of large-scale industry, the instruments of labour are converted from tools that workers use into machines that workers tend. High-tech equipment is used to minimize labour costs and maximize productivity.

Just as women and young people were drawn into paid labour in the early days of the industrial revolution in England, we see parallels in the foodservice industry today. As Marx stated,

The labour of women and children was, therefore, the first result of the capitalist application of machinery! That mighty substitute for labour and for workers, the machine, was immediately transformed into a means for increasing the number of wage-labourers by enrolling, under the direct sway of capital, every member of the worker's family, without distinction of age or sex. Compulsory work for the capitalist usurped the place, not only of the children's play, but also of independent labour at home within customary limits, for the family itself.[2]

One hundred and fifty years later, all family members are again being drawn into waged work. While the pressures on young family members to enter paid work take a form different from that of their nineteenth-century predecessors, the effect is very similar.

REDESIGNING THE WORKER

Mechanization alone does not guarantee increased profits to the employer. In order to ensure that it will, management must address itself to what an employee does on the job, and how he or she does it. Mechanization must be used to replace workers, and to get the remaining ones to work more intensively, if it is to be money-saving.

The project of "redesigning the worker"[3] began in the twentieth century. Frederick Taylor, in 1911, laid down the management principles acknowledged to be the basis of modern foodservice management. Taylor sought to establish the right of management to determine what workers ought to be doing by dividing all jobs into a series of simple tasks and determining how these should be accomplished. The work of Taylor and, following him, Frank B. Gilbreth,[4] formed the basis of what is now known as time and motion study.

This effort to streamline work through increasing managerial authority was supported by an ideology that imparted positive value to such developments. "Efficiency" was originally a technical term in philosophy: by the eighteenth century it had found its way into physics, where it referred to the ability of a physical force to cause an effect. By the end of the century, it had become associated with work. "Efficiency" was now a concept charged with moral connotations that seemed to supply a common denominator for taking the measure of workers and machines within coordinates derived from the physical sciences.[5] Rather than looking to the independent worker as a model of virtue, the new philosophy promoted obedience and the ability to take orders. In place of dictatorial and arbitrary whims exercised by employers, "science" would reign. Scientific management would simultaneously promote material wealth and social harmony. Thus, "social problems could be reduced to problems in applied physics."[6]

Taylor's problem was that while there was a clear idea of what one might expect of a machine, limits to workers' efficiency are not so evident. Therefore, standards for workers' performance needed to be established. As machines replaced the skills that formerly lay in the hands of workers, and a body of workers existed that could be coerced into working for reduced wages, workers were still not working hard enough to suit employers. Underwork or "soldiering" remained a problem. This "evil" of underwork, in Taylor's view, was caused by two things: "the natural instinct and tendency of men to take it easy and second from more intricate thought and reasoning caused by their relations with other men, which may be called systematic soldiering."[7]

Taylor's method consisted of two parts – first an analysis of the work process through a detailed definition of what the worker is supposed to be doing, and second, a reorganization of the work itself to "eliminate unnecessary motions and substitute fast for slow and inefficient motions for the men." This involved the development of "one method and one implement which is quicker and better than any of the rest," which could be discovered through "scientific" study.[8]

Many aspects of work traditionally done by workers were to be taken over by management: planning was separated from doing. Less skilled and cheaper labour could be employed, and tighter controls on how fast the work was done could be maintained, as

managers came to determine what workers *ought* to be doing. Taylor
viewed this replacement by the manager of the authority of worker
and foreman over how the work is done as the application of
"science."

Taylor sought to eliminate "soldiering" through task management,
rather than through the old system of initiative and incentive. In
Taylor's scheme, both workers and management would benefit as
higher pay would be offered to workers in return for their compliance
with the new system. This outlay of higher wages would be more
than offset by the increase in productivity. However, the system is
based on a belief in the stupidity of the common labourer. It involves
breaking down group solidarity by training each person individually.
Taylor is quite explicit on this point. "The idea then, of taking one
man after another and training him under a competent teacher into
new working habits until he continually and habitually works in
accordance with scientific laws, which have been developed by
someone else, is directly antagonistic to the old idea that each workman can best regulate his own way of doing the work. And besides
this, the man suited to handling pig iron is *too stupid to properly train
himself.*"[9]

Taylorism proved to be too limited and rigid a system for widespread implementation and in its initial form met with considerable
resistance from both workers (who resisted deskilling) and foremen
(who resented the erosion of their supervisory powers). Nevertheless, as Littler points out, the overall approach of Taylor's system
and the ideological integration this approach provided were very
widespread in the United States.[10]

In the foodservice industry, the impact of engineering methods
developed by Taylor (and following him, Gilbreth), are very much
in evidence. One foodservice manual, *Increasing Productivity in Foodservice*, describes Taylor's principles as "the foundation of modern
management thought."[11] Frederick Taylor is deemed the principal
researcher in modern scientific management and, the manual as-
serts, years of tests have proved him right.

The foodservice manual stresses the importance of carefully planning what employees should be doing at all times in order to increase
productivity. However, this is not accomplished so easily, as

one of the problems in providing alternate duties, or switching employees
to different jobs in order to achieve greater utilization, is the natural resistance of employees to change. The usual reaction of the employee is to
say, "You've got me doing two people's work." Management has to be
ready for such a reaction by being able to explain why increased productivity

is in the interest of the employee. An effective argument for introducing methods that will increase the American worker's productivity – and one that workers are familiar with – is the need for American products to be able to compete in a world market. To keep the American standard of living at the desired level requires the improvement in productivity that will keep America's products competitive. [12]

These arguments have a contemporary ring to them. They are commonly used as employer strategies to explain to workers why they must accept less in wages and benefits. "Competitiveness" in the 1990s means competitiveness with non-unionized workers in the United States and even poorer workers in the third world. Rather than guaranteeing decent wages and benefits for workers as in the European common market, for example, the strategy is to ensure that there is no limit placed on employer's profits. The reasoning is as follows: greater efficiency will hold down menu prices, enabling more people to eat away from home. Higher sales volumes will result in greater utilization of labour and even greater efficiency.

Harry Braverman's Labor and Monopoly Capital explains the significance of these developments. Using Marxist theory, he looks at what has happened to the labour process in the twentieth century. He describes how technology has been used not to create new skills, but to fragment and deskill jobs. The division of mental and manual labour – that is, between someone (management) who plans how the work ought to be done, and those (the workers) who do the work – is the basis for the division of labour and key to understanding how Taylor's ideas came to dominate production in many industries in the twentieth century.

Braverman also describes the development and impact of what he calls "the universal market" in the era of monopoly capitalism. The introduction of social services that could make people's lives easier and facilitate social solidarity instead has had the opposite effect. "As the advances of modern household and service industries lighten the family labour, they increase the futility of family life, as they remove the burdens of personal relations, they strip away its affections; as they create an intricate social life, they rob it of every vestige of community and leave in its place the cash nexus." These new service industries employ non-unionized, unskilled workers in a situation in which "training prerequisites for most of these occupations are minimal, a job ladder leading upward is virtually non-existent, and unemployment rates are higher than average." [13]

While Braverman's thesis can't be applied to all work situations in the twentieth century, his insights remain quite useful to certain industries, particularly in the service sector. Since the publication of his book in 1974, cheaper and easier-to-use technology makes it possible to monitor work in new ways. In many areas of the post office, at supermarket checkout counters, telephone operator systems, and in other data input functions, each work move is timed and workers' movements tightly controlled. Employers, with the help of management consultants and technical support, have perfected the treatment of workers as human machinery. With careful planning, workers can perform almost as well as robots. They may be more difficult to deal with, but then, in minimum wage part-time jobs, they are not quite as expensive to maintain.

OPERATIONS RESEARCH AT BURGER KING

Computer technology has allowed the fast food industry to monitor aspects of its operations in ways previously undreamed of. During the 1970s, the development of small microprocessor chips enabled electronic cash registers to be linked to an in-store computer that collects information on unit operations. As a consequence, the number of menu items sold, inventory levels, inventory dollar values, cost of sales, and labour costs per hour can now be calculated and monitored through built-in programs easily accessed by store managers. By the mid-1970s, computerized equipment began to be introduced into Burger King restaurants.

The computerized cash register is the single most important piece of equipment in an individual outlet. A Point of Sale Management System links the various parts of the store together and daily relays sales information by modem from all stores to the Burger King headquarters in Miami. The system includes the cashiers' keyboards, printers that print up the order at each keyboard, a microprocessor housed in the master station, and kitchen printers located at different work stations. When the cashier rings in an order, information is stored in the microprocessor and the order prints out on the appropriate printer in the kitchen.

The manager's terminal contains the following parts of the restaurant operation, which can be tracked automatically:

• Inventory input and raw product costing.
• Cash reconciliation, which balances the accounts.
• Sales mix report. Each menu item sold is listed by item, class, and price. The product mix or total number of each menu item sold can be traced, along with its dollar value, and the percentage of total sales it represents. The food cost to the store for each item

can be easily ascertained, as can the cost of all sales, and percentage cost of sales.
• Hourly sales. This includes customer counts, dollar sales, and average sales per customer.
• Cash sales by station. This helps monitor workers' productivity.

Through the easy and instant accessibility of this information, control on inventory can be maintained and labour costs manipulated, leading to an increased cash flow. In 1978, with the help of the newly available computerized cash registers, Burger King introduced a system that called upon store managers to plan staffing needs according to hourly sales projections.

In 1980, Burger King started deploying mainframe technology to assist its operations research, which is responsible for determining the workflow most profitable for Burger King. Operations research has been an important activity of large corporations since World War II. While the roots of this endeavour can be traced back to the introduction of scientific management, it developed in its present form through military research during World War II. During the industrial boom of the 1950s and 1960s, it became apparent that similar techniques could be used in civilian settings.

Burger King decided to use the new computer technology to help plan how to get fewer workers to do the job and still maintain the three-minute maximum waiting time for the customer, thus increasing productivity. The more sophisticated system was needed because by the late 1970s operations at Burger King were becoming more complex: there were twenty-five distinguishable kitchen designs, a "drive-thru," and a larger selection of sandwiches. Burger King was presented with the dilemma of all retailers; it had to reduce production costs as much as possible without hurting business through too long a service delivery time.[14]

The use of computers helped to solve this problem; arithmetic calculations could be performed quickly and in such volume that dealing with the complex problems Burger King faced was greatly facilitated.[15] As the director of Burger King Industrial Engineering and Operations Research explained, Burger King's approach to labour deployment is

based on the fact that fast-food restaurants operate like manufacturing plants today–not restaurants... We take raw materials, turn them into a variety of quality products, package them, and deliver them. It's just like a factory, except that production and speed of service are key. The computer tells us where to put people to get the best possible service and how to use the least number of persons at any given time for the least possible cost... while maintaining speed of service. [16]

In each restaurant raw material is received, processed, sold, and consumed. However, a combination of elements must be considered: customer arrival patterns, product production, cashier interactions, what people are likely to order at various times, inventory rules, time motion studies, and corporate rules about servicing time.

Speed of service (called SOS at Burger King) is crucial to a restaurant's profitability. Restaurant sales during peak hours are often so high that total sales are limited only by production capabilities. If customers generally have lunch between noon and one, for example, then the more lunches that can be served during that period, the more profit accrues to a restaurant.

There is a tradeoff between the cost incurred by keeping customers waiting, and the cost of providing the meal. The first is calculated not only by the number of customers who leave because service is too slow, but the estimated number who will not return in the future. This must be balanced against the cost of wages and productivity of the servers. If people stationed at various positions in the store are not working at what is considered to be their optimal capacity, then what must be calculated is the loss to Burger King in unrealized labour, and also loss in potential profit if what those workers could have produced had been sold. This idea can be stated mathematically. [E(TC) stands for estimated total cost, E(SC) for estimated serving cost and E(WC) for estimated waiting cost.] The objective at Burger King is to estimate how minimize costs.

$$\text{Minimize } E(TC) = E(SC) + E(WC)\text{[17]}$$

While this calculation is useful when Burger King is operating at optimal capacity, it provides a static picture. Because customer arrivals fluctuate constantly, a new program called General Purpose Simulations Systems (GPSS), which could deal with varying volumes, was introduced. In GPSS, a model of the system is constructed and simulated experiments are conducted using that model. The simulation model divides the system into component parts, each of which exhibits predictable behaviour. Thus, a range of data, such as when customers come, timings of customer-cashier interactions, and time-motion studies of how long it takes to assemble a sandwich were gathered for forty different restaurants and entered into the computer. What emerged was a family of programs for each store layout with a complete distribution over time showing what would happen if a certain number of crew were put in various positions in the store. [18]

After generating all this information, Burger King then tested the results in a simulated situation. A model was constructed in a Miami warehouse and staffed with borrowed Burger King employees. The results were videotaped and compared to the computer projections. The model was judged to be successful. The new plan that emerged provided greater control than the scheduling system in effect since the late 1970s. Managers now predict hourly sales and a manual issued from head office indicates how many crew persons are allowed for each sales volume. Managers themselves decide where crew should be placed to maximize production. The results of the computer study are encompassed in a kit called Productivity Planning for Profit (PPP), which is distributed to store managers. The information on deploying workers contained in the kit is based on a service delivery time of three minutes, from the time a customer enters the restaurant, orders, pays for, and receives a meal.

The use of the kit relies on the ability of each local restaurant to make accurate sales projections. The operations department instructs them on how to do this most effectively. The most accurate method is to average previous sales for the particular time and day of the week from the three previous weeks. For example, staffing for lunch hour on a Friday will be determined by sales volume for the three previous Fridays during the noon to one o'clock rush hour. These forecasting procedures can of course be affected by special events (holidays, sporting events) or the vagaries of the weather.

With this method, sales projections are required for half-hour periods. These are compared with actual sales for each time period. Labour is divided into what is called direct (productive) and indirect (non-productive) hours. The actual production and sale of the menu is considered direct labour while the cleaning, maintenance, and minimal food maintenance necessary is indirect labour. (Food preparation includes stacking the fries into the fry racks, slicing the tomatoes, putting the condiments into the trays for the burger and sandwich boards, etc.) The positioning of workers according to expected sales volume is regulated, as is the number of staff. For example, if fifteen people are scheduled to work at a particular time, the number who should be placed at each work station (the cash registers, the fry area, etc.) is indicated by a chart given to all stores.

Managers must constantly try to reduce service time by getting employees to perform according to time-motion specifications. Instructions are given for how to time each individual worker and evaluate each operator's performance according to the standard indicated in the manual. Just as Taylor considered that workers were "soldiering" if they worked at less than their physiological maximum, so Burger King considers that it is entitled to the physiological maximum from its minimum-wage employees.

Thus Burger King uses the new technology to centralize planning. With the help of the computer, a detailed plan for organizing labour in all stores under all possible conditions has been developed. This plan, the result of a GPSS study completed in 1981, has been distributed to all stores. Each individual store then uses its computerized cash register to forecast sales. This local information is slotted into the grand master plan to receive the appropriate instructions for the particular outlet. Thus, the computer is used to develop and maintain a system of tight central control.

If computer projections are to be useful, than a ready supply of labour is necessary, one that can be called in to work when the volume of business is greater than expected or asked to "go home early" if the store is not busy. Careful attention must be paid to what workers can do. Standardization in all aspects of production is absolutely essential. The following will give some idea of just how the combination of scheduling policy, technology, and routinization of the work processes is set up.

Under the old labour schedule, which came into operation in 1979 and was still used during most of my fieldwork, only the number of workers allowed per sales volume was specified. Managers at the outlets would position workers, depending on the kitchen design and their own judgment. The new labour program cuts down on the number of workers allowed in order to lower labour costs by about 1.5 percent of gross sales, and also specifies where workers should be placed for maximum speed and efficiency. The principles remain the same but what is noticeable from the workers' point of view is that fewer people are around to do the same work.

The form the innovation took was called the "Shape Up" program, an effort to improve the "bottom line" at Burger King through training crew to work faster while enforcing consistency even more. At a crew meeting called to announce the new program, production leaders quizzed workers on the details of their shift. For example, "How many ounces of ketchup go on a burger?" During the new training, production leaders assisted at work stations as there were so few people on the floor.

One production leader reported that the changeover was very difficult. The scheduling manager described the implementation as follows:

The first two weeks were a nightmare. The kids did not like the new schedule. They had to work harder, and they did. Alan (a production leader) said the next time I saw the people at head office to tell them the new schedule stinks. Normally you'd put a weak person in with strong people to compensate. Now you have one person on whopper board, one person on specialties, one person on burgers, except for maybe Thursday night (when it's very busy).

It was really tight, and the kids did work. Now there were a few who just couldn't hack it, so those people would not get scheduled as frequently and it was unfortunate for them. Plus the kids were saying, "We want more hours, we want more hours." You're cutting back three to five people per night and you have to explain that.

After the reviews, we cut a lot of people. We asked people to leave, or gave them the opportunity to leave. [19]

Mr. Shape Up, a cartoon character, was introduced to promote the program. In the managers' newspaper, *Up Front*, Mr. Shape Up was called Burger King's answer to Superman. Mr Shape Up's civilian disguise was as a district manager. Shocked at the slovenliness of a restaurant he visits, the district manager jumps into the walk-in cooler and comes out as Mr. Shape Up with his cape flying. From reports, one did indeed need a cast of supermen and women to implement the new program.

Scheduling rules were laid out as follows:

• Schedule according to the minimum number of hours that an employee must work as required by law. Minimize the use of full time people where possible. Schedule longer than the minimum shift only when it results in a saving of hours.
• Minimize breaks if you must pay for them. Breaks are to be given out during slow periods and periods in which you had to schedule more people than needed because of minimum shift laws.
• Do not schedule to accommodate employees – schedule to the needs of your restaurant. Schedule on a daily basis using at least hourly increments. [20]

Not appearing for a shift is viewed as a serious matter, and after a warning, the employee will be fired. If a crew member calls in to say he or she is ill, management will call back to make sure the worker really is at home.

One of the common complaints of the young workers is that their school grades suffer because of their working hours and their inflexibility. One daytime worker said that she was sometimes late for her evening class because Burger King asked her to stay longer than her scheduled shift. More than one parent has intervened and insisted that their offspring leave the job. Some of the summer workers said they were leaving at the beginning of the school year because of past unfortunate experiences with neglected schoolwork.

The adult women workers objected to the irregularity as well. One of the workers described it as follows: "I don't know when to come in anymore. I never know if there will be time to shop or do the chores. When I start to leave at the scheduled time, they tell me not to because it's too busy. I come in early to relax a bit before starting work, and they rush me upstairs because they need me. I need longer hours, because I need the money, but they schedule me from 10:30 AM to 2:30 PM."[21]

When Sheila, another older worker was hired, the managers told her she would be working twenty-five hours a week, which would include lunch preparation (slicing the tomatoes and putting out the condiments). When she started work, however, she was told that she would only be needed for three hours a day and that someone else would be doing the preparation. Sheila was quite annoyed, but resented her coworker rather than the poor planning and misinformation of her managers.

Although managers vary the schedule at their discretion, workers are expected to always comply. I often overheard managers lecturing youngsters who failed to appear for a shift. Their tone was stern, and the message was that the person had let Burger King down. One must show responsibility if one wants to have a job, and such behaviour will not be tolerated. On the other hand, if the store is short staffed, managers call up workers for additional reinforcements. One young man said that the managers accused him of telling his sister to lie and say he was out of the house when they phoned. He said he was afraid to answer the phone, because it was very difficult to refuse the heavy pressure when managers requested him to work extra hours.

SCHEDULING MANAGERS AND PRODUCTION LEADERS

Production leaders' and managers' hours were also inconvenient and variable. When I first started working, the production leaders worked regular hours each day. In the evenings and on weekends the high school production leaders would be in charge. When the summer came, management decided to include all production leaders in a shifting schedule. Thus, the production leaders could never be sure of having a free weekend or evening and they were generally scheduled for eight-hour shifts. The two daytime production leaders soon quit. One of them, a young woman, asked for a raise and was refused, and subsequently left. Another young woman objected to being scheduled three Saturday nights in a row. One of the workers commented that management did that because she was so reliable.

Managers who work full time get two days off a week, but the two days are never the same. As the store is open from early morning till late at night, their shifts vary as well. Managers' meetings at Briarwood were scheduled weekly for Tuesday afternoons and all managers were expected to attend whether they were working that day or not. A look at the schedule for one of the assistant managers over a three-week period in July showed that he worked one full weekend out of the three. On the second weekend he worked on the Saturday and the third weekend he worked Sunday. In addition, his schedule included three all-night shifts (from midnight to 8 AM), and seven evenings, from 5 PM to closing (around 1 AM).

Burger King assistant managers at forty-four company-owned stores in Massachussetts and Connecticut sued for overtime pay in the early 1980s. They maintained that because so much of their time was spent in menial duties and because their tasks were regulated by head office, they did not perform true management duties and should not be properly classified as management. Therefore, they were entitled to compensation for overtime. The case was initiated by a US Labor Department complaint and won in a lower court but lost in the US Court of Appeals. It overturned a 1980 federal court decision that ruled that overtime pay had to be awarded to all assistant managers earning less than $250 weekly.[22]

GOOD DAYS AND BAD DAYS

Burger King plans its labour system with extraordinary detail. However, whether this tightly organized system is adhered to in real life is not completely predictable. Perhaps my own experiences will help to convey a sense of how this routinized labour process unfolds. Even in a very controlled situation, there are good days and bad days, good managers and bad managers. As I worked in the store, I kept a record of all that happened each day, though this was not without its difficulties, as I have mentioned earlier. The following are two excerpts from my fieldwork. One, I call A Bad Day, and the other, A Good Day.

Tuesday, 19 May – A Bad Day

In the morning, just after arriving, I hear that Kathy, the production leader, is going to train one of the new Chinese students on the "drive-thru," and I ask if I can listen and learn it

too.[23] She agrees, but Ira, one of the second assistant managers, tells me that I am to expedite (collect orders for the cashier). I explain that I am listening to the training session for the
"drive-thru." Linda, the head manager, comes over to me and
says I am blocking traffic at the takeout window. She orders me
to expedite, which I do. We bump into each other at one point,
and she rebukes me for carrying the order slip in my hand
(I should have stapled it to the bag first!).

Next thing I know, Helen, the second assistant manager,
comes over and tells me not to be offended (which I interpret
as meaning that I should be) but to go help out on the broiler-
steamer (the lowliest of low positions). So I go there. I am
standing on the side where the buns come out of the conveyor
belt, shoving the buns over as they come out of the toaster,
and then reaching with a pair of tongs to the other side to grab
the burgers as they come out of the conveyor broiler and put
them in the buns. Another worker, Judy, is on the other side
also assembling the cooked patties. I do not feel pleased at
being banished from the front, where the work is a little more
interesting.

Linda, the head manager, beckons me with her finger and I
go into her office. She reprimands me for not obeying the assistant manager when I was moved to a different station (although I had said nothing to Helen except a confused "okay")
and then tells me that my attitude is failing. I have a bad attitude and if my attitude doesn't improve she will have to dis-
continue my "program." I say that I'm just a little tired and go
back to the broiler-steamer. Then another manager moves me
over to assembling the whoppers.

I find that more interesting so I feel a little better. Sally, the
production leader, asks me to sweep the place, which I do.
Then Linda, the head manager, asks Darlene (a worker making
the small hamburgers) and me to wet-mop and dry-mop the
store. There is only one free mop, and Darlene is ordered to do
it and so I go on burger boards (making the small hamburgers).
I start thinking about a few weeks ago when David, Darlene's
brother, was being trained. Linda ordered him to sweep the
floor nine times in one day. David is only fifteen. Their father is
quite ill and can't work. Darlene, who had been living on her
own, moved back home, and David quit school to help make
ends meet. Darlene is convinced that the managers don't like
her. When Burger Bucks are given out for those who have performed well at their station, she says she is always passed over.

At lunch I tell Pat, one of the workers, about my run-in with the head manager. She is surprised that they would dress me down for having a a bad attitude, as I am generally pretty cheerful.

After the lunch rush, it is clean, clean, clean. I am asked to scrub the copper piping, and then to scrub down the base tiles all around the store, back and front. (Workers are always politely "asked" to do things. It is the kind of request that may not be refused.) So there I am crawling around the kitchen. Carmen, working at cash, asks me to help her expedite. I should refuse, as my hands are full of junk used for cleaning the steel; I don't. (A fellow workers' request may be refused, unless it is backed by a manager's authority. Production leaders fall somewhere between. They are supposed to be obeyed but it is possible to give them more flack than one dare give a manager.)

At supper, I am placed in the fry section, only I keep getting pushed around. I am asked to place the fries in the oil, which I find unpleasant work requiring a strong wrist. The other job on that station, placing the fries in the bags, is done by someone else who is faster than I am at scooping them up.

A manager asks me to fill a fry rack. I groan as it is my third one that day, and also it is a really greasy job. Each rack holds about thirty wire baskets. The manager suggests I must be really good at it, since I've done it so many times that day. So I do that, and then Ira, another second assistant manager, reprimands me because I put too many fries into each basket for deep frying. Ira says that too many fries will be cooked at once and remain unsold. He claims it's a thirty-dollar food loss, and he will be chewed out. (How on earth he calculated that, I don't know – I figure it's only a few dollars.)

This place is completely overrun with managers. In addition to the head manager, there is one first assistant, three second assistants, two training managers, and a swing manager. So that means as many as three, even four, managers plus two production leaders ordering a person around at any one time.

I end my work on the floor and go downstairs around 7 PM. Two of the three Abel brothers are there. They are young black men from Jamaica. They also complain about managers ordering people to do different things at the same time. Ben says the place is crazy and someone should write a book about what goes on. So I say I am, but I regret it because I think it makes them a little uncomfortable.

One of the young women comes downstairs with her dinner of hamburger and a plate of fries. Jay, the first assistant manager, comes down the stairs into the crew room and makes some snide comment to me about mingling with the common crew. Muriel comes down to ask if someone will take her shift Thursday. Juliette agrees and goes upstairs to the kitchen to find who made up the schedule and ask about changing it. The scheduling manager tells her that he'll be right down, but appears about thirty minutes later. When he finally comes downstairs, he rebukes Muriel for not giving him two weeks notice and she replies, "Well, how did I know you were going to schedule me then?" Thursday is her eighteenth birthday.

I am finally ready to go home around 7:45 PM. Juliette and her friend are late to meet some other pals in a nearby shopping mall, so I offer to drive them.

Wednesday, 2 June – A Good Day

Today was an eventful day. There were five new people on the floor, or 25 percent of the workers. I was placed up front expediting and everyone was busy showing the new ones how to do things. Elaine was not here, Margaret has likely found another job (I'll ask her friend, Maria), and Kathy wasn't there either; she's probably in her new foster home. Lucy will be leaving on Thursday to have her baby. Both Brenda and Dana have been made production leaders. That catapulted me, who has been there all of one month, into the position of experienced worker. I can do everything better and faster than the new people, and it feels sort of good to have that recognized. I was expediting up front today. I noticed myself sweeping the floor without being asked, pleased with myself that I can beat the managers to asking me to do it by doing it first.

I annoyed Maria, the cashier, in an argument about what size bag to put a big whopper in. It used to go into a 12-lb. bag, but now they have changed the rules. (These kinds of changes come from head office via a memo.) Now it's to be put in a small bag sideways, if there's nothing else with it. I insisted doing it the old way, but Maria turned out to be right.

I offered to collect the cash for the "drive-thru" as the new young woman placed there did not know how to make change. (In the "drive-thru," unlike the in-store cash, the worker needs to be able to make change because the items are entered and picked up with a short time lapse.) Carmen was quite patient, but the new woman couldn't get things straight. They really do put the pretty ones up front. Shirley, an older woman, was on the specialty board (making sandwiches). A new fellow, Colin, was on broiler-steamer and not looking happy at all. (He quit the next day.) The other new guy, Ron, was on whoppers but he had worked at Burger King before.

The managers had their meeting today, and Brenda was the production leader running the floor. I was asked to do preparation, and Sharon showed me how to slice the tomatoes with the machine so not so much is wasted near the core. She doesn't let the tomato quite rest on the bottom when it's sliced so the end piece that gets discarded is smaller. She told me she had figured that out herself. Sharon is a mother of three in her thirties. Her husband was laid off his job, and she really needs all the hours she can get. Sharon has a hard life. In addition to the eight hours a day she puts in at Burger King, she does everything at home too. She was eventually promoted to production leader and then fired for the cardinal sin, "bad attitude."

I took my time with the tomatoes and David (the fourteen-year-old who had dropped out of school) picked up on that and kept saying to me, "Aren't you done yet?" I, in turn, asked him how come they had changed his station from the dining room, was he was ruining people's appetites or what? When I finally finished I went downstairs for my break. It was good to sit down because I was tired. All I wanted to do was read the paper. I ate some disgusting food, ham and cheese and onion rings. Ugh.

In the evening I was placed with Ben on whoppers, but was then moved across to the burgers. This pleased me, because I got to hold the fort by myself. It's a challenge to see if I can keep up and fun to see how fast I can get. On whoppers, there are two people and the task breakdown is fairly standard. One person looks at the computer printout to see if there are specials (any variations on the standard – e.g., no ketchup, or extra tomatoes) and does the bottom, while the other does the tops and microwaves the whole burger. Alone, on burgers, I didn't have to coordinate efforts with anyone.

Only once today did two managers tell me to do different things at the same time; that's pretty good. Helen, the assistant manager, and Sheila, the production leader, were busy deciding who to send home this evening as it was pretty slow. Revising the schedule in this way is illegal as a number of people were sent home after only two hours. People are asked first, but I

doubt that they know the law well enough to refuse, and anyway the request is made in such a fashion that it's hard to refuse.

When I look at my notes and my reactions, I find it embarrassing that I took the rules so seriously. This certainly was the
case with my co-workers. If there was a dispute between the
rules and commonsense, it was no contest: the former would
prevail. The only minor hitch in Burger King's planning was
the extent of direct control required to maintain work intensity.
Unlike an automobile assembly line, the conveyor belt for the
burgers could not be speeded up, and so workers had to be
pushed to work quickly. This meant many low-level managers
exerting the only real control over their jobs that they had – the
freedom to push around those under them.

A FAIR DAY'S WORK

Burger King's system is based on the old notion that a fair day's
work consists of all that it is humanly possible to do within a given
period of time. When observing the Burger King workplace, it is
easy to see how, while the work itself is quite labour-intensive, the
machinery makes the cooking decisions. Thus the worker's job is to
assemble the product according to very specific rules and regulations. Under constant pressure to keep production as high as possible, store management often falls somewhat short of the cross
training that would make it possible to assign any worker to any
station in the store, as speed would temporarily decline. Nevertheless, the restaurant can function quite adequately even with a high
percentage of brand new workers.

The job ladder presented to workers does not represent significant
opportunity: becoming a production leader just means taking on
more work. Store managers, too, receive low pay, and make few
decisions. Their major area of authority is overseeing the crew to
ensure that people work hard. Braverman's contention that work
under monopoly capitalism has become deskilled seems amply il-
lustrated in this industry. Braverman makes a distinction between
training and skill; traditional concepts of skill involve a knowledge
of the processes as well as the manual dexterity required for production, while training implies acquisition of manual skills only.
"What is left to workers is a reinterpreted and woefully inadequate
concept of skill; a specific dexterity, a limited and repetitous
operation."[24]

However, even in Burger King, management has not completely monopolized knowledge. There is still a distinction to be made between doing a good job and doing a bad job. For one's own self-respect, doing a good job is important. In the Burger King workplace, however, this "worker knowledge" is disregarded in creating the structure of authority. Obedience is primary; there is a great deal of direct control along with a myriad of rules and regulations. Consequently, managers exercise their authority over workers in often contradictory ways. An age factor enters in as well; as one woman describes it, "I get sick of being pushed around by a bunch of teen-agers." There is a consensual aspect in translating labour power into labour; workers' cooperation is needed, even if it is just at the level of showing up on time. However, the kind of political power that can be exercised by a worker with scarce, not easily obtainable skills – someone like the chef in William Whyte's restaurant – is quite a bit greater than that of a worker who can be instantly replaced by another if she or he doesn't smile enough.

People try to make the best of situations over which they feel they have little control. In Burger King, people develop preferences for one station over another, or for one manager over another. They joke with and tease each other when they can, and this alleviates some of the tedium of the job. However, the fact that workers breathe life into a very limiting and boring work situation must be understood as only part of the reality; the other part is that Burger King's control over the conditions of production is never seriously challenged.

Photomontage   Richard Slye

CHAPTER SEVEN

Martialling Workers' Loyalty

In the previous chapter we saw that Burger King's profits rest on the availability of a shifting labour force, one that Burger King can call upon and dismiss as the need arises. By simplifying the work tasks and cross-training at all stations, Burger King has attempted to create a work situation that allows any worker to do any job in the restaurant. Just as almost all discretion is removed from the job, workers are told how important each of them is to the restaurant's success. Thus we see some of the contradictions involved in grafting a human relations approach to labour management onto a division of labour determined by the principles of scientific management. The organization of production at Burger King is geared to treating human labour as an undifferentiated, quantifiable input. At the same time, workers must be convinced of their individual importance in order to elicit their maximal output.

The management in the individual outlet faces a difficult task – it must contend with the constant need to find suitable workers, while keeping its labour costs low enough to be acceptable to higher levels of management. The single greatest challenge facing managers is dealing with the workforce that meet Burger King's criteria for availability – teenagers and married women. While young people are fast workers, they need to be impressed with certain basic job skills such as punctuality. A former manager described it as follows:

Let's think of, say a Roman ship that's being rowed by galley slaves on its way to war. You want them to work hard, your business needs them to work hard. How do you get them to smile? It's hard – after all, the work is rush, rush, rush, clean, clean, clean. Having those kids lined up begging to work. How do they do it?

Competitions – who can make the best hamburger, the fastest hamburger. Also the hiring practices. They want a certain kind of kid in there. Not the kid that everyone looks down on, that they make fun of. They want the captain of the football team working. Working at Burger King has to be the thing to do. Attitude matters. It doesn't matter how funny kids look. If they are happy, they give out a certain impression. The kind of person required is one that will relate well to other people. It's the people business.[1]

The adult women workers, normally hired to work daytime during the weekdays, are slower, but generally more reliable. The women are there strictly for the money and have few options. As the ex-Burger King manager quoted above said,

Let's face it – what other kinds of jobs are available? Where else can they go – to a variety store? They have responsibilities to their kids, want to see them off to school and be there for them when they get home in the after-noon. They have demanding husbands who come home from work at night and want to be looked after. The job at Burger King gives them a bit of extra money. They live nearby and even if the job isn't too pleasant, well it'll do.

The hiring, training, and supervision of the workforce are the most important functions of a Burger King manager. Motivation of em-ployees is explained to managers as "your action which creates the atmosphere, or the environment for your employees; benefits, signs also. Something you say or do to meet your employees' needs to get what you want and to make you and your employees happy."[2] In its newsletter to managers, called *Up Front*, Burger King stresses that the "manager is key ... who plays the biggest role in maintaining a high level of morale and job satisfaction among crew members? Who holds the key to a smooth running restaurant? You do, according to a study conducted by the Marketing Research Department."[3]

Voiced somewhat less positively, this same survey found that about half of the crew members were either only somewhat satisfied or not at all satisfied with their jobs. Workers who have been on the job longest are the least satisfied. The newsletter made a con-nection between satisfaction with the manager and a worker's sat-isfaction with the job. The clear message in the article is that a good manager is able to keep workers happy.

In a test for training managers that is part of the Basic Restaurant Operations Course, trainees are questioned about their knowledge of employees' "needs and wants." They were asked to rank the following items in order of importance.

Good working conditions
Personal loyalty to worker
Sympathetic understanding of personal problems
Promotion and growth
Good wages
Interesting work
Tactful discipline
Appreciation of work done
Job security
Feeling in the know of things going on[4]

Contrary to what one might suppose, managers are told that the three most important things for workers are: first, appreciation of work done; second, feeling in the know of things going on; and third, sympathetic understanding of personal problems. Good wages are fifth on the list, promotion and growth ninth, and last on the list is good working conditions. Thus the same message is made clear in the training course: only a bad manager has an unhappy crew. It is within each manager's power to provide for employee "needs and wants" as defined by the company. (The manager whose manual I read gave the "wrong" answer. He foolishly thought people take jobs for the money!)

"Science" is invoked to explain why managers should believe what they would expect to be otherwise, namely that people take jobs because they want and need the wages. This science is a particular brand of psychology, and is commonly referred to in management literature for the restaurant business, as well as in general management manuals.

Burger King has adapted the work of Abraham Maslow, the social psychologist and Frederick Herzberg, the industrial psychologist, in a most innovative manner.[5] Maslow and Hertzberg's writings are from the 1950s and early 1960s, a time when companies had an interest in preventing high worker turnover. It was particularly suited for those situations where bureaucratic control was in effect.[6] Companies were willing to grant concessions in order to win workers' loyalties. These psychologists stressed that material incentives would not be sufficient. People needed less tangible rewards as well as those listed in the satisfier column above.

Management psychology in the Basic Restaurant Operations Course begins with a chart credited to to the work of Abraham

Maslow. The chart displays what is called a "hierarchy of needs." These are:

1   Physiological needs
2   Safety needs
3   Social needs (to love and be loved)
4   Self actualization – the need to grow and become what one is capable of becoming

When one level of needs is met, it is argued, one begins to experience the necessity of meeting a new and higher level of needs. While radicals such as the late Abbie Hoffman, of Yippie fame, found inspiration in Maslow's work for a political and cultural challenge to the status quo, Maslow's work has also been adapted for corporate use.[7] The work of Frederick Herzberg is presented in a chart that identifies "work dissatisfiers" and "work satisfiers."

Work Dissatisfiers	*Work Satisfiers*
1 Company policy	1 Achievement
2 Supervision	2 Recognition
3 Working conditions	3 Work itself
4 Interpersonal relations	4 Responsibility
5 Salary as defined as changes in the amount of pay	5 Advancement

Herzberg points out that the absence of work dissatisfiers is not sufficient to motivate people. Motivation requires the presence of work satisfiers.

Rather than using work satisfiers as a supplement to decent wages and working conditions, (see the Dissatisfier column), Burger King encourages managers to believe that the findings of "science" show that the things over which managers have no control do not really matter to workers anyway. The managers' challenge is to provide feelings of achievement and recognition to the crew without being able to do much about altering the dissatisfiers. Considering the other requirements of a manager, to abide by stringent scheduling rules and put the needs of the restaurant before the interests of workers, this is a hard task.

At first glance it seems as if Burger King's use of the work of Maslow and Herzberg is a distortion that violates the integrity of their work. However, Russell Jacoby in *Social Amnesia* gives a convincing explanation of why the ego psychology of the neo- and post-Freudians is so easily adapted to corporate use. He maintains that these psychologists "mirror rather than penetrate surface phenomena ... Personality and identity, becoming and authenticity move to the fore as unadvertised specials of the affluent society which already is a bargain hunter's delight."[8]

In Jacoby's view, dividing material needs from psychic needs is itself a mystification. The fulfillment of psychic needs and spiritual values – "authenticity" and "fulfillment" – become commodities to be shopped around for. When "work" is separated from "free time," when material structure is seen as something different from the psychological world, when producers are separate from consumers, then our discontent becomes diverted from the source of the problem to superficial or surface matters, the symptoms of the problem.

Thus, Jacoby maintains, the work of post-Freudians such as Maslow is misleading. At a time when mass society is threatening subjectivity itself, their theories tell us that we can all be free right now – "without the sweat and grime of social change." Collective action is rejected in favour of individual "how-to manuals: ... while business dominates mind and body, one is admonished to mind one's own business."[9]

The concepts are less than critical: they are bland checks that endorse the prevailing malpractices with cheery advice on inner strength and self-actualization. Maslow's "peak experience" is the misery of everyday life condensed. Liberation is a banal existence plus enthusiasm ... The alchemists of liberation transmute the base wares of capitalism into the treasures of humanity.[10]

A psychology that concentrates on workers' needs and wants, defined in terms of isolated individuals, is very useful for training Burger King managers. Thus, crew members can be motivated by adequate manager leadership. Worker satisfaction is an individual phenomenon defined not through decent pay scales and working conditions, but in the less tangible area of psychological concepts. A manager doing his or her job will solve the problem of employee discontent through adequate communication. Store signs, crew meetings to tell crew about new policies, RAP (real approach to problem) sessions where selected crew members are invited to express their grievances, all contribute to building what is called good communication. "Employees who understand what is going on and who feel a part of store life, develop a sense of loyalty and pride. As a result they work harmoniously with management."[11]

THE MANY FUNCTIONS OF TEAMWORK

Identification of crew members with the restaurant and pride in the restaurant is fostered through a division between "us" and "them."

"Us" includes both managers and workers, while "them" refers to the customers. The image of "teamwork" of all restaurant staff is promoted. Signs in the crew room exhorting the crew to more closely adhere to regulations would often end with "Let's Keep Briarwood Number One!"

The service nature of the industry is used in the attempt to keep workers hard at work for their "team." Making money for Burger King is equated with treating customers properly, the responsibility of crew. A handout to cashiers to help in their training makes this explicit:

"Customer service and cultivating the good will of our customer requires the teamwork and cooperation of every person in a Burger King restaurant ... We have the best food products to serve and a pleasant, attractive place to eat. But without the personal attention to good service that only you can give, our customers may not return... Be fast and friendly, with a "smile." Make the customer's visit a happy one."

Following this introduction is a declaration of service to the customer. Some excerpts are as follows:

A customer is not dependent on us. We are dependent on him ...
A customer is not just money in the cash register. He is a human being with feelings, like our own ...
A customer is a person who comes to us with his needs and his wants. It is our job to fill them ...
A customer deserves the most courteous attention we can give him. He is the life-blood of this and every business. He pays your salary. [12]

The theory is that when customers feel and see a good attitude, they sense concern for them and their needs. This makes them like Burger King and want to return. Burger King urges employees to be pleasant, cheerful, smiling, and courteous at all times with customers, fellow workers, and supervisors. They should also show obvious pride in their work and employment. But as Arlie Hochschild points out in *The Managed Heart*, a book about stewardesses, when spontaneous warmth becomes part of the job, workers become estranged from their own smiles. When job requirements involve appearing to love it, companies lay claim not just to their workers' physical motions, but to their *emotions* as well.

At Burger King, identifying crew members as individuals is seen to be important both for crew morale and for the customers. "Guests like to think of you as a person, not some sort of robot." To this end, the crew must make sure the name tag identifying them is on straight, and its safety catch fastened, before greeting the "guests." Burger King encourages its employees always to look their best, blurring the distinction between people's work and non-work lives. "Know how you have more fun at parties and on dates when you're sure you look your best? Same thing goes at your job. Except maybe it's more important to look great – because you're meeting more people."

Athletic analogies are used to explain managers' jobs to them. One area manager for Burger King describes the functions of a manager as: "In many ways, managing a restaurant is like coaching a team. They stay on the sidelines and send in the play."[13] Burger King workers are called "crew." Working quickly is presented as a challenge similar to an athletic contest. The object is "winning," which, I suppose, is serving the customer as quickly as possible, while abiding by Burger King rules and regulations.

During a rush in the restaurant, anywhere from two to four managers may be on the floor offering helpful comments such as, "Let's go team," or "Let's get with it." Cheating is not abiding by Burger King rules. If one does not give the customer the specified amount of fries, pickles, and lettuce, or doesn't heat a sandwich to the specified temperature, then one is "cheating" the customer. If one gives out too many fries, or too many tomatoes, one is "cheating" the restaurant. (This was explained to me by a manager who chastised me for putting more than the specified one-ninth ounce of mustard on a hamburger. She said I was cheating both the store and the customer. The customer was not being given "satisfaction" because not only was there too much mustard on the hamburger, but I had placed it in the centre, instead of spreading it around in a thin circular motion as recommended in the Manual of Operating Data.)

A Burger King Olympics is held annually. A "Best Darn Team" is selected for each area. Each store sends a crew member from each station to compete. The person who can perform the work on her station fastest while abiding by rules and regulations has the honour of making the Best Darn Team for her area. A small cash bonus is also included. There are also regular contests within the store, which pit employees against each other and keep people working hard. An employee of the month is selected. In addition to having her picture displayed above the ordering counter, she receives a twenty dollar bonus.

Each year, from September to December, "Burger Bucks" (or Burger King "funny money") are handed out daily. They are given to crew members who have "kept up" during rush times and those

who have done extra jobs. The cashier whose money balances the
most times in a month receives a bonus of fifty Burger Bucks, for
example. A sign posted in the crew room explains the value of Burger
Bucks:

Burger Buck Bonanza
Only 3 weeks left to earn $Burger Bucks
What are they?
Burger King funny money you earn for doing extra jobs.
What are they good for?
Save them to buy prizes at our auction sale.

Burger Bucks serve to foster competitiveness and resentment
among workers. Charges of favoritism are common with respect to
the way they are dispersed. Some of my fellow workers complained
that a particular manager would pass over them even though they
had "kept up" during a rush. In December, management hosts a
party in which Burger Bucks are redeemable for various items –
many of them with a Burger King insignia.

COMMUNICATION

Managers are told that communication is one of the most valuable
tools for controlling workers. A handout in the Basic Restaurant
Operations Course advises: "Employees who understand what is
going on and who feel a part of the store life, develop a sense of
loyalty and pride. As a result, they work more harmoniously with
management." "Keeping crew in the know" is seen as very important
in maintaining good communication. To this end, crew meetings
are held regularly to keep crew informed about company policy and
to enlist their support. One meeting I attended asked for suggestions
about how to solve the ever-present problem of keeping the crew
room clean. The enthusiastic suggestions elicited from workers involved docking pay and taking away the "privilege" of a free meal.
Interestingly, no one suggested including crew room maintenance
along with other tasks of running the restaurant, like keeping the
dining room and the customers' bathroom clean. It was assumed
that crew room maintenance should be a voluntary activity.

The crew meeting also included a skit given by the managers acting
out what "bad" crew members do and concluding with a discussion

of how a "good" crew member should look and act. The bad crew member had mustard on his uniform, and made hamburgers with too many condiments. Everyone enjoyed the managers' antics. This particular meeting was also designed to announce the new labour system, the Shape Up program. Crew were told that the new program was being implemented to improve production and service, making Burger King a better restaurant for everybody.

The RAP session, or real approach to problems, is one way management keeps informed of any discontent in the restaurant. A group of eight or ten employees is selected to gather in the manager's office and discuss what they like and don't like about their jobs. As described in the Basic Restaurant Operation Course for new assistant managers, managers must expect to deal with complaints involving scheduling, pay, and assignment to work stations in these RAP sessions.

KEEPING MORALE HIGH AND
COSTS LOW

Burger King efforts to martial loyalty are focused on creating the kind of morale that will keep work intense and productivity high. The attempts to ensure long-term commitment are minimal. Thus the semi-annual reviews for crew members result in pay raises averaging ten cents per hour, hardly a monetary incentive conducive to long-term commitment. The promise of upward mobility is offered through promotion to production leader. A production leader's working conditions, however, are actually worse than those for crew, and they achieve little monetary gain. Production leaders are responsible for making sure the work goes smoothly, the kitchen remains clear, and not too much food is wasted. They can ask workers to sweep or mop, and temporarily reassign them from one work station to another. Often the production leaders end up working very hard themselves at a work station. They must field the resentment of workers, who object to being ordered around by those they see as their peers, and they also face the reprimands of managers if there is a hitch in the process.

Every six months for a company-owned restaurant, and every year for a franchise, outlets are inspected by a group of officials from the area office. The inspection is called ROC, Restaurant Operations Consultation, and is designed to keep close watch on lower-level management and to ensure that there is tight centralized control in each outlet.

Every aspect of operations is looked into and noted on a thirty-nine-page 9 × 14 form. Overall operations can receive a maximum rating of 1,000. Less than 699 points is unsatisfactory. Of the nine sections in the graded part of the review, "product quality" and "customer service" receive the most emphasis. Product quality refers to obeying Burger King standards for cooking and the temperature at which the meal is served. Customer service includes the length of time it takes to serve customers. The new form, developed since the Shape Up Program, has reduced these standards to two and one-half minutes. As in the training sessions, cheerful service, suggestive selling, and clean restrooms are all considered important.

Preparations for the day of the big test, when the big brass from the area office come around, reinforce the notion of crew and store management operating as a team. In the period prior to the inspection, crew are encouraged to work hard cleaning everything in sight. On the day of the inspection, only the most competent crew members are scheduled, and the event is treated as a kind of performance. A high score is seen as a victory for everyone in the store.

The most effective way of ensuring an intense work pace is built into the service nature of the business. As we have seen, all Burger Kings are designed with an open kitchen. Not only can customers see what is going on, but workers know when the restaurant gets busy. When a worker sees people lined up at the counter waiting for their food, the pressure to work harder is enhanced. According to Donald Smith, the Burger King president who implemented this design: "The benefit is that the crew and management in that unit know that they are on display and there is a certain showmanship that is part and parcel with trying not to look bad and trying to put on a show. Productivity is amazingly upgraded in that type of atmosphere... whether it is a McDonald's or a Wendy's that is wide open to a customer's view."[14]

Burger King social activities are planned to help foster an identification with the company and keep morale high. During my fieldwork a group of teenagers, most of whom were production leaders, "volunteered," with a bit of managerial prodding, to form a "social committee." It was their job to organize and sign up workers for various Burger King events – skating parties, dances, bowling, baseball. These activities were presented as entirely for the benefit of Burger King crew and as such, it was accepted that they would be funded by crew members.

The social committee had some difficulties. The first problem was lack of sufficient interest from other crew members. Helen, the second assistant manager, made it clear that it was up to the production leaders on the committee to whip up the necessary enthusiasm. Various ways of raising money were suggested, such as a car wash, wiping windows, mowing lawns. All of these were vetoed by the first assistant manager. Burger King will sponsor community activities to improve community relations and encourage more business, but funding crew events does not fit into that category.

The social committee finally decided to organize a garage sale. Eileen, a production leader, generously offered her parents' garage, but the parents vetoed the idea. Finally, Maria, an older Italian woman who was vociferous in her criticisms of Burger King, volunteered the use of her lawn, since she lived close by. She felt that she was helping out the youngsters. Signs were put in the crew room to encourage people to bring things in for the big day, but the sale never happened because not enough workers brought in things to sell. Some money was raised through fines levied for renting uniforms when people either forgot theirs or came in to work with dirty ones. For the most part, individual crew members paid their own way to the social events. Thus those who signed up for the Burger King baseball team were charged $12.52 each for their Burger King team jersey.

The events themselves were fairly popular among the part-time teenagers who worked evenings. The ballgames drew about fifteen players for each game. Helen, the second assistant manager, was expected to attend these Sunday morning games, whether or not it was her scheduled day off. More elaborate activities were planned as well. A Burger King dance was planned at the local Holiday Inn. The cost was $17.50 a person or $30.00 per couple. A disc jockey, door prizes, roses for the first fifteen "girls," the selection of a ballroom king and queen, were some of the promised events of the evening. The social committee entered into plans for the dance with great enthusiasm. They decided that the "boys" on the committee would rent tuxedos for the occasion. One of the male production leaders told me it was going to cost him between $62 and $72, depending on the style he chose. Few of the daytime workers attended these events; certainly none of the women with families participated.

The only event formally sponsored by Burger King was an annual picnic. For this day, store personnel from another store staffed the outlet so that all crew members could go. Transportation to the park and lunch for the crew members was provided by management. This act of generosity had some strings attached, however. A crew room notice advised everyone that they must show up in a bright yellow Burger King T-shirt.

> Hop on the Wagon T-Shirts Are available for everyone.
> Get two T-Shirts; the first one free And Buy the Second
> for $1 for a friend.
>
> This money will go to the crew fund
> to make our picnic more enjoyable
> You must wear a T-Shirt to come to the
> picnic or pay a fine if you show up
> without one.

A great deal of pressure was put on all crew members to attend the picnic. A few of the daytime workers objected, saying that Burger King had no right to make them lose a day's pay which they could ill afford. Management backed down and allowed these workers to work. Others said that if they had to take a day off, they had better things to do than attend a picnic.

Nevertheless, almost all of the part-timers and about three-quarters of the full-timers did attend, some with their children. The picnic was held at a conservation area about 45 minutes from the restaurant. People with cars brought them for transportation. The lunch consisted of barbecued hot dogs and hamburgers, fruit, and soft drinks. After the rituals of throwing people into the water, we were coerced into playing games. Different kinds of relays were held with prizes given out for the winners. Announcements were made in the middle of the games: best new trainee, best employee, and (a surprise), the assignment of a new manager to the store.[15] The day ended with a best bathing suit contest. The contestants, of course, were all young women and the distinction between the "best bathing suit" and a ranking of the bodies of the young women modelling them was one of semantics only.

Because the labour scheduling system assigns different groups of workers to work together each day, workplace social relations can only develop from shared commonalities based on other aspects of workers' lives. These common ties based on gender and age influence the way in which workers relate to each other; they are used by Burger King to promote activities geared to its particular labour force.

GENDER, RACE, AGE, AND THE WORKPLACE

The reasons people come to work at Burger King often have to do with their gender, race, or age. That is, they are people who must handle all the family responsibilities, or who must still be in school full time, or those with fewer job opportunities. These characteristics are outside the traditional discourse of class position and are related to peoples' lives off the job. They often apply to immigrants, visible minorities, women, or teenagers.

Labour market theorists describe the workings of two labour markets in which workers compete for jobs. The primary labour market has wage, employment, and promotion policies that will ensure a stable labour force.[16] In the secondary labour market employers use the cultural hierarchies of workers and exploit them by assigning jobs on the basis of age, race, and sex; women and minority groups often find themselves locked in low-skilled, irregular work.[17] More privileged workers use these cultural hierarchies to their advantage and have in the past objected when women or visible minorities attempted to take on certain jobs. It used to be common for blacks to be janitors or dishwashers, but rarely waiters or cooks. In the New York restaurant chain I worked in as a teenager in the 1950s, there were no black waitresses. In sub-basement B, where food preparation took place, about half the workforce were visible minorities who worked as kitchen "aids." Thus, certain features of particular workers – their gender, race, or age – come into play as an explanation of the jobs to which they are assigned. In recent years, the number of secure, well-paying jobs in the primary sector has been shrinking, and the number of poorly paid, low-skilled job opportunities has increased. Despite equal pay laws, and some minor changes in human rights legislation, women and visible minorities remain in job ghettoes. While labour market theorists describe how certain groups do not compete on an equal basis with others, they can't tell us very much about what happens at work.

"Plant sociology," the tradition of examining industrial behaviour within the workplace, looks carefully at what happens at work in order to see what interventions will produce cooperative working relationships and greater productivity. They assume there is no inherent conflict of interest between workers and their employers. Marxists such as Harry Braverman were critical of this research. Braverman claimed that these industrial sociologists, concerned with avoiding signs of dissatisfaction on the part of the worker, completely overlooked the nature of the work itself, and how it has been degraded. Braverman starts from the premise that the nature of capitalism necessarily produces a workplace where the interests of the workers are opposed to the interests of employers, in a workplace that is becoming increasingly coercive.

Michael Burawoy's significant contribution to the discussion of the labour process was to focus on the human side of work in a way that questioned the premises of the plant sociologists and some Marxists, such as Braverman. In Burawoy's view, neither cooperation nor conflict are inevitable developments; both need to be investigated. He considers workers' positions in production or actual jobs to be primary. In *The Manufacture of Consent* he explores social relations at work to see how they determine workers' dispositions and social configurations. He concludes that how people relate to each other is influenced by the kind of work they do and the organization of the workplace in which they find themselves.

Burawoy's analysis is thought-provoking and goes a long way towards turning around a view of workers as powerless dupes, helplessly manipulated by forces outside their control. He addresses the problem of how a capitalist mode of production came to be the dominant mode. How is it that workers work hard enough to produce surplus value, or profit for their employers? How do workers come to actively support a work situation that is inherently exploitative?

Burawoy's research addresses some very large questions about how capitalism operates. But he ignores other factors that operate in a working environment. In what way are certain environments "for men only," while others, such as Burger King, are the domain of women and teenagers? He observed how workers get caught up in games of "making out" (the shopfloor lingo for "making the rate"), if necessary risking life and limb in the process of fulfilling quotas informally set by the workgroup. However, the reader may wonder whether his observations apply to *all* workers' response to work, or just male responses to a male workplace. Burawoy noted that workers expressed racist attitudes through jokes but claimed that this did not interfere with their ability to cooperate with each other in doing the work. However these are artificial distinctions. For example, women now view verbal sexual harassment as a workplace abuse not to be tolerated.

By taking the workplace and the labour process as his point of departure, Burawoy ignores the special interests of white men in maintaining their privileged position in the workplace. Feminist criticisms of Marxist theory need to be considered. In his concern to develop theory that underlines the importance of the kind of work we do and how that work is organized, Burawoy relegates considerations related to gender, race, and age to minor factors. This is not good enough. Feminist writers such as Heidi Hartmann have charged that most of Marxism and sociology is sex-blind in its analysis of production. Unfortunately, even as fine a theorist as Burawoy is no exception.[18]

That sexism and racism enter the workplace is not likely to be contested by any observant person. The question is, what effect does it actually have on how workers do their work? When I entered the Burger King workplace, very impressed with the work of Michael Burawoy, I wanted to know what the "manufacture of consent" would look like in this kind of a workplace. I knew that it would not be the same as the machine shop in Chicago he studied. I nevertheless assumed, however, that in a fast food restaurant there were bound to be forms of cooperation between workers and some mediating power that workers would have over management directives. After all, workers, even fast food workers, are not automatons.

I looked and looked, but never found this active participation in determining the labour process that Burawoy described. Workers at Burger King do not have even a limited arena in which they can delude themselves into thinking of the labour process as a game in which they participate via commonly agreed-upon rules. Control of the game and setting the rules of playing are the prerogative of Burger King alone. If one does not choose to play by Burger King's rules, one must leave the game entirely. While workers in Burger King, like the skilled machinists studied by Burawoy, enjoy "keeping up," this is not the same as "making out" or making the rate. Thus it is not consent that is produced, but acquiescence.

This acquiescence, however, is very limited. If Burger King finds workers relatively easy to dispense with, so too most workers find jobs at Burger King easy to leave. The commitments of workers to their lives off the job don't reinforce their obligations to stay at the job for very long. Thus, other obligations place some limits on Burger King's capacity to exploit its labour force.

The most clearly observable forms of gender, age, and race inequalities emerge in why people work in this kind of a situation. As in other industries characterized by high turnover and absence of unionization, women, visible minorities, and young people are overerrepresented.[19] I also noted how once this cheap labour is recruited, it is interchangeability rather than gender, age, or race which becomes the major consideration in assigning people to work stations. Interchangeability of workers is desirable for a fluid production team where all workers can do all the jobs. Another current, however, runs counter to the first goal; local management places the prettier younger female workers at the cash register, the adult women in the back, and the young men at jobs where slightly more strength is required.

The overriding determinant is to keep replacement costs as low as possible. Some young men and adult women do work up front, women do the heavier jobs when young men are not around, and teenaged women are sometimes assigned to the fry station. Management policy from Burger King headquarters actively encourages this versatility because if any worker can do any job, then the cheapest workers can be used.

I heard accounts of overt racism at Burger King. One of the young black women who was fed up with the job and was quitting told me that one of the managers had called her a "nigger." I was shocked, and asked another young black fellow in the crew room if he could confirm what she said. "Sure," he said, "Big Ira and Donny routinely refer to Ben as 'nigger.'" I asked my informant why no one had complained to management. He said that if they wanted the job, the best course of action was to do nothing and not "make waves."

Although this kind of crude racism is not Burger King Canada policy, charges are made of racial discrimination in the industry as a whole. Few management posts are held by members of racial minorities. McDonald's black franchisees have claimed they are offered only the less lucrative locations. The NAACP (the National Association for the Advancement of Colored People), a fairly conservative organization of blacks in the US, charged Shoney's, a large restaurant chain in the United States with a systemwide "antiblack" policy.[20]

In early 1990, a coalition of fifty church, labour, and community groups in Philadelphia banded together to launch a boycott of McDonald's because of discriminatory wage policies practised in McDonald's outlets. The coalition, called the Campaign for Fair Wages, was acting on documentation that the starting pay of fast food workers in the inner city averaged almost one dollar less than that of suburban workers. Seventy-five percent of the inner city fast food workforce is black, compared to only 37 percent in the suburbs. The campaign coalition targetted McDonald's, because they are the largest and most profitable chain. McDonald's management maintains that its franchisees are simply making "sound business judgements," an argument that left the boycott leader unmoved. Rev. M. Lorenzo, of the Campaign for Fair Wages, responded that "every worker deserves a living wage, even those whose employers operate in markets swollen with people cut off from jobs and opportunities ... The fast food chains should be aware that their profits come from those of us living in these communities." The Campaign for Fair Wages raises some challenging questions.[21]

There is no reason to believe that racism is any more prevalent in the restaurant industry than in other sectors of society. However, the matter of fact responses of the young men and women crew members of colour at Burger King took me aback. For them, although unpleasant, it seemed to come as not particularly surprising or shocking that some Burger King managers felt free to use racial slurs. Indeed, for the young woman who quit, the racial insults were only part of a work experience that she found generally demeaning.

The sexism evident in Burger King is also remarkable in how commonplace it is. While Burger King, unlike some other workplaces, made sure that these prejudices did not intrude upon profitability, if there was a choice, the young women would be put on display as cashiers. The female manager who told me that this was her deliberate policy assumed that this decision belonged in the "of course" category, not even worthy of questioning. At the Burger King picnic, there were no negative reactions to the bathing suit contest for the young women that was part of the scheduled events, and many young women volunteered to participate. It was good training ground for the battle of "catching" a husband.

Age and gender considerations sometimes affected the way in which workers did their jobs, and how they felt about them. Management's observations were that adult women workers were generally steadier and more reliable. In the dining room, in particular, there seemed to be a battle that had generational overtones. The two women who were assigned to the dining room during the weekdays complained that the part-time teenagers from the night before left the place in a mess. The day workers then had to rush around emptying garbage bags left from the night before and cleaning the tables and trays when they began their shifts. One of these women resented this so much that she insisted that the manager station her in the kitchen, or she would quit. Nevertheless, neither of these two women seemed to mind the dining room station as much as the young people did.

The women who prepared the condiments for the lunch rush also felt that loose ketchup bottle tops from the night before reflected the poor work habits of young people. There seemed to be shades of "mom looking after the kids" in the women daytime workers' views of the high school evening workers. My own observations were that the young workers worked very hard indeed, although some boys were rather sloppy about how they did their work. They did not always keep their work stations as clean and orderly as the adult women did.

The women workers had to cope with a gendered distribution of power in their families that they expressed in various ways. Weddings were very important topics of conversation. Why? The answer lies not just in the psychological realm of meeting emotional needs, and the "romance of romance." Without an opportunity to get higher education or proper skills training, what are these women's chances for a decent paying job? They think they are lucky to find a husband because they would be worse off without one. How can most women even think of having children unless there is a male breadwinner on the scene?

A few of the women described emotionally abusive relationships with a very unfair distribution of household labour. There was no room for them to try and negotiate a different kind of relationship. The challenge of paying the rent and providing for children even with two incomes was difficult enough. The alternative of one income (at a fast food job) or welfare was not to even be considered. An unhappy marriage was, for them, a more realistic choice.

Burger King, like all other capitalist businesses, operates by rules it did not invent but helps maintain. Sound business judgment means taking advantage of racial discrimination and sexual discrimination to hire workers at the lowest possible cost. Burger King is able to pay people so much less than a living wage and provide no work security at all because the labour force upon which it relies is treated as marginal. The question is how long the fast food industry can succeed in this approach – relying on the availability and hard work of a particular group of workers and counting on them not to challenge their working conditions.

HOW WORKERS COPE

Despite a job hierarchy that is virtually flat in terms of skill distinctions, the younger workers in particular differentiate between more or less favoured jobs at Burger King. Cashier and burger boards are the most favoured jobs. The burger boards are popular because of the challenge of working fast enough to "keep up." Some, saying that they "like people," prefer to be up front at the cash register. Broiler-steamer and dining room hostess are the least favoured work stations.

Although in an "upscale" restaurant hostessing is one step above waitressing, in a Burger King, this position is one of the least preferred. A hostess is isolated from other workers, wiping tables, and sweeping and mopping up constantly – she is more a combination janitor-busgirl than a hostess. The only part of this job some people find pleasant is dispensing the Burger King giveaways to small children. One grey-haired Irish woman who was regularly stationed in the dining room at Briarwood got fed up with the cheeky twelve-

NEWSFLASH! Unemployment Drops to Ten Year Low*

WHOOPIE!!!!

(*NEVER BEFORE HAVE SO MANY EARNED SO LITTLE FROM SO FEW.)

year-olds she had to deal with. "Some days I feel like putting my foot right into their faces," she declared.

Young people dislike being assigned to the dining room because in addition to working on their own, away from other crew members, they do not want to be wiping tables for any friends who happen to come to the restaurant. One young man was so unhappy that he threatened to quit if they wouldn't station him elsewhere. Another unpopular request is asking crew people to help sing "Happy Birthday." Most of the workers I knew hated to participate, despite the offer of a free piece of cake – they found the whole thing embarrassing. The adult women workers generally seem to be more accepting of where they are assigned, and a number of them take great care in ensuring that the work at their stations is done "right." One woman, who was regularly assigned to broiler-steamer, was always carefully rearranging the hamburgers in the steamer, so that the FIFO (first in, first out) rule would be observed. She made sure that anybody working with her did the same.

This care, while more noticeable among the adult women workers, is sometimes shared by younger ones. One young woman, assigned to the same station in the evening, proudly said that no one ever ran short of burgers when she handled that station. Another young woman refused to give a chicken sandwich to a crew person going on her break. She was afraid that a customer might be kept waiting, as the supply of cooked sandwiches was low. While it was virtually impossible to avoid working at capacity during busy times, it was also a point of honour to "keep up."

Boredom is the single most common reaction to working at any of the Burger King stations. One worker, a young mother of two who had dropped out of high school after grade ten, remarked in disgust in her second week of work, "A moron could learn this job, it's so easy." A survey conducted by Burger King indicated that about half of all crew members were dissatisfied with their jobs. The three stations most often mentioned as "boring" were broiler-steamer, dining room attendant, and drinks. [22]

Almost any crew member, in the space of a few hours, can learn any job that needs to be done. Placed at Burger King as part of the fast food supervisor's course I took at George Brown College, I learned all the stations in the store, with the exception of cash, by the end of the week. The manager was reluctant to place me on cash, perhaps because I wasn't a regular employee. Naturally, this station appeared to me to be somewhat more interesting then the others. Workers placed on cash all the time got sick of it and said they wished they could be moved back to production.

Managers attempt to maintain a high level of work intensity even when there are no customers in the store. Workers may not sit down (there are no chairs anyway), or even lean on the counters. As a result, slow times are the most deadening of all. No matter what station one is assigned to, it is generally agreed that the time goes more quickly when the restaurant is busy. Although the rush can be hectic and tiring, during busy periods staff is so intent on "keeping up" that the time passes more quickly.

During rush times, some managers can be quite irritating. A worker can have as many as two production leaders, and three managers – on some occasions, even four – with authority over her. The best strategy for survival, as one older worker put it, is to "Go the way the wind blows. Do what you're told until someone comes along and tells you to do something else." Managers sometimes run around the floor asking, "How's it going?" or "Are you having fun?" They pace back and forth, calling out helpful phrases like "Let's go, team!," or "Level 6, level 6," meaning that there should be ten of each kind of hamburger waiting in the chute. As the crew is already working as hard as possible, it is difficult to see the point of such exhortations. When it got very busy at Briarwood, the managers would help out on the work stations. Crew are not allowed to leave their stations without permission. Thus, if you want to have a drink, or need to use the bathroom, a production leader or manager must first give you permission to do so. Between the hours of noon and 1:30 PM, and 5 PM and 6 PM, no worker is allowed to ask for such permission.

When a production leader or a manager wants something done, they usually say, "Would you do this for me?" rather than give a direct order. Burger King's attempt to use a team analogy – the idea of people helping each other out – works. If the restaurant is busy and a worker is asked to stay longer than scheduled, it is very difficult to refuse. Despite the inconvenience, one feels that one would be making others work too hard if one insists on going home. I certainly felt that kind of obligation – not to Burger King, but to my fellow workers. When Maria offered her lawn for a garage sale for the Burger King crew activities, she felt she was helping out other people, not Burger King corporation.

When I was working on a station with another worker, we would sometimes try to switch around to make the work a little less tedious. If a manager noticed, we would be ordered to stay put. Managerial prerogative was all-important.

My experience was that Burger King's right to insist on whatever rules it wished to in the workplace was accepted. Burger King management has been quite successful in convincing workers that doing well means doing it "right" – the Burger King way. One worker was fired for "poor attitude" shortly after the Shape Up program was instituted. I expressed regret to her co-worker. (I was no longer working in the store.) Shirley said, "It's a wonder she wasn't fired a long time ago. She didn't like working here and everybody knew it. If she doesn't like working here, than she shouldn't be here."

Sometimes unpopular measures are introduced. When I first started my fieldwork, all workers could have a free drink, sandwich or burger and fries on each shift. Later, following orders from head office, management imposed a $2.50 limit on the retail price of the food we consumed each shift. One worker responded that, "If we don't like it, we can just stuff it." In other words, Burger King had the right to do as it pleased. Another worker, however, told me how she managed to get food practically for free for her friends. She would ring up an inexpensive item, such as fries or apple pie, and place a more expensive item such as a chicken sandwich in the bag along with the order. This could be done right under the manager's eye if she wasn't too close to the register.

A worker promoted to swing manager told me how she found a young woman worker crouched under the takeout counter eating a sandwich! The swing manager was amazed at such a feat and begged the youngster not to do it again. She didn't have the heart to turn her in, but also knew her own job was at stake if another manager discovered what this crewperson was up to.

Sometimes, other objections to Burger King were registered. One teenager I worked with complained, "Steve's always on my back, telling me to smile. Why should I smile? I do my work and that's good enough. There's nothing funny here." Lydia, a young woman from Hong Kong, once walked off the job in protest because management had not given her the time off to which she was entitled. She was an unusually fast worker, and management took advantage of that by leaving her on whoppers without a helper for long periods of time. She worked eight hours one Saturday without a break. After five hours without a break the next day, she simply walked out. She was, however, welcomed back.

Once, when paychecks were a day late, people were quite upset and some very inconvenienced. Burger King had no right to change payday without notice, they said. The most vociferous person on this issue was the same young woman who had zealously guarded her chicken sandwiches, refusing to give any to an employee for her lunch because she was afraid she would run short for the customers. Thus, this worker displayed the limits of her loyalty to Burger King. As an employee, she conscientiously placed customer needs ahead of fellow workers. However, her right as a worker to be paid promptly was a prerogative Burger King could not meddle with.

Objections to Burger King tended to be personalized. One teenaged woman, assigned to a work station she didn't like, declared she was put there because the manager of that shift, Big Ira, "hated" her. Another worker said of the head manager, "Tony doesn't like me. He never gives me any Burger Bucks although I never fall behind in my station. Pat gets them all the time." It seemed as if almost every worker, including myself, had a strong feeling that some managers picked on them, while other workers were favoured.

Resentment of the managers' control was sometimes expressed in terms of age. One worker named Judith said, "I was twenty-seven when I started work. They would talk to me in such a condescending manner, and these managers were nineteen or twenty. They still lived at home with their mothers, still rosy cheeked. I told them I didn't like the way they talked to me. They said I was being insubordinate."

Most workers do not work with the same people each shift. In the daytime, there is a smaller stable of workers so there is considerable overlap. In the evenings, the labour force is much more changeable. There is no predictability about when the high school students will be scheduled or who their co-workers will be. Unlike many workplaces, where a diverse group of people come together daily to share the common experience of production, Burger King does not provide its workers with a unifying experience based on working together with the same people.

This assessment does not mean that there is no socializing at the workplace. Most of the hiring is done locally, in the neighbourhood. Consequently, the teenage workers come from a few schools, and often recognize each other as classmates. Furthermore, approximately 20 to 25 percent of the workforce consists of related siblings. Thus, points of identification with other workers arise on the basis of age, student status, or family membership, rather than work experience. In the face of a work situation that is very atomizing, workers rely on other parts of their lives to connect to each other.

For all shifts, day and evening, the crew room at Briarwood was the centre for socializing. The tone of the place, and the content of the conversations was somewhat different during the day than at night. In the day, the talk would be about weddings, fixing up a home, children. We all followed the daily installments of Julie's wedding preparations. She was a young Italian woman who had interrupted her course at nursing school and gotten the job so that she could have "the wedding of her dreams." Booking the hall, shopping for the dress, the cost of the meal were all discussed. It was agreed that "even the ugliest girls glowed with beauty" on their wedding day. "But why do brides cry?" we mused. One worker said, "They cry with relief because they've found a husband." Other less happy tales were recounted. The older of the Portuguese sisters had a boyfriend who she had planned to marry, but the engagement was broken off. Her boyfriend had gotten someone else pregnant, and had to marry her.

The interaction in the crew room was generally quite enjoyable. Everyone was accepted and welcomed into the conversation; the older workers exchanged advice and experiences with each other and the younger workers. Julie was surprised when she learned how old I was (I have children about her age) and exclaimed that she had been talking to me as if I were her peer. Another older worker said, "We're the same as you inside, you know. Just with a bit more experience."

Both in the crew room, and on the floor, the evenings were louder and livelier. There was a lot more joking and horsing around. Keeping the crew room clean was a constant struggle. A sign that appeared in the crew room explains what it was sometimes like.

Attention Crew

The social committee has taken the time and effort to redo the crew room. It is beautiful and we would appreciate it being kept beautiful.

No food fights (ketchup).
Do not kick the base boards.
Do not flick ashes or cigarettes onto the floor.

Anyone caught violating these conditions will be penalized severely.

1st violation – Clean the whole crew room.
2nd violation – Will be banned from this room for a week.

Thank you for your cooperation.
The Social Committee

People talked about school tests. They discussed plans for the weekend, places to go. Sometimes the teenaged women talked about clothes they had bought or would buy. We all knew who was saving up for a stereo and discussed the latest cassette tapes. In short, the crew room was an interesting place. Once, a young woman who did part-time modelling brought her entire makeup kit to the store and made up the face of another worker. The head manager, who was fairly easy going, happened into the crew room and asked, "What is this, a beauty salon?", but didn't try to stop the activity. Another time, Lily, a production leader who was proficient at making French braids, braided the hair of everyone whose was long enough. I was pleased by how lovely she made my hair look.

As Julie's wedding day grew near, some of the workers organized a surprise bridal shower for her. All of the daytime workers came, although some had been working just a few weeks, and hadn't had the time to get to know her very well. Each person came with an offering of food, and elaborate presents representing approximately half a week's earnings. Sometimes adult women workers made plans to go out together on the weekends, but this was rare. A few of the women who left Burger King kept in touch with workers still in the store. Otherwise, the crew room was the site for regular social contacts between workers.

As we have seen, the social activities initiated by Burger King are attended by the teenagers. They have more free time, and seem to form friendships with each other that extend beyond the workplace more readily than the adult women workers. Here again, in the jostling in the crew room, the flirting, and the teasing, the forms of interaction between workers are clearly marked by age and gender.

In a traditional restaurant such as the one William Whyte studied, which I described in Chapter 2, the cliques were based on the "status hierarchy" in the restaurant – for example, the waitresses in the upstairs dining room formed a group in Whyte's description of Stouffers' restaurant. They ate together and socialized together. In Burger King, workers manage to organize a social life despite the shifting work groups. However, these social groupings are based on common interests from outside work, rather than the division of labour in the workplace.

Burawoy attempts to introduce "real workers" into the workplace, and to show that their daily struggles influence the shape of the labour process – for example in the case where it becomes more profitable to introduce new technology than to deal with an organized, resistant labour force. However, these "real workers" are apparently stripped of gender and racial characteristics when it comes to what actually goes on at work. Gender and racial oppression are seen to be shaped by class (true enough), but for Burawoy class domination is "the more basic principle of organization of contemporary societies".[23]

One glance at a Burger King workplace, or at the fast food industry in general, indicates how firmly the industry relies on a particular sexual division of labour for both its market and its labour force. How would the expansion of the industry have occurred without the nuclear family to draw from? The work women do within the family unit makes the conditions of paid work Burger King offers the best choice they have. It is not possible to rule out the gendered nature of experience, or, in many situations, the profound impact of racial and ethnic divisions. At Burger King, because of gender and age characteristics, most workers do not view their work as necessarily central to their lives. This affects their response – what they do when they are unhappy with Burger King's rules.

VOTING WITH THE FEET

The most typical response to dissatisfaction with the workplace at Burger King is to leave it. Workers quit or are fired with great regularity. Dissension with Burger King practices or policies results in either passive measures such as not showing up for scheduled shifts, or arguments with the managers. Both usually result in termination.

While turnover at Briarwood occurred regularly throughout the year, it was particularly high during certain periods. Many workers quit in September when school started, and after Christmas, there was often a major shift in the workforce. The assistant manager in charge of training estimated that out of ten workers hired, two or three of them would leave before the initial two-week pay period was up. Estimated turnover rates for the fast food industry are 300 percent per year.[24]

Mr. Banks, director of operations for Burger King Canada, said that out of a group of new employees, the largest group will work at Burger King for one to three months. About 30 percent will stay up to half a year, and about 15 percent for a year or more. He estimated that 10 to 15 percent of new workers do not make it to the end of the first two-week pay period, a somewhat lower dropout rate than the 20 to 30 percent indicated by Briarstone's training manager.[25]

The turnover rate among the younger people was greater than among the adult women workers. In October, over half (56 percent) of the workers at Briarwood who had been there for a year or more were over eighteen, although only one-fourth of the crew as a whole were over eighteen. When I returned to the restaurant some time after my fieldwork was completed, I was surprised to find four workers that I knew there. Three of these were adult women, while one was a teenager, now promoted to production leader. Manager turnover in company-owned Burger Kings is also very high. One industry executive's estimate was as high as 100 percent annually.[26]

Burger King company policy is to shift managers frequently from outlet to outlet. Mr. Banks in the Canadian head office, indicated that this practice was to prevent managers from "becoming stale". Given the stringent scheduling rules, it is probably easier for managers to pursue measures to keep labour costs low when they are dealing with a workforce with whom they have not had a chance to get too familiar. The store had four new head managers in the course of one year, and more than one complete turnover in assistant and swing shift managers. I know that at least two of them left the company. It is not clear how many of the other managers were promoted, given lateral transfers, or left the company.

Workers leave their jobs at Burger King for a variety of reasons. Sometimes, they get better-paying jobs. One of the Portuguese sisters working at Briarwood in the daytime enviously described a friend whose office job allowed her to sit down all day for full minimum wage. She eventually found an office job herself. One young man was expecting to get a job in a factory where his friend worked for $5.50 an hour. Another young woman said she liked working at Burger King because of all the socializing, but would be quitting because she had a chance to earn more money.

Other workers quit for a variety of reasons. One part-time worker who wanted some time off quit. After taking a vacation, she was eventually rehired, as she had left on fairly good terms. As seniority leads to only very minimal pay differentials and there are no benefits beyond what Burger King must legally provide, this intermittent work involves few sacrifices. One young woman was leaving the job because she said she was being asked to work too many weekend evenings and it was ruining her social life. Two workers left to have babies. Most often, a combination of reasons led people to leave. Lydia, the young black woman, disliked the job because of the low pay, the racism, and too many managers ordering her around.

As already mentioned, turnover among production leaders is fairly high. Two production leaders left because management refused them raises and because of the inconvenience of irregular scheduling. Two others quit because they expected promotions to management which were not forthcoming.

It was sometimes unclear whether people quit or were fired. Judith, promoted to night coordinator, supervised other workers on the late night "drive-thru" until 4 AM. After that, she did the bookwork and the inventory until 6 AM. Inventory involved going into the walk-in freezer and counting boxes. "I would come out of there and my fingers were numb, and my glasses would fog up. It was freezing. If you missed something, you had to go back in and count it over again." The "final straw" for her was having to count the wasted products as well, which, she said, was supposed to be the job of the night manager. "The managers would take off to make last call at the tavern and leave me to count all the wastes. So when I told them that they weren't doing their job, they said I was being insubordinate. That's what happened. So when it came to my review, they said that I was doing my job well, but was being insubordinate to the other managers." After this, she was demoted to crew. "I said, in essence you're firing me. He said, no, I'm not firing you. I'm just demoting you. I said, you are taking my job away from me."

She understood the demotion to be an invitation to leave, which she did. In thinking about what happened, she also thought her demotion might have had something to do with asking for time off, as she was pregnant and not feeling well. She thought the charge of insubordination might have been an excuse, and the real reason was unwillingness to give her the time off she had requested and really needed.

In another instance an unusually pretty young woman named Cheryl was accused of laziness by management. She had dropped out of school because, according to her, the other girls gave her a hard time for being too popular with the boys. In her case, she didn't work as hard as her co-workers. She had been laid off for not showing up for work by calling in sick. She was called in again to work, but announced she was quitting. Lily, who got into an argument with a manager for ordering her around, was not fired. The manager warned her that if she didn't do as she was told, she might lose her job. At that point she said, "Fine, I quit."

Pressure from families sometimes results in young people leaving Burger King. Poor grades was one common effect of being a Burger King worker, which was why so many people left Briarwood in September. Others stayed on, but parents didn't necessarily share Burger King's sense of priorities for their youngsters' lives. One production leader I knew, Cecil, a young man in eleventh grade, had finals coming up, papers due for the end of term, and was scheduled to work an eight-hour shift on Saturday night. His father would not allow him to come to work and called Burger King to tell them that. Cecil was called in the next week and four managers berated him for his lack of commitment to Burger King. The young man either quit or was fired.[27]

I asked Helen, one of assistant managers, why people are fired. She said it was rare for anyone to be fired for poor performance. One woman left because she was making more on Mother's Allowance than she could with a Burger King salary; three others quit for various reasons; and nine people were fired. Most of these were "no shows."

IS QUITTING THE ONLY OPTION?

As we have seen, the most common reaction to dissatisfaction with working conditions in a fast food outlet is to leave. Are there any options available other than these individual reactions?

What are the possibilities of workers in the fast food industry getting together to improve their pay and working conditions? The outlet where I worked was not unionized, nor did I hear anybody talk about the possibility. It is very difficult, but not impossible, to organize in fast food restaurants. The companies have so many resources available to them that the battle between a few workers in one outlet and a huge company resembles a modern-day Goliath versus David match. Collective bargaining legislation, developed for large industrial situations where many full-time workers can join together, does not help much in situations where the bargaining units are small and the company is large. AFL-CIO Food and Beverages Trades Department President Robert Harbrant maintains that the National Labor Relations Act (NLRA) and National Labor Relations Board (NLRB) now stand for something quite different. They were put in place in the United States in the 1930s under the Roosevelt administration, and were seen as regulatory mechanisms to make sure that labour was treated fairly. Now in an administration dominated by a pro-business orientation, Harbrant maintains they are more aptly called "No Longer Really Applicable" and "Now Largely Representing Business." United States laws and regulatory bodies for some time now have not been used to ensure an even-handed dispensation of justice in the workplace.[28]

Despite the formidable odds, there have been successful organizing drives in a few places. Most of the unionization in the restaurant sector in Canada has occurred in places where the meal service is connected to a hotel chain. There have been a few near successes. In the 1970s, union organizing drives in McDonald's, Ponderosa, and Winco Steak n' Burger outlets in London, Ontario signed up the majority of workers in the outlets they targetted. However, the companies challenged the certification on the question of what constitutes a bargaining unit and won. Since not all the outlets owned by the same company were organized, the labour relations board decided that the union did not have a majority. Workers at a McDonald's outlet in Shawnigan, Quebec, became members of the Confederation of National Trade Unions and were certified in the late 1970s. The union accreditation was challenged, however, on the basis that managers were included in the bargaining unit. By the early 1980s, the Shawnigan McDonald's had lost its union.

The most impressive bargaining effort took place in Detroit in the early 1980s. It was spearheaded by a community activist organization called ACORN, the Association of Community Organizations for Reform Now, which launched an independent union, the United Labor Union (ULU). They geared their organizing efforts to young, exploited low-wage earners. In response to their presence in the Detroit area, a number of fast food chains began raising wages.

The ULU began with locals in four cities: Detroit, Philadelphia, Boston, and New Orleans. Recruitment focussed on the idea that food workers deserve "dignity" and "respect" rather than bread and butter pitches, an approach that struck a receptive cord. The exec-

utive director of the Ohio State Restaurant Association indicated that
the approach seemed to be working and certainly had their people
worried. The Detroit area organizer put it this way: "A lot of these
fast food operators think they can treat their teenage employees like
garbage just because they're young and inexperienced. The kids are
fed up with this kind of treatment and that's why they're joining
our union."[29]

The union kept initiation fees as low as possible, and often waived
them to sign up new members. The organizing drive itself was
sufficent to encourage some fast food chains to raise hourly wages.
The United Labour Union narrowly lost an election on 22 February
1980 and the union charged unfair labour practices, saying that the
company had spied on them, threatened workers, and offered them
inducements to remain non-union. Three years later, in 1983, the
charges were upheld and a bargaining order was issued.

After this delay, a new organizing drive was necessary. Of the
fifty or sixty people in the bargaining unit, a full one-third had been
there during the previous organizing drive. Given the generally high
turnover rate in the industry, this was a very large number. As one
organizer commented, "Not everyone is a high school kid looking
for money for Saturday night dances." In an area like Detroit, there
are many young men and women in their late teens and early twenties, out of high school, with nowhere else to go. Some are single
parents.

In August 1983, the union signed a three-year contract, which
managed to gain some protection for the workers. Scheduling and
hours had to take seniority into consideration, minimum shifts of
three hours were specified, and Martin Luther King day was a paid
holiday. However, the union was not able to make further inroads
into the industry, and after a few extensions of the contract, the
union was decertified. The lessons learned, according to one of
the organizers, was that it is not impossible to organize fast food
workers, and there is potentially lots of support for such an attempt.
However, the effort and the resources required are massive. US
labour legislation offers a myriad of opportunites for companies to
hold up the representation process indefinitely.

Looking back at the campaign one of the organizers remarked on
the positive legacy left by the long string of organizing attempts.
Young people are surrounded virtually from birth with the development of a corporate image carefully cultivated by the companies.
What three-year-old in North America doesn't know of Ronald
McDonald? Then young people enter their first job, and the lesson
they learn is that "the company can treat you any way they wish."

What an awful lesson to be taught to an entire generation of young people! Fast food companies use what they have learned about the importance of human relations to manipulate workers. Companies offer a controlled initiation of the dignity and self-respect workers want. However, the techniques they use – a name tag, for example – do not really give a worker individuality and the team imagery does not really make the crew person an equal member of a work collective that includes management. These organizing efforts make clear that workers will not settle for just a "feeling" of importance. They want decent wages and some control over their work. Through the ACORN-sponsored organizing drive, the young people had learned that they do have rights which they can fight for and that it is possible to fight the boss.[30] A Wendy's outlet in Windsor, Ontario, began an organizing drive in the fall of 1990. Like Detroit, Windsor has large unionized auto plants and a tradition of unionism. The workers approached the United Food and Commercial Workers, asking for assistance. Enough workers signed union cards to apply to the Ontario Labour Relations Board for certification as a bargaining unit. By early 1991, their union drive had succeeded, although a first contract still had to be negotiated.

Canada

CHAPTER EIGHT

Is This the Work Situation
of the Future?

There are different views of how we should live our lives and the kind of world we want to inhabit. Our private lives are linked to public concerns – what form do we want these connections to take? How does the growth and development of the fast food industry fit into these visions?

WHO BENEFITS?

The fast food industry is an example of how the market has entered the private realm of the family/household and transformed the work done there into business opportunities. The fast food industry, like any industry in a capitalist environment, is most interested in profit. Two methods of achieving this are the expansion of markets and the reduction of the price of labour – accomplished by reducing it to its most unskilled form. The fast food industry is a success story in both areas.

The fast food industry provides an example of how oligopoly made possible the transformation of the labour process and the development of specific control techniques. The restaurant industry is now dominated by large, transnational corporations. Whether the food served is healthy or not does not concern the large corporations that own the business, because quality is equated with standardization. With the help of huge advertising budgets, people of all ages are told that the food these corporations serve is desirable.

The oligopolic control of the industry continues, squeezing the small mom and pop restaurants out of business. Various ways to increase top-down control have been implemented for both the assembly and the sale of the meal. The hierarchy of skills required, from chef to dishwasher, characteristic of earlier restaurants, has been replaced by a crew of undifferentiated machine tenders in a fast food kitchen in which there are no pots and pans. These have been replaced by computerized machinery.

The product uniformity that facilitates mass marketing also permits the development of methods to control labour that can be applied in all Burger King outlets, wherever they are. The resources available to a corporation such as Burger King can be used to explore ways to intensify labour and reduce costs so that profits will increase. Workers find it hard to know who is responsible for making decisions about work patterns that affect the conditions of their work when these come from an invisible entity, located far away. The invisibility of the source of the control enables management to foster an image of individualism, masking the reality of the exploitation to which workers are subjected.

Production at Burger King is organized so that operations are standardized down to the smallest detail. With the help of computerized machinery that cooks the meal, and by cross-training workers to carry out a number of simplified tasks in assembling the product, Burger King can slot almost any crew person into any function in the store. However, the name tags workers wear are management's attempt to reassure them that they really are individuals. Workers are expected to work wearing a mass-produced smile that promotes the sale of the meal to the customer. They are expected to serve the customer cheerfully and energetically, using lines written in another country. Thus not only a worker's movements, but his or her emotions are considered to be at the disposition of Burger King management.

The workforce's main contribution to this process is its flexibility and hard work at minimum wages. Burger King workers are mostly drawn from a particular labour pool: stores are staffed for dinner hours and on weekends by teenagers who are still attending high school full-time; early afternoon shifts are taken primarily by women with young children in school. For women with family obligations, and for teenagers who can only work outside of school hours, the schedules offered by Burger King have advantages; besides, neither of these groups has a wide range of job opportunities. Wages and working conditions in this industry are based on the assumption that workers have access to support beyond their own earnings and therefore are "not really" workers. Companies benefit from the workers themselves not taking their jobs seriously. The conditions under which one works for "extras" as an addition to being a "housewife" or a student are not readily challenged. Therefore, the workers acquiesce to work arrangements which call them in for three-hour shifts at Burger King's discretion. As the labour supply is running low, companies are turning to older workers, often pensioners, to meet their demand for new workers.

The challenge for the fast food companies is to make money, lots of it, while retaining the pretence that they are doing the world a favour. This is the hypocritical essence of liberalism. While maintaining an image of benevolence, the reality is one of exploitation. However, even within the most standardized and boring jobs – those that permit the use of "interchangeable" workers – the workers themselves do not become human automatons. Workers bring to their jobs outlooks related to their experiences and responsibilities outside the workplace, not inherent in the job tasks themselves. Workers "fit in" to the Burger King workplace due to a common set of socialization practices that teaches them how to "get along," and does not expose them to the idea that they have many rights within the workplace. Their shared experiences (from school and home) provide the forms for cohesiveness between workers that enable them to create a social life at the workplace in spite of its transient nature.

There is little personal space at Burger King. The "working knowledge" or "tacit skills" Burger King workers bring to their jobs give them little room to manoeuvre in moderating management directives. Even physical needs such as drinking water or using the washroom are regulated. Scheduling procedures do not take workers' interests into consideration: the hours and days when workers are scheduled varies weekly according to Burger King's wishes.

The informal social life of the workplace is used by Burger King to create identification with the company and management pays a great deal of attention to the employee's social aspects. Thus a human relations "sales pitch" is presented as a substitute for decent wages and benefits at Burger King. The company does not offer sufficient incentives to effectively reduce turnover. Rather it seeks to embody the image of a happy loyal team or family, even with a constantly shifting group of workers. Loyalty is defined as obedience rather than longevity of tenure.

One of the preconditions of the development of a labour process using the "interchangeable worker" is the availability of a large pool of labour for part-time work. However, Burger King's claim on workers is limited by their other commitments. When job obligations conflict with their responsibilities to outside work, many workers soon come to understand that their interests and Burger King's are not the same. Their individual protests, which usually take the form of "voting with their feet," however, do not change management prerogatives in the organization of the workplace. Thus, while collective workplace resistance is kept to a minimum, the high turnover rate indicates the ultimate failure of the human relations approach in practice.

What are the advantages of this arrangement? For business, there are a number of ways in which profits are generated from the fast food industry. In addition, a population freed from domestic tasks has more time available for wage labour.[1] The commercial socialization of domestic labour, or market entry into household functions, is a major way of reducing the time and energy needed in non-waged areas. If food is purchased in a fast food restaurant or bought ready to eat in a supermarket; if one lives in a centrally heated apartment requiring minimal maintenance and if one drives rather than walks to work, then the total wage labour performed by the household can be increased. These changes also permit the development of other needs and activities frequently related to consumption and spending more money. Thus, for example, the average Canadian family spends several hours in front of the television each day where they learn of more ways to purchase a well-rounded, satisfying life. More people working in fast food also mean that more people have money to spend on eating out.

While enlarging the market increases the realm of potential profits, what are the advantages for workers in these industries that provide services for households? The job opportunities for women and young people are welcomed by many and have immediate and tangible benefits. The chance for women and young students to earn some money and thus become partially economically independent of their families is attractive. Women and young people working at Burger King during my fieldwork period wanted the chance to earn "their own" money. While they felt pressured to take jobs, they also enjoyed the autonomy earning wages brings.[2] Even when earnings were spent on necessities, decisions on how the money was to be used generally seemed to be in their hands. However, more than the push of economic incentive is required to understand why people take jobs at Burger King.

Adult women find the chance to be around other adults a welcome change from the isolating conditions of their work in the home. They bring their job training from the home into the workplace and approach their work with care and a sense of responsibility. They are conscientious, steady workers, and do not need to be told to keep the place clean and neat. The youngsters employed at Burger King display the exuberance and spirit common to teenagers; the crew room sometimes seems very much like a high school cafeteria. Teenagers are loyal fast food customers; in fact, managers must warn teenaged workers about using the place as a hangout. Burger King makes use of this desire to socialize in its encouragement of Burger King dances, skating parties, and baseball teams.

LIMITS TO MARKET ENTRY INTO THE FAMILY

There are contradictory elements in the push to reduce domestic labour. On the one hand, labour power – or workers – are needed by capital and are brought up and readied for work in the household through domestic labour where people are fed, clothed, and generally looked after. On the other hand, work inside the home presents an obstacle to accumulation, as so much of domestic labour occurs in non-waged forms and limits the availability of labour power or the ability to take waged jobs. If leisure time is to be successfully exploited for profit, then both domestic and waged labour cannot take up all one's waking hours.[3]

Socialization of domestic work through commercial industries has been one solution to this dilemma. There are nevertheless limits to the benefits of expanding the market into the household. While food and clothing can be mass-produced, other household activities cannot. Taking care of children is a very labour-intensive activity, and childbearing will continue to be an activity of individual women. In addition to economic and physiological barriers, the strong commitment to the family means people will resist too great an encroachment on their "private" lives.[4]

DRAWBACKS FOR WORKERS AND CONSUMERS

For the workers in a situation such as Burger King, there are drawbacks to the work, which is not particularly ennobling. As one worker put it, "Any trained monkey could do the job." Since workers are without the protection afforded by a collective agreement, they can be called in to work and dismissed as the need arises. There are virtually no fringe benefits. Only weekly schedules are planned and workers have no control over management scheduling decisions. A us study of the effects of such work on young people found that what teenagers learn at such age-segregated jobs is cynicism about work, rather than the hoped-for sense of responsibility and self reliance. Too many hours led to lowered school grades. Higher rates of alcohol and drug use, as well as lowered contact with their families, were also found amongst working teenagers.[5]

In this industry, the producers are connected to the consumers in ways that are unusually obvious and immediate. We don't see black South African miners when we buy a diamond, "the gift that is forever." However, the people who work in the fast food industry, along with their families, are also fast food consumers. And all of us live with the effects of the growth of this industry. The fast food industry has been an ecological disaster in a number of ways. The disposable styrofoam and plastic containers add to the already over-whelming mountain of garbage that cities increasingly have diffi-culties coping with. Certainly there are better uses for forests than providing paper and cups for a fast food meal.

The food is harmful to some people. Responding to health con-cerns of the population, many companies have introduced salad bars, but sprayed them with sulphites to make the vegetables stay fresh-looking. These chemicals are known to cause severe reaction in asthmatic customers.[6] In the US, the Center for Science in the Public Interest has petitioned the Food and Drug Administration and the US Department of Agriculture to list ingredient information on disposable wrappings. They pointed out that hundreds of thousands of Americans are allergic to fast food ingredients such as FD&C yellow dye No. 5 and corn-based sweeteners, while others need to avoid ingredients such as the coconut and palm oils or animal fats used for frying.[7] In Puerto Rico, an epidemic of early sexual development afflicting thousands of toddlers was linked by re-searchers to locally grown chicken containing high levels of estrogen. The industry has responded to some of these concerns, and will be forced to comply with others. McDonald's announced in 1990 that because of consumer objections that styrofoam was damaging to the environment, it was switching from styrofoam to paper containers (although they continued to maintain that the consumers were wrong). Both McDonald's and Burger King have decided to substi-tute vegetable for animal fat in their fryers. The National Academy of Sciences (NAS), an American government research institution, advised that fast food places should be obligated to provide nutri-tional profiles of their food. True to form, the NAS's suggestions were called "preposterous" and "unnecessary" by the National Res-taurant Association.[8]

US consumption of beef increased from 85 pounds per person per year in 1960 to 134 pounds per person twenty years later, in 1980. So the US started to import beef to meet the new demand. Beef production in Costa Rica increased two-fold from 1959 to 1972, but per capital consumption of beef declined from 30 pounds to 19. In Honduras, the figures are even worse. Beef production tripled be-tween 1965 and 1975, while consumption for Hondurans declined from 12 lbs. to 10 lbs. per person. An average American cat eats more beef annually than the average Central American![9] Twenty-five percent of all the beef consumed in the United States goes to the fast food industry. As the demand for beef increases, tropical forests are leveled for commercial purposes, threatening the destruction of the vitally important rainforests.

HAMBURGER DIPLOMACY

The fast food industry's image of benevolence and wholesomeness has effectively shielded North American customers from the reality of a very exploitative work situation. The successful international expansion of the industry has been helped along by clever advertising campaigns. Customers flock to the highest volume Burger King in the world, located close to the Parisian Arc de Triomphe. American fast food is a big hit in Japan, because of a trendy identification with American culture. Den Fujita, McDonald's partner in Japan, in his pitch to the Japanese claimed that "the reason Japanese people are so short and have yellow skins is because they have eaten nothing but fish and rice for 2,000 years. If we eat McDonald's hamburgers and potatoes for a thousand years, we will become taller, our skin will become white and our hair blond.[10]

The potentially lucrative Eastern Europe market is an enticing prospect. In the USSR, for example, some people see fast food technology and management methods as potentially useful in solving their country's critical distribution and service sector problems. McDonald's opened in Moscow in mid-1990. Soviet citizens envy the abundance of goods available in North America, and women in particular complain bitterly about the unavailability of time and energy-saving goods and services.

While George Cohon may sincerely believe that his hamburger diplomacy will "make the world a better place," a look behind the scenes of hamburger heaven makes one wonder if this is the best we can do. Consumers flock to fast food in Eastern Europe for reasons very similar to those in North America. The family dinner may be a pleasant experience, but no one wants to cook it. Women increasingly have neither the time nor the inclination to take on double duty, and eating out is easier than getting men to do their share. In part, fast food is a capitalist mediation of the battle between the sexes over the domestic division of labour. Taking the family out to dinner is a comfortable solution to challenging the unevenly distributed unpaid work women do in the home. But giving up the frying pan in favour of the fryer has generated new problems.

The linkages between family, community, and industry have been used by the large fast food companies to their advantage. They have invaded and taken over communal activities and public space for

their own private gain. Millions of dollars are spent to convince consumers of the relationship between fast food restaurants and charitable, community-minded endeavours. School picnics and community fairs are used as relatively cheap company promotions. Even school reading programs are market opportunities to sell more pizza and hamburgers. McDonald's has made an effort to impress people that its outlets are not just good places to buy hamburgers, but they are also good places for young people to work. "Working at McDonald's wasn't just a job, it was an event," declares a former worker in a McDonald's ad.[11]

Image and illusion permeate the industry, but certain aspects of social life cannot be marketed. Thus the counter person's smile and the cheery greeting welcoming the customer to a fast food outlet do not really make the server happy to be serving or turn the customer into a guest. The commercialization of human feeling is a new and insidious incursion into job requirements.[12] The cute cartoon-like characters that appeal to toddlers do not make fast food into wholesome family fare.

Another part of the illusion goes well beyond the responsibility of the fast food industry. Our young people are taught to honour the wishes and needs of unbridled market forces. They are taught that taking a job means either putting up with what the employer wants or leaving. However, our legal system guarantees workers' rights and privileges. Working for pay does not require boundless gratitude to an employer nor a complete suspension of all rights. Students need to be taught the truth – not just how to obey uncritically. Work-study arrangements such as one in North York, Ontario, where students are sent to fast food places for job training, need to be carefully scrutinized, as students need to learn more than management's side of what it means to be a worker. They need to enter the workplace with a sense of their own dignity and worth. The idea that employers can treat workers any way they want is a poor lesson.

There is no turning back to a mythological past of a nuclear family where mom cheerfully and uncomplainingly does all the domestic work with a little help from the children. No one wants to. Women and young people are happy to be free from the limiting patriarchal control of this situation. Even for men, such a setup has its limitations, as their worth gets measured by their ability to "bring home the bacon." However, the capitalist alternative – the free enterprise solution to the socialization of domestic labour – obviously has its drawbacks.

How does the development of this history fit in with more general trends? Both labour and business people are concerned about the disappearance of manufacturing jobs and the growth of the service sector. Toronto, for example, is losing its industrial base. By 1985, service sector employment in Canada's largest city constituted 66.5 percent of all employment. Some of these jobs, in services to business, pay very well indeed. However, the jobs paying livable wages in the middle of the wage spectrum are disappearing. Most of the new jobs are at the bottom of the wage distribution.

The change in the wage distribution of jobs is not confined to the service sector. Indeed, a Statistics Canada study found that industrial restructuring is the major cause of the shift to new jobs at both the top and bottom of the wage distribution. There are changes occurring in the whole economy – in full-time jobs, in all industries, and in all occupational groupings.[13] Young people are the big losers. Despite the shrinking supply of young workers in the 1981 to 1986 period, there has been a remarkable downward shift in their relative wages. Middle-aged and older workers' wages increased. Young women fared the worst. By 1986, almost 60 percent of full-time equivalent jobs held by young women aged sixteen to twenty-four were in the two lowest wage levels, compared to 34 percent for men. There is good reason to be concerned that this decline is a permanent one that will not be recouped as these workers age. The jobs younger workers hold are less often unionized and are in smaller firms. This is the first generation of young people since World War II facing a life that will not be as comfortable as that of their parents.

WHAT ABOUT THE FUTURE?

What are the alternatives? What would a non-capitalist attempt to eliminate the drudgery of privatized servicing of families look like? Is it possible to recognize and respect the non-work contributions people make in their homes and in their communities? What would a Canada look like where everyone had a right to jobs with decent wages and working conditions? How do we do more than wring our hands about the escalating health hazards in our diets, our workplaces, our lifestyles, adding up to the approaching ecological destruction of the earth?

This is a large and difficult but not a hopeless undertaking. In communities such as Markland Woods, Ontario, or Hartford, Connecticut, neighbourhood groups have objected to the construction of fast food outlets near their homes because they wanted a different kind of community. Residents of Barcelona voiced opposition to McDonald's attempts to turn one of honoured architect Gaudi's buildings into a hamburger place. When a high school senior from New Jersey stands at a formal podium dressed as "Ronald McToxic," issuing a plea to stop eating McDonald's because "the planet deserves a break today," it is clear the battle is far from over.[14] The children's crusade against polystyrene packaging appeared across North America, from Toronto to Texas. The attempts at unionization of fast food outlets in Detroit and in Windsor, Ontario, leave a legacy that won't be easily forgotten. It is possible to fight the boss. Every worker, young and old, has rights and can fight for them.

The fast food industry uses work processes that reduce labour to its simplest form in a workplace accompanied by unusually restrictive conditions. This kind of workplace may typify the workplace of the future for many. In the marketplace, however, we are all equal. Demands for equality for all persons have marked this century. We have formally recognized the equal worth of all citizens, regardless of race, ethnicity, gender, or age.

While the liberal pursuit of individual freedom has involved progress in some spheres – women and young people are no longer completely subject to the whims of the husband and father – there has been a price. Now, more than ever the free choice in taking on a job is limited by the nature of the jobs that exist. Capitalists have also progressed in their ability to dominate and control the workplace.

A feminist and a non-capitalist alternative will, like the fast food industry hype, weave together family, community, and workplace. However, the agenda is a different one. Our task is to describe and explain the linkages between domestic and paid labour in ways that will promote human liberation in all areas. We will find out how to accomplish this in the act of building bridges uniting people's interests as family and community members, workers, and consumers.

Unions historically have been the most effective vehicles for empowering workers and could have an important role to play in this process. However, they have not adequately addressed the problem of poorly paid, high turnover service sector workers. Embroiled in business union practices, they have provided only lipservice to the needs of these groups of workers. Despite the rhetoric, the resources have not been forthcoming. As the experience of the dedicated organizers in the independent United Labor Union illustrates, it is possible to speak to the experience of young workers and women in ways that make sense. Yet the difficulties are enormous. Unions themselves are struggling to stay afloat even in areas that have been their traditional strongholds. Labour legislation based on a model of one employer, one enterprise is suitable for large plants with full-time workforces, but makes organizing difficult in other situations. The culture itself is profoundly anti-union.

In various parts of the world, people are recognizing the importance of joining forces to control the power of transnational food companies. There is common ground in the interests of workers in fast food, consumers of fast food, environmentalists, and women and young people concerned about their dignity and their rights. The first job is to tell the news in a way that reflects the experience, knowledge, and interests of these various groups.

Notes

The following abbreviations or shortened references are used in the notes.

AROC   Advance Restaurant Operations Course (Burger King)
BK   Burger King
BMOC   Basic Manager's Operations Course (Burger King)
BROC   Basic Restaurant Operations Course
CFRA   Canadian Food and Restaurant Association
CHR   *Canadian Hotel Review* (1928–33). It changed its name to the *Canadian Hotel Review and Merchant* in 1934, and in 1935 became the *Canadian Hotel and Restaurant* magazine.
DBS   Dominion Bureau of Statistics
FSH   *Foodservice and Hospitality* magazine. It is a Canadian magazine published in Toronto. Before 1965, it was known as *Restaurants and Institutions.*
FP   *Financial Post*
G&M   *Globe and Mail*
MOD   Manual of Operating Data. Burger King's manual for restaurant operations.
NRN   *Nation's Restaurant News.* This trade newspaper is published in New York.
R&I   *Restaurants and Institutions.* The name was changed to *Foodservice and Hospitality* magazine in 1965.

INTRODUCTION

1 I almost got a higher status job as a waitress, like other white, native-born, young women. The management discovered at the last minute that I was left-handed, and so it was salads and sandwiches in sub-basement B of the kitchen or nothing!

2 My sons used to call this "adult power tripping," where adults get their way not because they know better, but simply because they are older and have economic power.

3 Statistics Canada, "Working for Minimum Wage," 9.

4 See Thompson, *The Nature of Work*, for a good review of this literature.

5 See the well-known work by Goldthorpe and Lockwood, *The Affluent Worker*.

6 The work of Edwards, Reich, and Gordon, *Labour Market Segmentation*, is a good example of this.

7 Despite Burawoy's criticisms of Braverman, both writers share a traditional Marxist approach that treats the working class as ungendered. See Burawoy, *Manufacturing Consent*, and Braverman, *Labor and Monopoly Capital*.

8 Joy Parr's book, *The Gender of Breadwinners*, Cynthia Cockburn, *Brothers*, and Sally Westwood, *All the Livelong Day*, are some recent contributions to this literature.

9 See the Statistics Canada study by Picot and Miles.

10 Marx, *The German Ideology*.

11 While workers are protected by the state by minimum wage laws and employment standards, the area of managerial prerogatives has been growing. It is accepted that workers can be told exactly how to do their jobs.

CHAPTER 1

1 In "In the Privacy of Our Own Home," Sedef Koc describes why domestic work contains the worst aspects of both the public and private spheres.

2 Canada, *Census of Canada 1986*, 93–111.

3 Canada, *Census of Canada 1986*, 93–111 and Canada, *Statistics Canada*, 71–001.

4 The figures were 73.9 percent for females fifteen to twenty-four years of age, 70.8 percent for those twenty-five to thirty-four, and 71.4 percent for those thirty-five to forty-four years of age. Canada, *Census of Canada 1986*, 93–111.

5 Armstrong, *Labour Pains*.

6 Canada, *Market Research Handbook 1983*, 63–224.

7 Canada, Statistics Canada, *Household Facilities and Equipment*, 1989, 64–202.

8 Fox, "Women's Domestic Labour and Their Involvement in Wage Work."

9 Detergents were developed during World War II to compensate for the shortage of materials available for soap manufacture. In 1946,

Proctor and Gamble introduced Tide, the "washday miracle." By the early 1950s, the synthetic, nonbiodegradable detergents had taken over the market. By 1966, over one billion dollars was grossed in the sale of soaps and detergents. For each dollar spent on laundry detergent, 36 percent went to advertise various products that *Printer's Ink* reported had "essentially the same chemical ingredients" (28 October 1966). Since that time, "easy care" synthetic fabrics have been developed so that more clothing can be laundered at home, and a host of new cleaning products (e.g., to remove spots, add brightness, soften) have been added to the washday stock. The latest development is the promotion of a new concept – environmentally sound laundry soap!

10 Canada, *Canada Yearbook*.

11 I must credit this phrase to Russell Baker, who used it in one of his weekly *New York Times* magazine columns in 1983.

12 A random issue of *Seventeen* magazine, from June 1983 contained the following: nineteen ads for hair care – shampoos, hair curlers, etc.; nine ads to do with smells – either adding them to one's body in the form of colognes and perfumes, or avoiding them with deodorants; fourteen ads for makeup, including products for lips, face, and nails; eleven ads for skin care – either skin cleansers, pimple treatment creams, or suntan lotions; and eight ads to do with menstruation.

Ads for clothes and shoes in this particular issue were less evident than those for body treatment, although there were two fashion articles and ten ads for underwear, shoes, and jeans. Articles in the magazine mirrored the concerns in the advertisements. Eight columns bore titles like "Dear Beauty Editor," "Looking Good," "Good Scents," "Skin Care," "Makeup," "Five Fabulous Ways to Wear Your Hair." Included in the half-dozen articles on other issues were "How To Survive Your Parents' Divorce" and "Fifteen Ways To Make $100 A Month" in which teenagers were told that the "number of ways you can earn money is limited only by your imagination." Products had names like "Love" or "Laughter" (both colognes) and ads for them implied that buying the product would automatically bring these things into one's life.

13 Cummings, *The American and His Food*.

14 Fox, "Women's Domestic Labour and Their Involvement in Wage Work." Cowan, in *More Work for Mother*, describes how refrigeration is another example of a development dictated by the power and interlocking interests of large companies. According to Cowan, an energy efficient gas-powered model refrigerator was developed in the late 1920s. General Electric, however, stood to benefit from the increased use of electric power the sale of electric refrigerators would bring. The gas-powered refrigerator company was no match against the resources of a powerful corporation such as General Electric.

15 Weinbaum and Bridges, "The Other Side of the Paycheck." Manufacturers seek to restore the challenge to the homemaker while maintaining sales of prepared products. In 1983, *Seventeen* magazine published a recipe for a cake that looks like a hamburger. Three different
canned or packaged mixes are used in the time-consuming ten-step
process.
16 President of the National Restaurant Association in *NRN*, 23 May
1988.
17 Social Planning Council of Metropolitan Toronto, 1984.
18 Quoted in Strasser, *Never Done*, 297.
19 These statements are supported by Canada, Statistics Canada *Family
Food Expenditure*, 62–554, September 1984.
20 Canada, Statistics Canada, 62–554, Table 10, 79.
21 *NRN*, June 1989.
22 Fox, "Women's Domestic Labour and Their Involvement in Wage
Work."
23 Armstrong, *Labour Pains*.
24 National Council On Welfare, *Women and Poverty*.
25 Businesses have moved into the nursing home and day care sectors,
too, but adequate resources and staffing for children or elderly people
is expensive; and of course, those who need them the most are often
the same people who can least afford to pay.
26 These figures varied significantly by sex and by region. Thus in 1979,
40.8 percent of Ontario male students, and 39.1 percent of Ontario female student were in the labour force, while in Quebec, the figures
were 20.3 percent and 14.1 percent respectively.
27 Hollingshead, *Elmtown's Youth*, 268.
28 Larter, FitzGerald, and Friendly, "Students' Attitudes to Work and
Unemployment," Research Report 151.
29 Higgins, "Socio-cultural Characteristics of Elementary and Secondary
Students."
30 Higgins, Statistics Canada. In A.B. Hollingshead's well-known study,
Elmtown's Youth, first published in 1949, the author notes how well-
placed parents help their children get better jobs.
31 In anecdotal reports, Hollingshead makes clear how important is the
money that working-class children earn, even if it is not contributed
directly to the family coffers. A working youngster buys her own
clothes and pays all her own expenses for school or entertainment.
32 Marsh, *Canadians In and Out of Work*; Piva, *Condition of the Working
Class in Ontario*; Fox, "Women's Domestic Labour."
33 John Bullen, slide presentation on the unwaged work of young people
in Ontario, Ontario Museum Association Heritage Conference, 1 February 1985, Toronto.

34 Craig Heron, talk for the Ontario Museum Association Heritage Conference, 1 February 1985, Toronto.
35 White, *Women and Part-Time Work*.
36 Ibid.
37 Burke, "The Growth of Part-Time Work in Canadian Social Trends."
38 White, *Women and Part-Time Work*, Table 1.
39 CRFA submission respecting "Part Time Work in the Food Service Industry."
40 *Advertising Age*, (8 October 1979) carries an ad picturing a bride that reads, "When she saids I do, she means I'll buy." Another ad features two old people with the caption, "Mom and Pop put in long hours at the store... not working, shopping."
41 See Ewen, *Captains of Consciousness*, for a fuller treatment of how this process occurs.
42 *NRN*, 23 May 1988, p. F16.

CHAPTER 2

1 Root and Rochemont, *Eating in America*; Stokes, *How to Manage a Restaurant or Foodservice*; Lundberg, *The Hotel and Restaurant Business*.
2 Lavellee, *Van Horne's Road*, 291.
3 See Root and Rochemont, *Eating in America*.
4 DeLottinville, "Joe Beef of Montreal," cover photo.
5 From the Christmas dining menu at Hotel Vancouver, 1909. Even the CNR hotels could not match Delmonico's, the first fine restaurant in New York. Here, visiting merchants hosted banquets for their guests. One dinner hosted by a visiting Englishman for tea and coffee merchants cost $20,000 in the 1870s. The menu boasted well over 200 choices of entrees alone! (There were 28 beef entrees, 46 of veal, 20 of mutton, 47 of poultry, 22 of game, 47 of fish, shellfish, turtle, and eels.) The selection of vegetable dishes, liqueurs, wines, and champagnes was no less impressive. At one of Delmonico's banquets, the restaurant created an artificial lake 30 feet long with four swans swimming in it (Lundberg, *The Hotel and Restaurant Business*).
6 There were 228 restaurants in Quebec, 203 in Ontario, and 173 in Nova Scotia. The census contains no special enumeration of restaurant workers. It is possible that some people classified as "servants" were in fact working in restaurants as unskilled workers (Canada, *1890–91 Census*).
7 Canada, *1911 Fifth Census*. Young women who were foreign-born went into domestic and personal service in greater proportions than into restaurant work. It is likely that young women from rural areas worked in restaurants. Domestic service was one of the few occupa-

tions that was even less desirable than restaurant work because of the limitations on personal freedom. Servant work was also plentiful.

8 *Toronto World*, 26 December 1884.

9 Grove, *The Search for America*, 37.

10 Ibid., 37.

11 Ibid., 41–2.

12 Ibid., 46.

13 Ibid., 52–3. In *Down and Out in Paris and London*, George Orwell describes a very similar sort of scene in a Paris hotel kitchen: the disgusting filth and stench and the pandemonium of a meal rush, where noise and quarreling among the staff helped them goad each other into working what he says is twice as fast as possible. In Lundberg, the kitchen at Delmonico's is similarly portrayed. Despite the "beastly and silly" (p. 56) nature of the work, the hotel keeps going because the employees take genuine pride in what they do, and in their efficiency. Orwell describes the elaborate caste system operating in such a place:

> Undoubtedly the most workmanlike class, and the least servile are the cooks. They do not earn quite as much as waiters, but their prestige is higher and their employment steadier. The cook does not look upon himself as a servant, but as a skilled workman ... He knows his power – knows that he alone makes or mars a restaurant, and that if he is five minutes late everything is out of gear. He despises the whole non-cooking staff, and makes it a point of honour to insult everyone below the head waiter. And he takes a genuine artistic pride in his work, which demands very great skill. It is not the cooking that is so difficult, but the doing everything to time. (56)

14 Personal communication, August 1983.

15 Personal communication, October 1984.

16 *R&I*, March 1951.

17 Wage scale from the Cooks, Waiters and Waitresses' Union: Local 362 of the Hotel and Restaurant Employees International Alliance, 20 January 1915. From Canada, Department of Labour, *Strikes and Lockouts in Canada*.

18 Cummings, *The American and His Food*.

19 Lundberg, *The Hotel and Restaurant Business*.

20 See Stewart Ewen, *Captains of Consciousness*, for a wonderful description of this development. In Canada, Craig Heron's thesis on Hamilton also refers to this development.

21 Gad and Holdsworth, "Building for City, Region and Nation," 272–73.

22 Frisken, "A Triumph for Public Ownership."

23 *CHR*, March 1928, 21.
24 *CHR*, 15 January 1938.
25 Ibid.
26 Personal communication, June 1983.
27 Canada, *1931 Census*, vol 11, 1934.
28 Aaron Ladowsky, personal communication, October 1984.
29 Canada, *1931 Census*.
30 Personal communication, 1983.
31 *FP*, 5 May 1934.
32 Leonard Marsh, *Canadians In and Out of Work*, is quoted in Copp's discussion of standard of living in Montreal at the onset of the depression in *The Anatomy of Poverty*, 36–43.
33 As there was no inflation during the 1930s, Marsh's estimates for the early part of the decade apply to the mid-1930s as well.
34 Canada, Department of Labour, *Strikes and Lockouts in Canada*, RG 27, vol. 360.
35 Ibid., vol. 356, Strike 89.
36 Ibid., vol. 360, Strike 60.
37 *FP*, 5 May 1934.
38 The article in *CHR*, 15 January 1938, 1, was entitled "Quebec Fair Wage Act Menaces Industry."
39 Mr. Ladowsky was rather vague about other appliances. Personal communication, October 1984.
40 *CHR*, 15 November 1938, 9.
41 Urquhart and Buckley, *Historical Statistics of Canada*.
42 There is some discrepancy between DBS figures reported in an article published in the *CHR* in 1948, which lists sales in 1939 as $50 million, and the DBS publication *Retail Trade*, which reports sales for the years 1930–61 and indicates 1939 sales were $69 million. The post-war sales figure is $270 million (DBS publication 63–510).
43 *CHR*, 15 June 1944.
44 Ibid., 15 March 1944.
45 Ibid., 15 June 1944, 16.
46 Ibid., 15 March 1944.
47 Ibid., 15 June 1944.
48 *Restaurant Business*, May 1976.
49 Personal communication, June 1984.
50 Bendix, *Work and Authority in Industry*, 294.
51 I say "supposedly" because there have been critiques made of the accuracy of the data used.
52 *The Sociological Eye*, 319.
53 Whyte, *Human Relations in the Restaurant Industry*, 3–4.
54 Ibid., 21.

55 Ibid., 28.

56 Ibid., 29.

57 Ibid., 31.

58 Canada, *1951 Census*, vol. 7.

59 According to *Restaurant Business*, May 1976.

60 *R&I*, September-October 1956, 37.

61 Urquhart and Buckley, *Historical Statistics of Canada*, 1965.

62 *CHR*, 15 September 1955.

63 Stone, *Urban Development in Canada*, 22.

64 The percentage change in the number of men engaged in non-urban occupations such as agriculture, hunting, fishing, or trapping increased dramatically (Stone). From a 5 percent rate of change before the war, the level increased to 37 percent for the decade between 1951 and 1961.

65 *CHR*, 15 September 1955, 23.

66 Ibid.

67 *R&I*, November-December 1956.

68 Ibid., August 1957.

69 Ibid., July 1959.

70 Ibid., June 1951.

71 Ibid., November-December 1951.

72 *CHR*, 7 December 1951, 28. A drive-in in Denver, Colorado, illustrates how the scientific approach was employed during the post-war period to reduce the turnover in carhops. Each young woman was sent to a twelve-week self-improvement and modelling course at Denver's School of Charm. Her parents were consulted, not only when she was hired, but if she got an unfavourable work report. The owners reported that parents were pleased that they took such an interest in their daughters (*Fast Food*, vol. 19, 1952, p. 36).

73 Pope, "Utilization," 193.

74 *R&I*, November 1957, 5.

75 *CHR*, 15 February 1957, 9. A limited menu, produced with a streamlined production process and served in paper plates and cups, was designed for the St. Joseph's Oratory in Montreal. Their self-service cafeteria was able to serve as many as 8,000 pilgrims a day (*R&I*, March 1957, 43–4).

76 *R&I*, February 1960, 46.

77 Ibid., March 1959, 47.

78 Ibid., February 1960, 64.

79 Ibid., May-June 1956, 96.

80 *FSH*, 23 October 1967, 5.

81 Ibid.

82 *R&I*, November 1957, 5.

CHAPTER 3

1 Interview done by *Institutions* magazine (1972) and quoted in Boas and Chain, *Big Mac*, 15–16.
2 *Canada's Hospitality Business Fact File*, 1987, and Canada, Statistics Canada, 63, 224.
3 *Village Voice*, 12 June 1990, 31.
4 Levitt, "Production Line Approach to Service," 44–6.
5 *FSH*, May 1988.
6 Marx, *Communist Manifesto*, 489.
7 Ibid., 372.
8 Over 1.3 billion US dollars was spent on television advertising in 1987 by the leading top ten restaurant chains in the United States (*NRN*, 28 March 1988).
9 *R&I*, April 1960, 25.
10 *FP*, 8 October 1983, S1.
11 Ibid., 3.
12 Ibid., 16 October 1982, F3.
13 Ibid., 8 October 1983, S8.
14 Ibid., S10.
15 *NRN*, 13 August, 1984.
16 *R&I*, April 1960, 25.
17 McDermott, "From Franchising to Microelectronics"; Luxenberg, *Roadside Empires*.
18 *R&I*, April 1960.
19 Personal communication, June 1983.
20 *CHR*, 15 May 1966, 40.
21 *R&I*, April 1960, 25.
22 *NRN*, 5 October 1982, 11.
23 By the 1980s, a prospective Burger King franchisee had to be prepared for a $400,000 investment, $150,000 of it in cash (*NRN*, 5 October 1982). Supported by personal communication from head office.
24 *FP*, June 1988.
25 *FHS*, February 1985, 17.
26 *FP*, 16 October 1982, S1.
27 *FHS*, September 1970.
28 Address by Mr. Sukornyk of Harvey's Restaurants to Canadian Restaurant Association, 23–4 February 1970.
29 *Fortune*, March 1980.
30 *FP*, 25 August 1984.
31 "Big Mac in the Hospital Ward," *G&M*, 29 March 1980, editorial.
32 George Oake, "See Dick, See Jane, Get Big Mac," Toronto *Star*, 23 September 1990, B1.

33 *NRN*, 28 March 1983, 33.
34 *NTN*, 15 May 1989.
35 This information itself represents a nice marketing coup. I read this figure in an article in *Toronto Life*, October 1981. The same information is described in *Big Mac* as resulting from a survey conducted by McDonald's advertising agency, with no explication of sample size or how the finding was made.
36 Newman, "The McWonderful World of George Cohon," 45.
37 *NRN*, August 1983, 36.
38 Ibid., 29 August 1983, 11; 7 April 1983; 6 June 1983; 23 May 1983; 23 April 1984.
39 *FSH*, September 1989.
40 Marx, *Communist Manifesto*, 13.
41 *Fortune*, 14 March 1988.
42 *G&M*, 29 May 1987.
43 *NRN*, 6 June 1988.
44 Ibid., 25 September 1984.
45 Ibid., 22 October 1990.

CHAPTER 4

1 Quoted in *Up Front* magazine, vol. 2, no. 6 (n.d.).
2 Pillsbury engages in three major businesses. The following, extracted from Pillsbury annual reports, is only a partial list of what is included:

- Consumer products bearing labels such as Green Giant, Poppin' Fresh, Hungry Jack, Ballard. Products include refrigerated foods, frozen foods, canned vegetables and dry grocery products such as cake and pancake mixes, and pasta. Plants are located in various parts of the United States, Latin America (Venezuela and Guatemala), Mexico, and Western Europe (Germany, France, and the United Kingdom).
- Agri-products. The company mills flour for sale to bakeries, restaurants, hotels, and institutions. It owns a breading manufacturing division, which sells coatings for fried products, Pioneer Foods which mills rice, and a sunflower seed operation. It also produces equipment for the commercial baking industry and engages in merchandizing of grain and feed ingredients which include Wickes, a processor of beans, peas, and lentils.
- Food services. In addition to Burger King, Pillsbury operates a number of other restaurant chains, such as Steak n' Ale and Poppin' Fresh Pie Shops.

3 *Fortune*, 14 May 1984, 194.

4 Ibid., "Burger King Puts Down its Dukes," June 1980.

5 Ibid., 16 June 1980.

6 Emerson, *Fast Food*.

7 Ibid.

8 BK survey, "Who Our Customers Are," n.d.

9 Emerson, *Fast Food*.

10 Carl Dibiase, "Restaurant Trends" in *NRN*, 18 February 1985.

11 *NRN*, 25 October 1982, 1.

12 Ibid., 28 March 1983.

13 Ted Richman, "A call for caution in comparative advertising," in *NRN*, 24 September 1984, 105. Another similar column, by Louis J. Haugh, appeared in *NRN*, 3 March 1984.

14 *NRN*, 25 October 1982, 1.

15 Carl Dibiase, "Restaurant Trends" in *NRN*, 18 February 1985.

16 Burger King Canada brochure, n.d.

17 Personal Communication, Mr. Banks, Director of Operations, Burger King Canada, November 1982.

18 *FSH* September 1984.

19 "Pillsbury Chief Executive Philip Smith Finds Takeover Bestows Lot of Dough," *G&M*, 22 December 1988, B13.

20 *FSH*, February 1985.

21 Burger King University brochure, n.d.

22 I visited Burger King University in January 1982.

23 Personal communication from Burger King, December 1981.

24 AROC course handout.

25 AROC course notes.

CHAPTER 5

1 Levitt, "Production-line Approach to Service," 46.

2 Karl Marx, *Communist Manifesto*, 27.

3 Mitchell, "Class and Situation Analysis."

4 Ibid.

5 Burger King, MOD.

6 Burger King hands out different toy each week. "The toys really draw the kids in, said one Burger King executive," *NRN*, 28 February 1983, 43.

7 Fast food supervisor course, George Brown College.

8 The emphasis on smiling is not unique to Burger King. An article in *Institutions* magazine (March 1980) was entitled "Smile Seminars, a Real Challenge to the Employer." See also Hochschild, *The Managed Heart*, for a description of how stewardesses are trained to sell "niceness" to their customers.

9 Service time has been reduced to two and one-half minutes since I did my fieldwork.

10 1979 Burger King marketing study from the Burger King University library.

11 *NRN*, 22 May 1989, F48.

12 The narrow staircase seems to be a common feature of restaurants. Orwell described one in *Down and Out in Paris and London*, as did Frederick Grove in his description from late nineteenth-century Toronto in *In Search of America*. The principle that all seem to share is that only the onstage performance (what the customer can see) matters.

13 BK Corp, *Up Front*, vol. 2, no. 2.

14 These have been replaced by video cassettes.

15 Mr. Banks of Burger King headquarters informed me that Dawmor has since been sold. Personal communication, November 1982.

16 Personal communication, February 1982. The name of the store manager has been changed.

17 It was more difficult to get to know the "part-timers." There were more of them, and because of the ad hoc scheduling system, I seldom worked with the same group.

18 *NRN*, 22 May 1989, F32.

CHAPTER 6

1 Peddersen, "Motivation and Foodservice Worker Productivity," 3.

2 Marx, *Capital*, vol. I, 517.

3 James Petersen used this term in chapter 1 of his Ph.D. dissertation, "The Origins of Canadian Gold Mining."

4 Pedderson, "Motivation and Foodservice Worker Productivity," 4.

5 Petersen, "The Origins of Canadian Gold Mining," 26.

6 Ibid., 28.

7 Taylor, *Principles of Scientific Management*, 19.

8 Ibid., 25.

9 Emphasis added. Ibid., 63.

10 Littler, *Development of the Labour Process in Capitalist Societies*, 174–95.

11 Peddersen et al., "Increasing Productivity in Foodservice," 4.

12 Ibid., 192.

13 Braverman, *Labor and Monopoly Capital*, 372.

14 Production costs can easily be lowered, but at the expense of service time. At the other extreme, service time can be lowered well below the projected three minutes, but at the expense of production costs. The challenge is to design a kitchen that finds the optimal point for the corporation. That point is the proper amount of production costs,

staff, and equipment alotted for a given "inter-arrival" time. If management knows how many customers are coming at a certain time interval, then production costs (meaning labour, since the price of raw materials is fixed) and production design (kitchen layout and the number of production lines) can be dynamically designed.

15 Hillier and Lieberman, *Introduction to Operations Research.*
16 *Restaurant Business*, October 1981, 110.
17 This equation is from Hillier and Lieberman, *Introduction to Operations Research.*
18 Personal communication, Luco Donno, Chief of Operations Research at Burger King, January 1982, Miami.
19 Personal communication, 8 March 1982.
20 These scheduling rules are from the MOD. They are also specified in the training filmstrip for managers on scheduling, and handouts from the Basic Manager's Operations Course.
21 Personal communication, Summer 1981.
22 *NRN*, 10 May 1982.
23 This kind of initiative is generally not welcomed. The "drive-thru," which involved working the cash register, was one of the few stations I had not been assigned to in my training period.
24 Braverman, *Labor and Monopoly Capital.*

CHAPTER 7

1 Personal communication, Vince Callaghan, former Burger King manager, 30 October 1981.
2 Basic Restaurant Operations Course, 1981.
3 "Survey Shows Manager is Key," *Up Front*, 2, no. 5.
4 BROC, 1981.
5 See Lundberg, *The Hotel and Restaurant Business*; Wyckoff and Sasser, *The Chain Restaurant Industry*; Solomon and Katz, *Profitable Restaurant Management*; Peddersen et al., *Increasing Productivity in Foodservice*. All refer to the work of Maslow and Herzberg in their restaurant manuals. So do standard management texts such as Hersey and Blanchard, *Management of Organizational Behavior.*
6 Edwards, *Contested Terrain.*
7 *Zeta* magazine, June 1989.
8 Jacoby, *Social Amnesia*, 48.
9 Ibid., 46, 51.
10 Ibid., 51.
11 BROC handout.
12 This paean to the customer is not a Burger King creation. I saw the identical saying in an automobile service garage.

13 *Up Front* 2, no. 6.
14 Emerson, *Fast Food, The Endless Shakeout*, 156.
15 The manager changeover was a bit of a scandal. The head manager, it seems, was using too much labour time and tried to change the statistics delivered to head office, to make her costs for labour seem impressively low, for which she would be rewarded. Of course, since the material is computerized, her alterations of the data were discovered, and she was relieved of her store. She was later hired to manage a franchised Burger King.
16 See for example, Doeringer and Piore, *Internal Labor Markets and Manpower Analysis*.
17 Edwards, Gordon, and Reich emphasize this in *Labour Market Segmentation*.
18 Hartmann, "Capitalism, Patriarchy and Job Segregation by Sex." A new literature in history and sociology is documenting how gender enters the workplace, and how men and women respond to their work in ways that reflect not just the organization of the work, but a sense of "manliness" or "femininity." The workplace culture is also affected by the gender of its inhabitants. (See the work of Joy Parr, *The Gender of Breadwinners*; Cynthia Cockburn, *Brothers*; and Sally Westwood, *All the Livelong Day* for good examples of this new literature.)
19 Garnsey, "Women's Work and Theories of Class and Stratification."
20 *NRN*, 16 October 1988.
21 Jim Woodward, "McDonald's Boycott Targets City-Suburban Wage Discrimination," *Labor Notes*, no. 133, April 1990, 5.
22 *Up Front*, vol. 2, no. 4.
23 Burawoy, *The Politics of Production*, 9.
24 George Brown fast food course advisory committee.
25 Personal communication, 21 November 1981.
26 A member of the George Brown advisory committee for the fast food course gave this estimate at a meeting.
27 This account was given me by the young man involved.
28 *NRN*, 22 November 1982.
29 Personal interview with Dale Ewart, now with Service Employees International Union (SEIU) in Detroit.
30 Personal interview with Dale Ewart.

CHAPTER 8

1 Companies also generate plenty of profit from their real estate holdings. Indeed, McDonald's is classified as a real estate company by the Canadian government in its securities listings.

2 While I have noted earlier how the use of women and children is not at all new, there is evidence that these groups have more control over their wages than in earlier times. Young girls in the New England mills (see Tentler, *Wage Earning Women*) for example, often did not see their wages, which were given directly to their families. In *Children in English Society*, Pinchbeck and Hewitt, on the other hand, note the independence of young working children on the streets of London. At Burger King, although many of the women and some of the young people contribute their wages to the family economy, it is nevertheless legally theirs. In studies such as the Minnesota Youth Poll (Hedin, Wolfe and Arneson, *Youth's Views on Money and Success*) youngsters describe having money in terms of the sense of freedom and self worth that it brings. Charlene Gannage's work quotes women garment workers on the importance of earning money. The body of literature on unemployment elaborates on how crucial a job, any job, is in terms of self-esteem. (See, for example, Sharon Kirsh, *Unemployment: Its Impact on Body and Soul*.)

3 See Vogel, *Marxism and the Oppression of Women*; also Ewen, *Captains of Consciousness*; Ewen and Ewen, *Channels of Desire*.

4 A profit and loss approach to childcare has been tried in the case of Mini-skools, which one critic has called "Kentucky Fried Children." However, it means reducing workers' salaries to a bare minimum and skimping on facilities and equipment. The guidelines set for adequate care for children by early childhood educators are expensive to implement. Even minimum childcare requires funding that governments are loathe to provide.

5 Ellen Greenberger and Laurence Steinberg, *When Teenagers Work: The Psychological and Social Costs of Adolescent Employment*.

6 *NRN*, 14 January 1985.

7 Ibid., 3 July 1985.

8 Ibid., 8 October 1990.

9 Joseph K. Skinner, "Big Mac and the Tropical Forest."

10 Report on Business, *G&M*, January 1987.

11 *Maclean's*, 27 January 1986.

12 See Hochschild, *The Managed Heart*.

13 Myles, Picot, and Wannell, "The Changing Wage Distribution of Jobs," 1981–86.

14 Ridgeway and Bischoff, "Fighting Ronald McToxic."

Bibliography

Acton, Janice, Penny Goldsmith, and Bonnie Shepard, eds. *Women at Work. Ontario 1850–1930*. Toronto: Women's Press, 1974.

Advertising Age. Selected issues, 1966–80.

Amann, Volker, Larry Boyce, Michael Hale, and Alex Mielnik. "Foodservice Industry Analysis," a study prepared for Business 2004, University of Toronto, located in the Faculty of Management Studies Library, University of Toronto. Mimeographed. Toronto, 1980.

Ames, Herbert Brown. *The City Below the Hill*. Originally published in 1897. Reprint, Toronto: University of Toronto Press, 1972.

Armstrong, Hugh and Pat Armstrong. *The Double Ghetto: Canadian Women and Their Segregated Work*. Revised Edition. Toronto: McClelland and Stewart, 1984.

Armstrong, Pat. *Labour Pains*. Toronto: Women's Press, 1984.

Barbie: The Magazine for Girls. Winter issue, 1985.

Baritz, Leon. *The Servants of Power: A History of the Use of Social Science in American Industry*. New York: John Wiley, 1965.

Barrett, Michelle. *Women's Oppression Today: Problems in Marxist Feminist Analysis*. London: Verso, 1980.

Barron's. Selected issues.

Baxandall, R., E. Ewen, and L. Gordon. "The Working Class Has Two Sexes," *Monthly Review* special issue on "Technology, the Labor Process and the Working Class," 28, no. 3(1976):1–9.

Beechey, Veronica. "Women and Production: A Critical Analysis of Some Sociological Theories of Women's Work." In *Feminism and Materialism: Women and Modes of Production*, edited by Annette Kuhn and AnneMarie Wolpe, 155–97. Boston: Routledge and Kegan Paul, 1978.

– "The Sexual Division of Labour and the Labour Process: A Critical Assessment of Braverman." In *The Degradation of Work? Skill, Deskilling and the Labour Process,* edited by Stephen Wood, 54–73. London: Hutchinson, 1982.

Bell, Daniel. *The Cultural Contradictions of Capitalism.* New York: Basic Books, 1978.

Bendix, Reinhard, *Work and Authority in Industry: Ideologies of Management in the Course of Industrialization.* Originally published in 1956. Reprint, Berkeley: University of California Press, 1974.

Benston, Margaret. "The Political Economy of Women's Liberation." *Monthly Review* 21, no. 4(1969):13–27.

Berger, Peter. *The Human Shape of Work.* New York: Macmillan, 1965.

Blauner, Robert. *Alienation and Freedom.* Chicago: University of Chicago Press, 1964.

Bluestone, Barry, and Bennett Harrison. *The Deindustrialization of America.* New York: Basic Books, 1983.

Blumer, Herbert. "Sociological Theory in Industrial Relations." *American Sociological Review* 12(1947):272–78.

Boas, Max and Steve Chain. *Big Mac.* New York: New American Library, 1977.

Bodemann, Y. Michal. "A Problem of Sociological Praxis: The Case for Interventive Observation in Field Work." *Theory and Society* 5(1978):387–419.

– "The Fulfillment of Fieldwork in Marxist Praxis." *Dialectical Anthropology* 4(1979):155–61.

Boorstin, Daniel J. *The Americans: The National Experience.* New York: Random House, 1965.

Braverman, Harry. *Labor and Monopoly Capital.* New York: Monthly Review Press, 1974.

Brenner, Johanna and Maria Ramas. "Rethinking Women's Oppression." *New Left Review* 144, March-April, 1984.

Briskin, Linda, and Lynda Yanz, eds. *Union Sisters.* Toronto: Women's Press, 1983.

Brown, J.A.C. *The Social Psychology of Industry.* Originally published in 1954. Reprint, Middlesex, England: Penguin, 1980.

Burawoy, Michael. "Towards a Marxist Theory of the Labour Process." *Politics and Society* 8, nos. 3–4 (1978).

– *Manufacturing Consent.* Chicago: University of Chicago Press, 1979.

– *The Politics of Production.* London: Verso, 1985.

Burger King Canada Inc. Brochure distributed by Head Office, Mississauga, Ontario, n.d.

Burger King Corporation. "The New Burger King Gift and Incentive Catalog." Miami, n.d.

– "Burger King – a World of Success." Miami, 1978.

– "Burger King University." Miami, 1979.

– "This Is Burger King." Miami, 1979.
– *Up Front*: A Publication Written Expressly for the Managers of Burger King Restaurants. Miami. Selected issues.
Burger King University Bulletin Board. October 1981 issue.
Butler, Elizabeth Beardsley. *Women and the Trades: Pittsburgh, 1907–1908*. In *The Pittsburgh Survey*, edited by Paul Underwood Kellog. 6 vols. New York: Charities Publications, 1909.
CBC. "Attacking Big Mac," Fifth Estate television show, 17 January 1978.
– "McDonald's" on Country Canada radio, 28 January 1979.
CRFA National Hospitality News. Selected issues, 1982–83.
Canada. *1890–91 Census of Canada* 2. Ottawa: Queen's Printer, S.E. Dawson, 1893.
– *1911 Fifth Census of Canada* 6. Occupations of the People. Ottawa: Queen's Printer, J. de L. Taché, 1915.
– *1921 Sixth Census of Canada* 4. Occupations. "Children in Gainful Occupations." Ottawa: Queen's Printer, F.A. Acland, 1929.
– *1931 Seventh Census of Canada* 11. Merchandising and Service Establishments, Part 2. Ottawa: Queen's Printer, J.O. Patenaude, 1934.
– *1931 Seventh Census of Canada* 7. Occupations and Industries. Ottawa: Queen's Printer, J.O. Patenaude, 1936.
– *1941 Eighth Census of Canada* 11. Merchandising and Service Establishments, Part 2. Ottawa: Queen's Printer, Edmond Cloutier, 1944.
– *1951 Ninth Census of Canada* 7. Distribution and Retail Trade. Cat no. 65–535. Ottawa: Queen's Printer, Edmond Cloutier, 1954.
– *1961 Census of Canada*. Retail Trade. Cat. no. 63–510. Ottawa: Queen's Printer, Edmond Cloutier, 1966.
– *1981 Census of Canada*. Labour Force Industry Trends. Cat. no. 92–925. Ottawa: Supply and Services Canada, 1983.
– *1981 Census of Canada*. Labour Force – Occupation by Labour Force and Work Activity. Cat. no. 92–919. Ottawa: Supply and Services Canada, 1983.
– *1981 Census of Canada*. Labour Force – Industry by Demographic and Educational Characteristics. Cat. no. 92–921. Ottawa: Supply and Services Canada, 1984.
– *1986 Census of Canada*. 93–111, 93–113, 93–152. Ottawa: Supply and Services Canada, 1989.
– Department of Labour, *Employment of Children and Young Persons in Canada*. Ottawa: Queen's Printer. December, 1930.
– Department of Labour. *Strikes and Lockouts in Canada, 1911–1960*.
– Dominion Bureau of Statistics. *Canada Yearbook*. Ottawa: Queen's Printer. Selected years.
– Labour Canada. "Labour Force Annual Averages." Cat. no. 71–529. Ottawa: Supply and Services Canada.

– Labour Canada. "Monthly Labour Statistics." Selected issues. Cat. no. 71–201. Ottawa: Supply and Services Canada.
– Labour Canada. *In the Chips: Opportunities, People, Partnerships*. Report of the Labour Canada Taskforce on Micro-Electronics and Employment. Ottawa: Supply and Services Canada, 1982.
– Labour Canada. *Commission of Inquiry into Part Time Work*. Ottawa: Supply and Services Canada, Wallace Commission, 1983.
– *Labour Force Statistics by Age*. Cat. no. 9603–101, 9603–512. Ottawa: Supply and Services Canada, 1945–67.
– Statistics Canada. *Canada Yearbook*. Selected years, 1970–1980. Ottawa: Supply and Services Canada.
– Statistics Canada. *Consumer Prices And Price Indexes*. Cat. no. 62–001 quarterly. Ottawa: Supply and Services Canada.
– Statistics Canada. *Historical Labour Force Statistics*. Cat. no. 71–201. Selected issues. Ottawa: Supply and Services Canada.
– Statistics Canada. *The Labour Force*. Cat. no. 71–001. Selected issues. Ottawa: Supply and Services Canada.
– Statistics Canada. *Labour Force Annual Averages*. Cat. no. 71–529. Ottawa: Supply and Services Canada.
– Statistics Canada. *Market Research Handbook*. Cat. no. 63–224. Selected issues, 1982–90. Ottawa: Supply and Services Canada.
– Statistics Canada. *Restaurant Statistics*. Cat. no. 63–001, 63–011. Ottawa: Supply and Services Canada.
– Statistics Canada. *Historical Compendium of Educational Statistics, Confederation to 1975*. Cat. no. 81–568. Ottawa: Supply and Services Canada, 1975.
– Statistics Canada. *Restaurant, Caterers and Taverns*. Cat. no. 529 occasional. Ottawa: Supply and Services Canada, 1976.
– Statistics Canada. *Out of School – Into the Labour Force*. Cat. no. 81–570E. Ottawa: Supply and Services Canada, 1977.
– Statistics Canada. *Restaurant, Caterers and Taverns*. Cat. no. 63–535 occasional. Ottawa: Supply and Services Canada, 1977.
– Statistics Canada. *Restaurant, Caterers and Taverns*. Cat. no. 63–536 occasional. Ottawa: Supply and Services Canada, 1978.
– Statistics Canada. *Urban Family Food Expenditures, 1978*. Cat. no. 62–548 occasional. Ottawa: Supply and Services Canada, 1980.
– Statistics Canada. *Family Food Expenditure in Canada, 1982*. Cat. no. 62–554 occasional. Ottawa: Supply and Services Canada, 1984.
– Statistics Canada. "Working for Minimum Wage." In *Perspectives* 75–001, Winter 1989.
Canada's Hospitality Business Fact File. Selected years. Toronto: *Foodservice and Hospitality* magazine.
Canadian Business. Selected issues, 1975–85.

Canadian Hotel and Restaurant: The Magazine for Foodservice and Lodging Management. Selected issues, 1928–84.

Canadian Restaurant Association. "Report on fast food." 1970. Mimeographed.

Canadian Restaurant Association, Ontario Region. Condensed proceedings of the seminar "Fast Food – Transition in the 70's," held 23–24 February at the Westbury Hotel. 1970. Mimeographed.

Canadian Restaurant and Foodservice Association. *Selling Service: A Manual for Hiring and Training Food and Beverage Service Personnel.* Toronto: CRFA, 1979.

– Part-Time Work in the Foodservice Industry. Submission to the Commission of Enquiry on Part Time Work, 1982.

Chandler, Alfred D. Jr. *The Visible Hand: The Managerial Revolution in American Business.* Cambridge, Mass.: Harvard University Press, 1981.

Charner, Ivan and Bryna Shore Fraser. *Fast Food Jobs.* Washington, DC: National Institute for Work and Learning, 1984.

Clawson, Dan and Richard Fantasia. "Beyond Burawoy: The Dialectics of Conflict and Consent on the Shop Floor." *Theory and Society* 5 (1983).

Cockburn, Cynthia. *Brothers.* London: Pluto Press, 1983.

Cole, Sheila. "Send Our Children to Work?" *Psychology Today* (July 1980).

Collins, Kevin. *Youth and Employment: A Source Book.* Ottawa: Canadian Council on Social Development, 1976.

Connelly, Patricia. *Last Hired, First Fired: Women and the Canadian Work Force.* Toronto: Women's Press, 1978.

Cook, Gail, ed. *Opportunity for Choice.* Ottawa: Information Canada, 1976.

Copp, Terry. *The Anatomy of Poverty: The Conditions of the Working Class in Montreal, 1897–1929.* Toronto: McClelland and Stewart, 1974.

Cowan, Ruth Swartz. *More Work for Mother: The Ironies of Household Technology from the Open Hearth to the Microwave.* New York: Basic Books, 1983.

Cummings, Richard O. *The American and His Food.* Reprint. New York: Arno, 1970.

DeLottinville, Peter. "Joe Beef of Montreal: Working Class Culture and the Tavern, 1869–1889." *Labour/Le Travailleur* (1981–82).

Denton, F.T., A.C. Robb, and B.G. Spencer. *Unemployment and Labour Force Behaviour of Young People.* Toronto: University of Toronto Press, 1980.

Directory of Restaurant and Fast Food Chains in Canada. Toronto: Monday Report on Retailers, 1982.

Doeringer, P.B. and M.J. Piore. "*Internal Labour Markets and Manpower Analysis.* Lexington, Mass.: D.C. Heath, 1971.

Drucker, Peter. "The Coming Rediscovery of Scientific Management." In *Toward the Next Economics and Other Essays,* edited by Peter Drucker. New York: Harper and Row, 1981.

Durkheim, Emile. *The Division of Labor in Society*. Translated by George Simpson. New York: Free Press. 1969. (First published in French in 1893. English edition first published in 1933.)

Edwards, Richard. *Contested Terrain: The Transformation of the Workplace in the Twentieth Century*. New York: Basic Books, 1979.

– M. Reich, and D.M. Gordon, eds. Labor Market Segmentation. Lexington, Mass.: D.C. Heath, 1975.

Eichler, Margrit. *Families in Canada Today*. Toronto: Gage, 1983.

Elder, Glen H. Jr. *Children of the Great Depression: Social Change in Life Experience*. Chicago: University of Chicago Press, 1974.

Elger, Tony. "Braverman, Capital Accumulation and Deskilling." In *The Degradation of Work? Skill, Deskilling and the Labour Process*, edited by Stephen Wood. London: Hutchinson and Co., 1983.

Emerson, Robert L. *Fast Food: The Endless Shakeout*. New York: Lebhar Friedman Books, 1979.

Engels, Friedrich. *The Origins of the Family, Private Property and the State*. Originally published in 1891. Reprint, New York: International Publishers, 1972.

Ewen, Stuart. *Captains of Consciousness: Advertising and the Social Roots of the Consumer Culture*. Toronto: McGraw-Hill, 1976.

– and Elizabeth Ewen. *Channels of Desire: Mass Images and the Shaping of American Consciousness*. Toronto: McGraw-Hill, 1982.

Fast Food. Selected issues, 1950–55.

Ferree, Myra Marx. "Sacrifice, Satisfaction, and Social Change." In *My Troubles Are Going To Have Trouble With Me*, edited by Karen Brodkin Sacks and Dorothy Remy. New Brunswick, New Jersey: Rutgers University Press, 1984.

Field, Debbie. "A New Look at Co-Worker Harassment." In *Union Sisters*. Toronto: Women's Press, 1983.

Financial Post. Selected issues, 1978–85.

Foodservice and Hospitality – Canada's Hospitality Business Magazine. Selected issues, 1955–1985.

Foodservice Technology International. January-February 1982.

Forbes. Selected issues, 1980–85.

Fortune. Selected issues, 1970–85.

"Franchising – Special Report." *Financial Post*, 16 October 1982, F1–F12.

"Franchising – Special Report." *Financial Post*, 8 October 1983, S1–16.

"Franchising – Special Report." *Financial Post*, 25 August 1984, S1–S10.

Frisken, Frances. "A Triumph for Public Ownership." In *Historical Essays on Toronto*, edited by Victor L. Russell. Toronto: University of Toronto Press, 1984.

Fox, Bonnie. "Women's Domestic Labour and Their Involvement in Wage Work: Twentieth Century Changes in the Reproduction of Daily Life." Ph.D. dissertation, University of Alberta, 1980.

Friedman, Andrew. *Industry and Labor*. London: MacMillan, 1977.

Friedmann, Georges. *The Anatomy of Work*. London: Heinemann, 1961.

Gad, Gunter and Deryck Holdsworth. "Building for City, Region and Nation." In *Forging a Consensus: Historical Essays on Toronto*. Toronto: University of Toronto Press, 1984.

Gannage, Charlene. *Double Day, Double Bind: Women Garment Workers*. Toronto: Women's Press, 1986.

Gardiner, Jean. "Women in the Labour Process and Class Structure." In *Class and Class Structure*, edited by Alan Hunt, 155–163. London: Camelot Press, 1978.

Garnsey, Elizabeth. "Women's Work and Theories of Class and Stratification." In *Classes, Power and Conflict: Classical and Contemporary Debates*, edited by Anthony Giddens and David Held. Berkeley: University of California Press, 1982.

Garson, Barbara. *All the Livelong Day: The Meaning and Demeaning of Routine Work*. New York: Penguin, 1977.

Gendreau, Nicoli. "Short Term Variations in Student Labour Force Participation Rates, 1966–73." Cat. no. 71–523. Ottawa: Statistics Canada. November 1974.

Gerstein, Ira. "Domestic Work and Capitalism." *Radical America* 7, nos. 4–5(1973):101–28.

Giddens, Anthony. *Emile Durkheim*. New York: Penguin, 1979.

Glazer, Nona Y. "Servants to Capital: Unpaid Domestic Labor and Paid Work." *Review of Radical Political Economics* 16, no. 1(1984):61–88.

Glenn, Evelyn Nakano, and Roslyn L. Feldberg. "Proletarianizing Clerical Work: Technology and Organizational Control in the Office." In *Case Studies on the Labor Process*, edited by Andrew Zimbalist, 51–72. New York: Monthly Review Books, 1979.

Globe and Mail. Selected issues, 1980–88.

Goffman, Erving. *Behaviour in Public Places*. New York, Free Press, 1963.

Gorz, Andre. *Farewell to the Working Class: An Essay on Post Industrial Socialism*. Originally published in France in 1980. Reprint, Boston: South End Press, 1982.

– *Paths to Paradise: On the Liberation From Work*. London: Pluto Press, 1984.

Gouldner, Alvin. *Patterns of Industrial Bureaucracy*. New York: Free Press, 1954.

Gramsci, Antonio. *Selections from Prison Notebooks*. New York: International Publishers, 1971.

Greenberger, Ellen, and Laurence D. Steinberg. "Early Adolescents at Work: Effects of Part-Time Employment on Literacy and Maturity." Research proposal to study the costs and benefits of early work experience to adolescent development. Program in Social Ecology, University of California, Irvine, 1978.

– When Teenagers Work: The Psychological and Social Costs of Adolescent Employment. New York: Basic Books, 1986.

Grove, Frederick Philip. A Search for America: The Odyssey of an Immigrant. Originally published in 1927; first draft 1894. Reprint, Toronto: McClelland and Stewart, 1971.

Hartmann, Heidi. "Capitalism, Patriarchy and Job Segregation by Sex." In Classes, Power and Conflict, edited by Anthony Giddens and David Held, 446–69. Berkeley: University of California Press, 1982.

Hayden, Dolores. The Great Domestic Revolution: A History of Feminist Designs for American Homes, Neighbourhoods, and Cities. Cambridge, Mass.: MIT Press, 1981.

Hedin, Diane, Howard Wolfe, and Janis Arneson. Minnesota Youth Poll no. 4. Youth's Views on Money and Success. St Paul, Minnesota: Center for Youth Development and Research, University of Minnesota, 1978.

Heron, Craig and Bob Storey. On The Job: Confronting the Labour Process in Canada. Montreal: McGill Queen's, 1986.

Hersey, Paul and Ken Blanchard. Management of Organizational Behavior: Utilizing Human Resources. New Jersey: Prentice Hall, 1982.

Herzberg, Frederick. Work and the Nature of Man. New York: World Publishing Company, 1966.

– "One More Time: How Do You Motivate Employees." Harvard Business Review 46, no. 1(1968): 53–62.

Higgins, Bruce. "Socio-cultural Characteristics of Elementary and Secondary Students." Cat. no. 81–561. Ottawa: Statistics Canada, 1974.

Hightower, Jim. Eat Your Heart Out. New York: Crown Publishers, 1975.

Hillier, Frederick S. and Gerald J. Lieberman. Introduction to Operations Research. San Francisco: Holden-Day, Inc., 1980.

Hochschild, Arlie Russell. The Commercialization of Human Feeling. Berkeley: University of California Press, 1983.

Hodgins, J. Herbert, David B. Crombie, Eric Crawford, and J. B. Herestic. Women at War. Toronto: MacLean, 1943.

Hollingshead, A. B. Elmtown's Youth. Originally published in 1949. Reprint, New York: John Wiley Science Editions, 1961.

Hughes, Everett Cherrington. Men and Their Work. Glencoe, Illinois: The Free Press, 1958.

– The Sociological Eye, vol. 2. Chicago: Aldine-Atherton Inc., 1971.

Humphries, Jane. "The Working Class Family, Women's Liberation and Class Struggle." Review of Radical Political Economics, Special women's issue, 9(1977):25–42.

Institutions. Selected issues, 1976–81.

Jacoby, Russell. Social Amnesia: A Critique of Contemporary Psychology from Adler to Laing. Boston: Beacon Press, 1975.

Jaggar, Alison. *Feminist Politics and Human Nature*. New Jersey: Rowman and Allanheld, 1983.

Johnson, Leo. "The Political Economy of Ontario Women in the Nineteenth Century." In *Women at Work*, edited by Janice Acton et al., 13–33. Toronto: Women's Press, 1974.

Katz, Michael. *The People of Hamilton, Canada West: Family and Class in a Mid-Nineteenth Century City*. Cambridge, Mass.: Harvard University Press, 1975.

Kealey, Greg, *Canada Investigates Industrialism: The Royal Commission on the Relations of Labour and Capital, 1889* (abridged). Toronto: University of Toronto Press, 1973.

Kelly-Gadol, Joan. "The Social Relation of the Sexes: Methodological Implications of Women's History." In *The Signs Reader: Women, Gender and Scholarship*, edited by Elizabeth Abel and Emily K. Abel, 11–26. Chicago: University of Chicago Press, 1983.

Kerr, Clark and Lloyd Fisher. "Plant Sociology: The Elite and the Aborigines." In *Common Frontiers of the Social Sciences*, edited by Mirra Komarovsky. Glencoe: Free Press, 1957.

Kirsh, Sharon. *Unemployment: Its Impact on Body and Soul*. Toronto: Mental Health Association, 1983.

Koc, Sedef. "In the Privacy of Our Own Home." *Studies in the Political Economy of Canada* 28 (Spring 1989).

Kottak, Conrad P. "Rituals at McDonald's." In *The American Dimension: Cultural Myths and Social Realities*, edited by Susan P. Montague and W. Arens, 129–38. Sherman Oaks, California: Alfred Publishing Co., 1981.

Kroc, Ray. *Grinding It Out: The Making of McDonald's*. New York: Berkley Books, 1977.

Kuhn, Annette and Annemarie Wolpe, eds. *Feminism and Materialism: Women and Modes of Production*. Boston: Routledge and Kegan Paul, 1978.

Kusterer, Ken. *Know How on the Job*. Boulder, Colorado: Westwood Press, 1978.

Landsberger, Henry. *Hawthorne Revisited*. Ithaca, New York: Cornell University Press, 1958.

Larter, Sylvia, John Fitzgerald and Martha Friendly. "Students' Attitudes to Work and Unemployment," part I, no. 151. Toronto: Research Department, Board of Education for the City of Toronto, 1978. Mimeographed.

Lavellee, Omar. *Van Horne's Road*. Toronto: University of Toronto Press, 1974.

Laventhol and Horwath, management consultant. "Report on the Canadian Foodservice Industry." Toronto, 1972. Mimeographed.

Leepson, Marc. "Fast Food, U.S. Growth Industry." *Editorial Research Reports* 7(1978).

Lenin, V.I. *The Emancipation of Women: From the Writings of V.I. Lenin*. New York: International Publishers, 1972.

Levitt, Theodore. "Production-line Approach to Service." *Harvard Business Review* 50, no. 5(1972):41–52.

Littler, Craig R. *The Development of the Labour Process in Capitalist Societies*. London: Heinemann Educational Books, 1982.

– and G. Salaman. "Bravermania and Beyond: Recent Theories of the Labour Process." *Sociology* 16, no. 2 (1982).

Lundberg, Donald E. *The Hotel and Restaurant Business*. Revised Edition. Boston: Cahners Books, 1979.

Lupton, Tom. *Management and the Social Sciences*. Third Edition. New York: Penguin, 1983.

Luxenberg, Stan. *Roadside Empires: How the Chains Franchised America*. New York: Viking Books, 1985.

Luxton, Meg. *More Than a Labour of Love*. Toronto: Women's Press, 1980.

– "Two Hands for the Clock: Changing Patterns in the Gendered Division of Labour in the Home." *Studies in Political Economy* 12(1983):27–44.

Lynd, Robert and Helen Merrell Lynd. *Middletown: A Study in Modern American Culture*. New York: Harcourt and Brace, 1929.

– *Middletown in Transition: A Study in Cultural Conflicts*. New York: Harcourt, Brace and World, Inc., 1937.

McDermott, Pat. "From Franchising to Microelectronics: An Analysis of Corporate Strategy." Ph.D. dissertation, University of Toronto, 1982.

McDonald's Corporation Annual Reports. Oak Brook, Illinois: McDonald's Corporation. Selected years 1971–84.

McLelland, R.M. *An Overview of the Canadian Foodservice Market, 1976–77*, Food Policy Group Report, Consumer and Corporate Affairs, Canada. Ottawa: Minister of Supply and Services, 1978.

Mandel, Ernest. *An Introduction to Marxist Economic Theory*. New York: Pathfinder Press, 1973.

Manwaring Tony, and Stephen Wood. "The Ghost in the Machine: Tacit Skills in the Labor Process." *Socialist Review* 74(1984):57–86.

Marsh, Leonard. *Canadians In And Out Of Work*. McGill Social Research Series no. 9, 1940.

Marx, Karl. *The Communist Manifesto*, edited by Samuel H. Beer. Originally published in 1848. Reprint, New York: Appleton Century Crofts Inc., 1955.

– *Selected Writings in Sociology and Social Philosophy*, edited by T.B. Bottomore and Maximilien Rubel. Translated by T.B. Bottomore. London: Watts and Co., 1956.

– *Capital: Volume III*. Moscow: Progress Publishers, 1971.

– *The Poverty of Philosophy*. New York: International Publishers, 1975. Written in 1846–47.

- *Capital: Volume I.* Translated by Ben Fowkes. Originally published in 1867. Reprint, New York: Vintage Books, 1977.
- *Capital: A Critique of Political Economy* vol. I. Edited by Frederich Engels. Reprint, Moscow: Progress Publishers, 1977.
- and Friedrich Engels. *The German Ideology.* Originally published in 1848. Reprint, New York: International Publishers, 1977.
Maslow, Abraham H. *Motivation and Personality.* New York: Harper and Row, 1954.
Mayo, Elton. *The Human Problems of an Industrial Civilization.* New York: Macmillan, 1933.
Meissner, Martin, Elizabeth Humphreys, Scott Meis and William Scheu. "No Exit for Wives: Sexual Division of Labour." *Canadian Review of Sociology and Anthropology* 12(1975):424–40.
Might's Toronto City Directory. Selected years, 1876–1916. Toronto: Might Directories.
Mitchell, J. Clyde. "Class and Situation Analysis." *Sociological Review* 38(1983):187–211.
Moberg, David. "Work and American Culture: The Ideal of Self Determination and the Prospects for Socialism." *Socialist Review* 50/51(1980):5–19.
Monday Report on Retailers. *Directory of Restaurant and Fast Food Chains in Canada.* Toronto, 1981.
Monthly Review. Special issue on "Technology, the Labor Process, and the Working Class," vol. 28, no. 3 (1976).
Moody's Industrial Manual. New York: Moody's Investor's Service, Inc., 1983.
Mulvaney, Charles Pelham. *Toronto: Past and Present; A Handbook of the City.* Toronto: W.E. Caiger, 1884.
Myles, J., G. Picot and T. Wannell. "The Changing Wage Distribution of Jobs, 1981–1986," Canada, Statistics Canada, *Monthly Labour Statistics,* 1988.
National Council of Welfare. *Women and Poverty.* Ottawa, 1979.
Nation's Restaurant News. Selected issues, 1970–1985.
Newman, Peter C. "The McWonderful World of George Cohon." *Toronto Life,* October 1981.
Newspaper Advertising Bureau. "Eat and Run: A National Survey of Fast Food Chain Patronage." July 1978.
New York Times. Selected issues, 1980–84.
Noble, David. *America By Design? Science, Technology and the Rise of Corporate Capitalism.* New York: Knopf, 1977.
- *Forces of Production: A Social History of Industrial Automation.* New York: Knopf, 1984.
Ontario Legislative Assembly. *Committee on Child Labour.* 1907.
Ontario Ministry of Labour, Women's Bureau. Factsheets nos. 1–5 distributed by the Women's Bureau.

Orwell, George. *Down and Out in Paris and London*. Originally published in 1933. Reprint, New York: Berkley Publishing, 1961.

Osterman, Paul. "Education and Labor Markets at the Turn of the Century." *Politics and Society* 9, no. 1(1979):89–102.

Parr, Joy. *Labouring Children*. Kingston, Ontario: Croom-Helm, McGill-Queen's University Press, 1980.

Peddersen, Raymond B. "Convenience Foods, Disposables and Automation." In *Increasing Productivity in Foodservice*, by Raymond Peddersen et al., 181–90. Boston: Institutions/Volume Feeding Magazine, 1973.

– "Motivation and Foodservice Worker Productivity." In *Increasing Productivity in Foodservice*, by Raymond Peddersen et al., 1–56. Boston: Institutions/Volume Feeding Magazine, 1973.

– Arthur C. Avery, Ruth D. Richard, James S. Osenton, and Harry H. Pope. *Increasing Productivity in Foodservice*. Chicago: Institutions/Volume Feeding Magazine, 1973.

Perrow, Charles. *Complex Organizations*. Second Edition. New York: Random House, 1979.

Petersen, James. "A History of Canadian Goldmining." Ph.D. Thesis, University of Toronto, 1976.

Pillsbury Corporation. *Annual Reports*. Minneapolis: The Pillsbury Company, selected years, 1979–84.

Pinchbeck, Ivy and Margaret Hewitt. *Children in English Society*. 2 vols. London: Routledge and Kegan Paul, 1969.

Pitfield, McKay, Ross and Co. Ltd. "The Canadian Restaurant Industry." Toronto, 1969. Mimeographed.

Piva, Michael J. *The Condition of the Working Class in Toronto, 1900–21*. Ottawa: University of Ottawa Press, 1979.

Pope, Harry H. "Utilization – Prerequisite to Increasing Productivity, A Summary." In *Increasing Productivity in Foodservice*, by Peddersen, et al. Boston: Institutions/Volume Feeding Magazine, 1973.

Printer's Ink. Selected issues, 1966–72.

Restaurant Business. Selected issues, 1966–82.

Restaurants and Institutions. Selected issues, 1928–65, when it became *Foodservice and Hospitality*.

Review of Radical Political Economics 16, no. 1 (1984). Special issue, "The Political Economy of Women."

Ridgeway, James and Bischoff, Dan. "Fighting Ronald McToxic." *Voice* 12 June 1990.

Rinehart, James W. *The Tyranny of Work*. Toronto, Longman Canada Ltd., 1975.

Rivzi, Saiyed H. and Charlene Brown. "The Fast Food Sector in Canada." *Food Market Commentary* 4, no. 3(1981):24–31.

Roberts, Helen. *Doing Feminist Research*. London: Routledge and Kegan Paul, 1981.

Roethlisberger, F.J. and W.J. Dickson. *Management and the Worker*. Cambridge: Harvard University Press, 1939.

Root, Waverly and Richard de Rochemont. *Eating in America: A History*. New York: Ecco Press, 1976.

Rothchild, Emma. "Reagan and the Real America." *New York Review of Books* 5 February 1981.

Sacks, Karen Brodkin and Dorothy Remy, eds. *My Troubles are Going to Have Trouble with Me*. New Brunswick, New Jersey: Rutgers University Press, 1984.

Seccombe, Wally. "The Housewife and Her Labour under Capitalism." *New Left Review* 83(1974):3–24.

– "The Expanded Reproduction Cycle of Labour Power in Twentieth Century Capitalism." In *Hidden in the Household. Women's Domestic Labour Under Capitalism*, edited by Bonnie Fox. Toronto: Women's Press, 1980.

Seventeen Magazine. Selected issues, 1980–83.

Skinner, Joseph K. "Big Mac and the Tropical Forest." *Monthly Review*, December 1985.

Smith, Dorothy. "Women, the Family and the Productive Process." In *Introduction to Sociology*, edited by J. Paul Grayson. Toronto: Gage, 1983.

Smith, Joan. "The Paradox of Women's Poverty: Wage Earning Women and Economic Transformation." *Signs* 10, no. 2(1984):291–310.

Social Planning Council of Metropolitan Toronto. *Caring for Profit: The Commercialization of Human Services in Ontario*. Toronto, 1984. Mimeographed.

Solomon, Kenneth I. and Norman Katz. *Profitable Restaurant Management*. Englewood Cliffs, New Jersey: Prentice-Hall, Inc.

Standard and Poor's Industry Surveys. April 1984. Survey for 26 January 1984.

Stokes, John W. *How to Manage a Restaurant or Institutional Food Service*. Dubuque, Iowa: Wm. C. Brown, 1967.

Stone, Leroy. *Urban Development in Canada: One of a Series of 1961 Census Monographs*. Prepared for the Census Division, Dominion Bureau of Statistics. Ottawa: Queen's Printer, 1967.

Stopard, John M. *World Directory of Multinational Enterprises*, 1982–3. Detroit: Dale Research Company, 1984.

Strasser, Susan. *Never Done*. New York: Pantheon Books, 1982.

Taylor, Frederick Winslow. *The Principles of Scientific Management*. Originally published in 1911. Reprint, New York: Norton, 1967.

Tentler, Leslie. *Wage Earning Women: Industrial Work and Family Life in United States, 1900–1930*. New York: Oxford University Press, 1979.

Thernstrom, Stephan. *Poverty and Progress: Social Mobility in a Nineteenth Century City*. Cambridge: Harvard University Press, 1964.

Thompson, Paul. *The Nature of Work: An Introduction to Debates on the Labour Process*. London: Macmillan Press, 1983.

Tilly, Louise H. and Joan W. Scott. *Women, Work and Family.* New York: Hold, Rinehart and Winston, 1978.

Toronto Star. Selected issues.

Toronto World. 26 December 1884.

Turbin, Carole. "Reconceptualizing Family, Work and Labor Organizing: Working Women in Troy, 1860–1890." *Review of Radical Political Economics* 16, no. 1(1984):1–16.

us Department of Commerce, Bureau of Industrial Economics, *U.S. Industrial Outlook, 1984: Prospects for Over 300 Industries.* 1984.

Urquhart, M. C. and K. A. H. Buckley. *Historical Statistics of Canada.* Toronto: Macmillan, 1965.

Vaughn, Charles L. "Growth and Future of the Fast Food Industry." *The Cornell Hotel and Restaurant Administration Quarterly* 17, no. 3 (1976).

Vogel, Lise. *Marxism and the Oppression of Women: Towards a Unitary Theory.* New Brunswick, New Jersey: Rutgers University Press, 1983.

Warner, William Lloyd. *The Social System of the Modern Factory.* Vol. 4 of the Yankee City Series. New Haven: Yale University Press, 1945.

Weber, Max. "A Research Strategy for the Study of Occupational Careers and Mobility Patterns." In *Max Weber,* edited by John Eldridge. London: Michael Joseph, 1971.

– "Science as a Vocation." In *From Max Weber: Essays in Sociology,* edited by H.H. Gerth and C. Wright Mills. Originally published in German in 1919. New York: Galaxy, 1962.

Weinbaum, Batya and Amy Bridges. "The Other Side of the Paycheck: Monopoly Capital and the Structure of Capitalism." In *Capitalist Patriarchy and the Case for Socialist Feminism,* edited by Zillah Eisenstein. New York: Monthly Review Press, 1979.

West, Jackie. "Women, Sex and Class." In *Feminism and Materialism,* edited by Annette Kuhn and AnnMarie Wolpe. London: Routledge and Kegan Paul, 1979.

– "A Political Economy of the Family in Capitalism: Women, Reproduction and Wage Labour." In *Capital and Labour: a Marxist Primer,* edited by Theo Nichols. Glasgow: Fontana, 1980.

Westwood, Sallie. *All Day Every Day: Factory and Family in the Making of Women's Lives.* London: Pluto Press, 1984.

White, Julie. *Women and Part-Time Work.* Ottawa: Canadian Advisory Council on the Status of Women, 1983.

Who Owns Whom. North America. London: Dun and Bradstreet, 1984.

Whyte, William Foote. *Human Relations in the Restaurant Industry.* New York: McGraw Hill, 1948.

– *Money and Motivation: An Analysis of Incentives in Industry.* New York: Harper and Row, 1955.

– *Men at Work.* Homewood, Illinois: Dorsey Press, 1961.

Williams, Claire. *Opencut: The Working Class in an Australian Mining Town.* Sydney: George Allen and Unwin, 1981.

Willis, Paul. *Learning to Labour: How Working Class Kids Get Working Class Jobs.* New York: Columbia Press, 1980.

Wood, Stephen. *The Degradation of Work?: Skill, Deskilling and the Labour Process.* London: Hutchinson, 1982.

Woods, Gordon and Co. *Foodservice Industry in Canada, 1951–1961.* n.d.

Woodward, Jim. "McDonald's Boycott Targets City-Suburban Wage Discrimination." *Labor Notes* 133(1990).

Wyckoff, D. Daryl and W. Earl Sasser. *The Chain-Restaurant Industry.* Toronto: Lexington Books, 1978.

Zaretsky, Eli. *Capitalism, the Family, and Personal Life.* New York: Harper and Row, 1976.

Zimbalist, Andrew. *Case Studies on the Labor Process.* New York: Monthly Review Press, 1979.

Index